GMAT® Math Workbook

Ninth Edition

Other Kaplan Books on the GMAT

Kaplan GMAT Premier
Kaplan GMAT Strategies, Practice, and Review
Kaplan GMAT Verbal Workbook
Kaplan GMAT 800
Kaplan GMAT Math Foundations
Kaplan GMAT Verbal Foundations
Kaplan GMAT in a Box

GMAT®

MATH WORKBOOK

Ninth Edition

The staff of Kaplan Test Prep

PUBLISHING

New York

© 2015 by Kaplan, Inc.

Published by Kaplan Publishing, a division of Kaplan, Inc.
395 Hudson Street
New York, NY 10014

Printed in the United States of America

10 9 8 7 6 5 4 3 2 1

ISBN: 978-1-61865-892-0

Kaplan Publishing print books are available at special quantity discounts to use for sales promotions, employee premiums, or educational purposes. For more information or to purchase books, please call the Simon & Schuster special sales department at 866-506-1949.

CONTENTS

How to Use This Book. vii

A Special Note for International Students. ix

PART ONE: GETTING STARTED

Chapter 1.   Introduction to GMAT Math. 3

PART TWO: MATH CONTENT REVIEW

Chapter 2.   Arithmetic 11

Chapter 3.   Algebra 109

Chapter 4.   Geometry 147

PART THREE: QUESTION TYPE REVIEW

Chapter 5.   Problem Solving 259

Chapter 6.   Data Sufficiency 327

How to Use This Book

Kaplan has prepared students to take standardized tests for more than 70 years—longer than the GMAT has even been around. Our team of researchers and editors know more about preparation for the GMAT than anyone else, and you'll find their accumulated knowledge and experience throughout this book.

The GMAT is a standardized test, and so, while no two test administrations are identical, they all cover the same content. This is good news for you; it means that the best preparation you can have will focus on the sort of questions you are likely to see on test day. All of the exercises in this book are made up of such questions.

The main focus of this book is on reviewing the math concepts you need to get a good score on the GMAT. Strategic reviews, exercises, and practice tests with explanations will help you brush up on math skills you may have forgotten since high school.

If possible, work through this book a little at a time over the course of several weeks. There is a lot of math to absorb, and it's hard to do it all at once. Cramming just before the test is not a good idea—you probably won't absorb much information if you pack it in at the last minute.

STEP 1: CHECK OUT THE BASICS

The first thing you need to do is find out exactly what is on the math sections of the GMAT. In Part One, "Getting Started," you'll see background information on the Quantitative section, what it covers, and how it's organized.

STEP 2: MATH CONTENT REVIEW

Once you have the big picture, focus on the content. Part Two of this book, "Math Content Review," does just that. It gives you a complete tour of the math that you will see on test day. There's a chapter for each of the three major content areas—arithmetic, algebra, and geometry. Since each chapter builds on the material in earlier chapters, it's best to go over them in order.

The material in the math content review is divided into subjects. Each subject begins with a review, followed by practice questions organized by level of difficulty: basic, intermediate, and advanced. This way, you'll be able to pinpoint the math concepts you need to review and quickly get your skills up to speed.

We suggest that you quickly skim the content review that introduces a section and then try the exercises. If you find them difficult, go back to the content review before moving on. If you do well on the exercises, try the basic problem set that follows. Once you are satisfied you have a good grasp on the basics, try the intermediate and advanced problem sets. Answers and explanations for the practice problems follow the chapter. Read the explanations to all the questions—even those you got right. Often the explanations will contain strategies that show you how you could have gotten to the answer more quickly and efficiently.

STEP 3: BECOME FAMILIAR WITH THE GMAT QUESTION TYPES

The math section of the GMAT has two question types: Problem Solving and Data Sufficiency. It's important to learn them now, well before test day. You will be limited in time during the actual test, so you cannot waste time then trying to figure out what you are being asked. Take the time to learn this question type well.

Now you're ready to begin preparing for the math section of the GMAT. Good luck!

A Special Note for International Students

The MBA (Master of Business Administration) has become a degree of choice for businesspersons around the globe. Variations of U.S.-style MBA programs exist in Asia, Europe, and the Americas. In recent years, hundreds of thousands of international students have studied business and management in the United States.

As the United States increases its participation in the global economy, U.S. business schools are reaching out to attract exceptional international candidates into their graduate programs. However, competition for admission to prestigious programs is intense, and international students need to plan carefully if they wish to enter a top U.S. graduate management program.

If you are not from the United States but are considering attending a graduate management program at a university in the United States, here is what you'll need to get started.

- If English is not your first language, you'll probably need to take the Test of English as a Foreign Language (TOEFL®) or show some other evidence that you are proficient in English. Most top graduate business schools require a minimum TOEFL® iBT score of 100 (600 PBT). The ability to communicate in English, both verbally and in writing, is extremely important to your success in an American MBA program.
- You may also need to take the GMAT® (Graduate Management Admissions Test). Some graduate business programs may require you to take the GRE® (Graduate Record Examination) as well.
- Since admission to many graduate business programs is quite competitive, you may wish to select three or four programs you would like to attend.
- Select a program that meets your current or future employment needs rather than simply a program with a big name. For example, if you hope to work in the hotel and tourism industry, make sure the program you choose specializes in that distinct area.
- You need to begin the application process at least a year in advance. Be aware that many programs offer only August or September start dates.
- Finally, you will need to obtain an I–20 Certificate of Eligibility from the school you plan to attend if you intend to apply for an F-1 Student Visa to study in the United States.

KAPLAN INTERNATIONAL CENTERS*

If you need more help with the complex process of business school admissions, assistance preparing for the TOEFL or GMAT, or help improving your English skills in general, you may be interested in Kaplan's English language and test preparation courses for international students, available at Kaplan International Centers/Colleges around the world.

Kaplan's English courses were designed to help students and professionals from outside the United States meet their educational and career goals. At locations throughout the United States, Canada, Ireland, the United Kingdom,

Malta, Australia, and New Zealand, international students use Kaplan's programs to help them improve their academic and conversational English skills; raise their scores on the TOEFL, GMAT, GRE, and other standardized exams; and gain admission to the schools of their choice. Here is a brief description of some of Kaplan's programs for international students.

General and Intensive English

Kaplan's General and Intensive English classes are designed to help you improve your skills in all areas of English and to increase your fluency in spoken and written English. Classes are available for beginning to advanced students, and the average class size is 13 students.

TOEFL and Academic English (TAE)

This course provides you with the skills you need to improve your TOEFL score and succeed in an American university or graduate program. It includes advanced reading, writing, listening, and spoken English practice and test-taking strategies, as well as academic skills work. You will also receive training for the TOEFL iBT using Kaplan's exclusive online test simulations and feedback.

GMAT Preparation for International Students (IGMAT)

The Graduate Management Admissions Test (GMAT) is required for admission to many graduate programs in business in the United States. Hundreds of thousands of international students have taken Kaplan's IGMAT course to prepare for the GMAT. This course includes the skills you need to succeed on each section of the GMAT, as well as access to Kaplan's exclusive online practice materials.

OTHER KAPLAN PROGRAMS

Since 1938, more than 3 million students have come to Kaplan to advance their studies, prepare for entry to American universities, and further their careers. In addition to the above programs, Kaplan offers courses to prepare for the SAT®, GRE®, IELTS, Cambridge, MCAT®, DAT®, USMLE®, NCLEX®, and other standardized exams at locations throughout the United States, Canada, and the United Kingdom.

Applying to Kaplan International Centers/Colleges

To get more information or to apply for admission to any of Kaplan's programs for international students and professionals, please visit our website at: **kaplaninternational.com.**

Getting Started

Chapter 1:
Introduction to GMAT Math

Been there, done that. If you're considering applying to business school, then you've already seen all the math you need for the GMAT. You would have covered the relevant math content in junior high. In fact, the math that appears on the GMAT is almost identical to the math tested on the SAT or ACT. You don't need to know trigonometry. You don't need to know calculus. No surprises—it's all material you've seen before. The only problem is, you may not have seen it lately. When was the last time you had to add a bunch of fractions without a calculator?

No matter how much your memories of junior high algebra classes have dimmed, don't panic. The GMAT tests a limited number of core math concepts in predictable ways. Certain topics come up in every test, and, chances are, these topics will be expressed in much the same way; even some of the words and phrases appearing in the questions are predictable. Since the test is so formulaic, we can show you the math you're bound to encounter. Some practice on testlike questions, such as those in the following chapters, will ready you for the questions you will see on the actual test.

Here is a checklist of core math concepts you'll need to know. These concepts are vital, not only because they are tested directly on every GMAT administration, but also because you need to know how to perform these simpler operations in order to perform more complicated tasks. For instance, you won't be able to find the volume of a cylinder if you can't find the area of a circle. We know the math operations on the following list are pretty basic, but make sure you know how to do them.

GMAT MATH BASICS

Add, subtract, multiply, and divide fractions. (Chapter 2)

Convert fractions to decimals, and vice versa. (Chapter 2)

Add, subtract, multiply, and divide signed numbers. (Chapter 2)

Find a percent using the percent formula. (Chapter 2)

Find an average. (Chapter 2)

Plug numbers into algebraic expressions. (Chapter 3)

Solve a simple algebraic equation. (Chapter 3)

Find the areas of rectangles, triangles, and circles. (Chapter 4)

HOW MATH IS SCORED ON THE GMAT

The GMAT will give you a scaled quantitative score from 0 to 60. (The average score is 37.) This score reflects your performance on the math portion of the test compared to all other GMAT test takers.

You will also receive an overall score that reflects your performance on both the math and the verbal portions of the test. This is a scaled score from 200 to 800.

TEST OVERVIEW

The GMAT is a Computer Adaptive Test, or CAT. You take this test on a computer at special centers. Here's a quick overview of the math section.

There are 37 questions to be done in 75 minutes.

Approximately two-thirds of the questions will be in the Problem Solving format, and the remaining questions will be in the Data Sufficiency format.

About 10 of the questions in the GMAT CAT math section will be experimental questions. These are questions that are being tested for use in future tests, and are not scored. However, there is no way of telling the experimental questions from the scored questions around them, so you should treat all questions as if they are scored.

Problem Solving Questions

In Problem Solving questions, you are given a question (and sometimes an accompanying chart or diagram) and asked to choose the correct answer from a list of five answer choices. Here's a sample Problem Solving question.

Example:

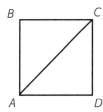

If the perimeter of the square *ABCD* is 8, what is the area of triangle *ACD?*

- ⟨ ⟩ 1
- ⟨ ⟩ 2
- ⟨ ⟩ 4
- ⟨ ⟩ 6
- ⟨ ⟩ 8

Answer: If the perimeter of square *ABCD* is 8, each side must be $8 \div 4 = 2$. The area of the square is then $2 \times 2 = 4$. The area of the triangle is half of this, or 2.

Data Sufficiency Questions

In Data Sufficiency, a question is followed by two statements containing certain data. Your task is to determine whether the data provided by the statements are sufficient to answer the question. All Data Sufficiency questions have the same five answer choices.

Here's a sample Data Sufficiency question.

Example: Is x even?

> (1) x is a multiple of 6.
> (2) x is a multiple of 5.

> ○   Statement (1) <u>by itself</u> is sufficient to answer the question, but statement (2) by itself is not.
> ○   Statement (2) <u>by itself</u> is sufficient to answer the question, but statement (1) by itself is not.
> ○   Statements (1) and (2) <u>taken together</u> are sufficient to answer the question, even though <u>neither</u> statement <u>by itself</u> is sufficient.
> ○   <u>Either</u> statement <u>by itself</u> is sufficient to answer the question.
> ○   Both statements (1) and (2) <u>taken together</u> are <u>not sufficient</u> to answer the question in the stem.

Answer: Since all multiples of 6 are even, but multiples of 5 may or may not be even, statement (1) is BY ITSELF sufficient to answer the question, but statement (2) by itself is not in this case. So the answer is choice 1.

The Data Sufficiency chapter has more examples of those questions.

MATH CONTENT

GMAT math is basically junior high school level math, but a bit harder.

Arithmetic—About half of all questions.

Algebra—About a quarter of all questions.

Geometry—About a sixth of all questions.

Graphs, logic questions, and other miscellaneous question types occur from time to time.

About half of all questions are presented in the form of word problems.

COMPUTER ADAPTIVE TESTING

The GMAT is a little different from the paper-and-pencil tests you have probably seen in the past.

You make your way through the GMAT CAT by pointing and clicking with a mouse. The test is preceded by a short tutorial that will show you exactly how to use the mouse to indicate your answer and move through the test. If you have used a computer and mouse before, you will probably find the procedure to be very simple.

How a CAT Finds Your Score

These computer-based tests "adapt" to your performance. This means the questions get harder or easier depending on whether you answer them correctly or not. Your score is not directly determined by how many questions you get right, but by how hard the questions you get right are.

When you start a section, the computer:

• Assumes you have an average score.
• Gives you a medium-difficulty question.

If you answer a question correctly:

• Your score goes up.
• You are given a harder question.

If you answer a question incorrectly:

• Your score goes down.
• You are given an easier question.

After a while you will reach a level where most of the questions will seem difficult to you. At this point you will get roughly as many questions right as you get wrong. This is your scoring level. The computer uses your scoring level in calculating your scaled score.

Another consequence of the test's adaptive nature is that for the bulk of the test you will be getting questions at the limit of your ability. While every question is equally important to your final score, harder questions generate higher scores and easier questions lower scores. You want to answer as many hard questions as possible. This is a reason to concentrate your energies on the early questions. Get these right and you are into the harder questions, where the points are. The sooner you start to see harder questions, the higher your final score is likely to be.

There are a few other consequences of the adaptive nature of the test that you should consider.

• There is no preset order of difficulty; the difficulty level of the questions you're getting is dependent on how well you have done on the preceding questions. The harder the questions are, the better you are doing. So, if you seem to be getting only hard questions, don't panic: It's a good sign!
• Once you leave a question, you cannot return to it. That's it. Kiss it good-bye. This is why you should never rush on the CAT. Make sure that you have indicated the right answer before you confirm it and move on. The CAT rewards meticulous test takers.

- In a CAT you must answer a question to move on to the next one. There's no skipping around. If you can't get an answer, you will have to guess in order to move on. Consequently, intelligent guessing can make the difference between a mediocre and a great score. Guess intelligently and strategically—eliminate any answer choices that you determine are wrong and guess among those remaining. The explanations to the questions in this book will demonstrate techniques for eliminating answer choices strategically.

- One final, important point. There is a penalty for unanswered questions on the CAT. Every question you leave unanswered will decrease your score by a greater amount than a question that you answered incorrectly! This means that you should answer all the questions on the test, even if you have to guess randomly to finish a section.

Math Content Review

Chapter 2:
Arithmetic

Most of the problems you will see on the GMAT involve arithmetic to some extent. Among the most important topics are number properties, ratios, and percents. You should know most of the basic definitions, such as what an integer is, what even numbers are, etc.

Not only do arithmetic topics covered in this unit appear on the exam, they are also essential for understanding some of the more advanced concepts that will be covered later. For instance, many of the rules covering arithmetic operations, such as the commutative law, will be important when we discuss variables and algebraic expressions. In addition, the concepts we cover here will be needed for word problems.

NUMBER OPERATIONS

Number Types

The number tree is a visual representation of the different types of numbers and their relationships.

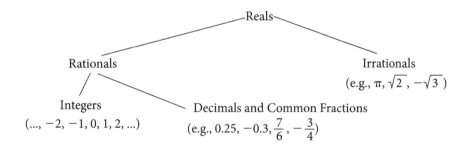

Real Numbers: All numbers on the number line; all the numbers on the GMAT are real.

Rational Numbers: All numbers that can be expressed as the ratio of two integers (all integers and fractions).

Irrational Numbers: All real numbers that are not rational, both positive and negative (e.g., π, $-\sqrt{3}$).

Integers: All numbers with no fractional or decimal parts: multiples of 1.

Order of Operations

PEMDAS = **P**lease **E**xcuse **M**y **D**ear **A**unt **S**ally—This mnemonic will help you remember the order of operations.

P = Parentheses
E = Exponents
M = Multiplication
D = Division } in order from left to right
A = Addition
S = Subtraction } in order from left to right

Example: $30 - 5 \cdot 4 + (7 - 3)^2 \div 8$

First perform any operations within **Parentheses**. (If the expression has parentheses within parentheses, work from the innermost out.)	$30 - 5 \cdot 4 + 4^2 \div 8$
Next, raise to any powers indicated by **Exponents**.	$30 - 5 \cdot 4 + 16 \div 8$
Then do all **Multiplication** and **Division** in order from left to right.	$30 - 20 + 2$
Last, do all **Addition** and **Subtraction** in order from left to right.	$10 + 2$ 12

Laws of Operations

Commutative law: Addition and multiplication are both **commutative**; it doesn't matter **in what order** the operation is performed.

Example: $5 + 8 = 8 + 5; 2 \times 6 = 6 \times 2$

Division and subtraction are **not** commutative.

Example: $3 - 2 \neq 2 - 3; 6 \div 2 \neq 2 \div 6$

Associative law: Addition and multiplication are also **associative**; the terms can be **regrouped** without changing the result.

Example:

$$(a + b) + c = a + (b + c) \qquad\qquad (a \times b) \times c = a \times (b \times c)$$
$$(3 + 5) + 8 = 3 + (5 + 8) \qquad\qquad (4 \times 5) \times 6 = 4 \times (5 \times 6)$$
$$8 + 8 = 3 + 13 \qquad\qquad\qquad 20 \times 6 = 4 \times 30$$
$$16 = 16 \qquad\qquad\qquad\qquad 120 = 120$$

Distributive law: The **distributive law** of multiplication allows us to "distribute" a factor among the terms being added or subtracted. In general, $a(b + c) = ab + ac$.

Example:

$$4(3 + 7) = 4 \times 3 + 4 \times 7$$
$$4 \times 10 = 12 + 28$$
$$40 = 40$$

Division can be distributed in a similar way.

Example:
$$\frac{3+5}{2} = \frac{3}{2} + \frac{5}{2}$$
$$\frac{8}{2} = 1\frac{1}{2} + 2\frac{1}{2}$$
$$4 = 4$$

Don't get carried away, though. When the sum or difference is in the **denominator**, no distribution is possible.

Example: $\frac{9}{4+5}$ is NOT equal to $\frac{9}{4} + \frac{9}{5}$.

Fractions

$$\frac{4}{5}$$
4 ← numerator
fraction bar (means "divided by")
5 ← denominator

Equivalent fractions: The value of a number is unchanged if you multiply the number by 1. In a fraction, multiplying the numerator and denominator by the same nonzero number is the same as multiplying the fraction by 1; the fraction is unchanged. Similarly, dividing the top and bottom by the same nonzero number leaves the fraction unchanged.

Example:
$$\frac{1}{2} = \frac{1 \times 2}{2 \times 2} = \frac{2}{4}$$
$$\frac{5}{10} = \frac{5 \div 5}{10 \div 5} = \frac{1}{2}$$

Canceling and reducing: Generally speaking, when you work with fractions on the GMAT you'll need to put them in **lowest terms**. That means that the numerator and the denominator are not divisible by any common integer greater than 1. For example, the fraction $\frac{1}{2}$ is in lowest terms, but the fraction $\frac{3}{6}$ is not, since 3 and 6 are both divisible by 3.

The method we use to take such a fraction and put it in lowest terms is called **reducing**. That simply means to divide out any common multiples from both the numerator and denominator. This process is also commonly called **canceling**.

Example: Reduce $\frac{15}{35}$ to lowest terms.

First, determine the largest common factor of the numerator and denominator. Then, divide the top and bottom by that number to reduce.

$$\frac{15}{35} = \frac{3 \times 5}{7 \times 5} = \frac{3 \times 5 \div 5}{7 \times 5 \div 5} = \frac{3}{7}$$

Addition and subtraction: We can't add or subtract two fractions directly unless they have the same denominator. Therefore, before adding, we must find a common denominator. A common denominator is just a **common multiple** of the denominators of the fractions. The **least common denominator** is the **least common multiple** (the smallest positive number that is a multiple of all the terms).

Example: $\frac{3}{5} + \frac{2}{3} - \frac{1}{2}$. Denominators are 5, 3, 2. $\text{LCM} = 5 \times 3 \times 2 = 30 = \text{LCD}$

Multiply the numerator and denominator of each fraction by the value that raises each denominator to the LCD.

$$\left(\frac{3}{5} \times \frac{6}{6}\right) + \left(\frac{2}{3} \times \frac{10}{10}\right) - \left(\frac{1}{2} \times \frac{15}{15}\right)$$

$$= \frac{18}{30} + \frac{20}{30} - \frac{15}{30}$$

Combine the numerators by adding or subtracting and keep the LCD as the denominator.

$$= \frac{18 + 20 - 15}{30} = \frac{23}{30}$$

Multiplication:

Example: $\frac{10}{9} \times \frac{3}{4} \times \frac{8}{15}$

First, reduce (cancel) diagonally and vertically.

$$\frac{{}^2\cancel{10}}{{}_3\cancel{9}} \times \frac{{}^1\cancel{3}}{{}_1\cancel{4}} \times \frac{{}^2\cancel{8}}{\cancel{15}_3}$$

Then multiply numerators together and denominators together.

$$\frac{2 \times 1 \times 2}{3 \times 1 \times 3} = \frac{4}{9}$$

Division: Dividing is the same as multiplying by the **reciprocal** of the divisor. To get the reciprocal of a fraction, just invert it by interchanging the numerator and the denominator. For example, the reciprocal of the fraction $\frac{3}{7}$ is $\frac{7}{3}$.

Example: $\frac{4}{3} \div \frac{4}{9}$

To divide, invert the second term (the divisor), and then multiply as above.

$$\frac{4}{3} \div \frac{4}{9} = \frac{4}{3} \times \frac{9}{4} = \frac{{}^1\cancel{4}}{{}_1\cancel{3}} \times \frac{\cancel{9}^3}{\cancel{4}_1} = \frac{1 \times 3}{1 \times 1} = 3$$

Complex fractions: A complex fraction is a fraction that contains one or more fractions in its numerator or denominator. There are two ways to simplify complex fractions.

Method I: Use the distributive law. Find the least common multiple of all the denominators, and multiply all the terms in the top and bottom of the complex fraction by the LCM. This will eliminate all the denominators, greatly simplifying the calculation.

Example:

$$\frac{\frac{7}{9}-\frac{1}{6}}{\frac{1}{3}+\frac{1}{2}}=\frac{18\cdot\left(\frac{7}{9}-\frac{1}{6}\right)}{18\cdot\left(\frac{1}{3}+\frac{1}{2}\right)}$$

LCM of all the denominators is 18.

$$=\frac{\frac{^{2}18}{1}\cdot\frac{7}{9_{1}}-\frac{^{3}18}{1}\cdot\frac{1}{6_{1}}}{\frac{^{6}18}{1}\cdot\frac{1}{3_{1}}+\frac{^{9}18}{1}\cdot\frac{1}{2_{1}}}$$

$$=\frac{2\cdot7-3\cdot1}{6\cdot1+9\cdot1}$$

$$=\frac{14-3}{6+9}=\frac{11}{15}$$

Method II: Treat the numerator and denominator separately. Combine the terms in each to get a single fraction on the top and a single fraction on the bottom. We are left with the division of two fractions, which we perform by multiplying the top fraction by the reciprocal of the bottom one. This method is preferable when it is difficult to get an LCM for all the denominators.

Example:

$$\frac{\frac{7}{9}-\frac{1}{6}}{\frac{1}{3}+\frac{1}{2}}=\frac{\frac{14}{18}-\frac{3}{18}}{\frac{2}{6}+\frac{3}{6}}=\frac{\frac{11}{18}}{\frac{5}{6}}=\frac{11}{18}\div\frac{5}{6}=\frac{11}{_{3}18}\times\frac{6^{1}}{5}=\frac{11}{15}$$

Example:

$$\frac{\frac{5}{11}-\frac{5}{22}}{\frac{7}{16}+\frac{3}{8}}=\frac{\frac{10}{22}-\frac{5}{22}}{\frac{7}{16}+\frac{6}{16}}=\frac{5}{_{11}22}\times\frac{16^{8}}{13}=\frac{40}{143}$$

Comparing positive fractions: If the numerators are the same, the fraction with the smaller denominator will have the larger value, since the numerator is divided into a smaller number of parts.

Example: $\frac{4}{5}>\frac{4}{7}$ i.e.:

If the denominators are the same, the fraction with the larger numerator will have the larger value.

Example: $\frac{5}{8}>\frac{3}{8}$ i.e.:

KAPLAN

If neither the numerators nor the denominators are the same, express all of the fractions in terms of some common denominator. The fraction with the largest numerator will be the largest.

Example: Compare $\frac{11}{15}$ and $\frac{13}{20}$.

$$\frac{11}{15} = \frac{11 \times 4}{15 \times 4}$$
$$= \frac{44}{60}$$

$$\frac{13}{20} = \frac{13 \times 3}{20 \times 3}$$
$$= \frac{39}{60}$$

Since $44 > 39$, $\frac{11}{15} > \frac{13}{20}$.

A shorter version of this method is to multiply the numerator of the left fraction by the denominator of the right fraction and vice versa (cross-multiply). Then compare the products obtained this way. If the left product is greater, then the left fraction was greater to start with.

Example: Compare $\frac{5}{7}$ and $\frac{9}{11}$.

Compare 5×11 and 9×7.

Since $55 < 63$, $\frac{5}{7} < \frac{9}{11}$.

Sometimes it is easier to find a common **numerator**. In this case, the fraction with the **smaller** denominator will be the **larger** fraction.

Example: Compare $\frac{22}{19}$ and $\frac{11}{9}$.

Multiply $\frac{11}{9} \times \frac{2}{2}$ to obtain a common numerator of 22.

$$\frac{11}{9} = \frac{11 \times 2}{9 \times 2} = \frac{22}{18}$$

Since $\frac{22}{19} < \frac{22}{18}$, $\frac{22}{19} < \frac{11}{9}$.

As before, the comparison can also be made by cross-multiplying.

$22 \times 9 < 11 \times 19$, so $\frac{22}{19} < \frac{11}{9}$.

Mixed Numbers: Mixed Numbers are numbers consisting of an integer and a fraction. For example, $3\frac{1}{4}$, $12\frac{2}{5}$, and $5\frac{7}{8}$ are all mixed numbers. Fractions whose numerators are greater than their denominators may be converted into mixed numbers, and vice versa.

Example: Convert $\dfrac{23}{4}$ to a mixed number.

$$\dfrac{23}{4} = \dfrac{20}{4} + \dfrac{3}{4} = 5\dfrac{3}{4}$$

Example: Convert $2\dfrac{3}{7}$ to a fraction.

$$2\dfrac{3}{7} = 2 + \dfrac{3}{7} = \dfrac{14}{7} + \dfrac{3}{7} = \dfrac{17}{7}$$

Decimal Fractions

Decimal fractions are just another way of expressing common fractions; they can be converted to common fractions with a power of ten in the denominator.

Example: $0.053 = \dfrac{53}{10^3}$ or $\dfrac{53}{1,000}$

Each position, or **digit**, in the decimal has a name associated with it. The GMAT occasionally tests on digits, so you should be familiar with this naming convention:

Comparing decimal fractions: To compare decimals, add zeros to the decimals (after the last digit to the right of the decimal point) until all the decimals have the same number of digits. Since the denominators of all the fractions are the same, the numerators determine the order of values.

Example: Arrange in order from smallest to largest: 0.7, 0.77, 0.07, 0.707 and 0.077.

$$0.7 = 0.700 = \dfrac{700}{1,000}$$

$$0.77 = 0.770 = \dfrac{770}{1,000}$$

$$0.07 = 0.070 = \dfrac{70}{1,000}$$

$$0.707 = 0.707 = \dfrac{707}{1,000}$$

$$0.077 = 0.077 = \dfrac{77}{1,000}$$

$$70 < 77 < 700 < 707 < 770; \text{ therefore, } 0.07 < 0.077 < 0.7 < 0.707 < 0.77$$

Addition and subtraction: When adding or subtracting one decimal to or from another, make sure that the decimal points are lined up, one under the other. This will ensure that tenths are added to tenths, hundredths to hundredths, etc.

Example: 0.8 + 0.08 + 0.008 =

$$\begin{array}{r} 0.8 \\ 0.08 \\ +\ 0.008 \\ \hline 0.888 \end{array}$$

Answer: 0.888

Example: 0.72 − 0.072 =

$$\begin{array}{r} 0.72 \\ -\ 0.072 \\ \hline \end{array} \quad = \quad \begin{array}{r} 0.720 \\ -\ 0.072 \\ \hline 0.648 \end{array}$$

Answer: 0.648

Multiplication and division: To multiply two decimals, multiply them as you would integers. The number of decimal places in the product will be the total number of decimal places in the factors that are multiplied together.

Example: 0.675 × 0.42 =

$$\begin{array}{r} 0.675 \\ \times\ 0.42 \\ \hline 1350 \\ 2700 \\ \hline 0.28350 \end{array}$$

(3 decimal places)
+ (2 decimal places)
———————
(5 decimal places)

Answer: 0.2835

When dividing a decimal by another decimal, multiply each by a power of 10 such that the divisor becomes an integer. (This doesn't change the value of the quotient.) Then carry out the division as you would with integers, placing the decimal point in the quotient directly above the decimal point in the dividend.

Example: 0.675 ÷ 0.25 =
        67.5 ÷ 25 =

Multiply each decimal by 100 by moving the decimal point two places to the right (since there are two zeros in 100).

$$\begin{array}{r} 2.7 \\ 25\overline{)67.5} \\ 50 \\ \hline 17\ 5 \\ 17\ 5 \\ \hline 0 \end{array}$$

Answer: 2.7

NUMBER OPERATIONS EXERCISE

Solve the following problems. (Answers are on the following page.)

1. $\dfrac{1}{2} + \dfrac{1}{3} + \dfrac{1}{4} =$

2. $\dfrac{12}{25} + \dfrac{13}{5} =$

3. $\dfrac{6}{21} + \dfrac{7}{3} =$

4. $\dfrac{1}{16} - \dfrac{3}{4} + 1\dfrac{7}{8} =$

5. $4\left(\dfrac{1}{3} + \dfrac{1}{12}\right) =$

6. $\dfrac{1}{2}\left(\dfrac{1}{3} + \dfrac{1}{4}\right) =$

7. $\dfrac{1}{24}(36 + 60) =$

8. $0.021 + 0.946 + 1.324 =$

9. $\left(\dfrac{12}{16} - \dfrac{3}{6}\right)^2 =$

10. $1.69 \times 0.002 =$

11. $30.17 \times 1.01 =$

12. $7 + 5 \times \left(\dfrac{1}{4}\right)^2 - 6 \div (2 - 3) =$

13. $4(1.24 - (0.8)^2) + 6 \times \dfrac{1}{3} =$

14. $\dfrac{\dfrac{5}{6} + \dfrac{3}{2} + 2}{\dfrac{1}{3} + \dfrac{4}{9} + 4} =$

15. $\dfrac{0.25 \times (0.1)^2}{0.5 \times 40} =$

ANSWER KEY—NUMBER OPERATIONS EXERCISE

1. $\dfrac{13}{12}$ or $1\dfrac{1}{12}$

2. $\dfrac{77}{25}$ or $3\dfrac{2}{25}$

3. $\dfrac{55}{21}$ or $2\dfrac{13}{21}$

4. $\dfrac{19}{16}$ or $1\dfrac{3}{16}$

5. $\dfrac{5}{3}$ or $1\dfrac{2}{3}$

6. $\dfrac{7}{24}$

7. 4

8. 2.291

9. $\dfrac{1}{16}$

10. 0.00338

11. 30.4717

12. $13\dfrac{5}{16}$

13. 4.4

14. $\dfrac{39}{43}$

15. 0.000125

NUMBER OPERATIONS TEST

Solve the following problems and select the best answer from those given. (Answers and explanations are at the end of this chapter.)

1. $3.44 =$

    ○ $\dfrac{14}{25}$

    ○ $\dfrac{33}{25}$

    ○ $3\dfrac{11}{50}$

    ○ $3\dfrac{11}{25}$

    ○ $3\dfrac{22}{25}$

2. $6\dfrac{3}{4} - 6.32 =$

    ○ 0.33

    ○ 0.39

    ○ 0.43

    ○ 0.57

    ○ 0.68

3. $0.125 + 0.25 + 0.375 + 0.75 =$

    ○ $1\dfrac{5}{8}$

    ○ $1\dfrac{1}{2}$

    ○ $1\dfrac{3}{8}$

    ○ $1\dfrac{1}{4}$

    ○ $1\dfrac{1}{8}$

4. Which of the following is less than $\dfrac{1}{6}$?

    ○ 0.1667

    ○ $\dfrac{3}{18}$

    ○ 0.167

    ○ 0.1666

    ○ $\dfrac{8}{47}$

5. $\dfrac{(0.02)(0.0003)}{0.002} =$

    ○ 0.3

    ○ 0.03

    ○ 0.003

    ○ 0.0003

    ○ 0.00003

6. $1 + \dfrac{1}{2} + \dfrac{1}{4} + \dfrac{1}{6} + \dfrac{1}{8} =$

    ○ $\dfrac{25}{24}$

    ○ $\dfrac{13}{12}$

    ○ $\dfrac{35}{24}$

    ○ $\dfrac{47}{24}$

    ○ $\dfrac{49}{24}$

KAPLAN

7. $\dfrac{12}{\frac{1}{4}} =$

    ○ 48

    ○ 3

    ○ $\dfrac{1}{3}$

    ○ $\dfrac{1}{16}$

    ○ $\dfrac{1}{48}$

8. Which of the following lists three fractions in ascending order?

    ○ $\dfrac{9}{26}, \dfrac{1}{4}, \dfrac{3}{10}$

    ○ $\dfrac{9}{26}, \dfrac{3}{10}, \dfrac{1}{4}$

    ○ $\dfrac{1}{4}, \dfrac{9}{26}, \dfrac{3}{10}$

    ○ $\dfrac{1}{4}, \dfrac{3}{10}, \dfrac{9}{26}$

    ○ $\dfrac{3}{10}, \dfrac{9}{26}, \dfrac{1}{4}$

9. $\dfrac{7}{5} \cdot \left(\dfrac{3}{7} - \dfrac{2}{5} \right) =$

    ○ $\dfrac{1}{165}$

    ○ $\dfrac{1}{35}$

    ○ $\dfrac{1}{25}$

    ○ $\dfrac{9}{15}$

    ○ 1

10. Which of the following fractions is closest in value to the decimal 0.40?

    ○ $\dfrac{1}{3}$

    ○ $\dfrac{4}{7}$

    ○ $\dfrac{3}{8}$

    ○ $\dfrac{5}{9}$

    ○ $\dfrac{1}{2}$

11. $\dfrac{\frac{1}{6} + \frac{1}{3} + 2}{\frac{3}{4} + \frac{5}{4} + 3} =$

    ○ $\dfrac{1}{3}$

    ○ $\dfrac{1}{2}$

    ○ $\dfrac{5}{8}$

    ○ $\dfrac{2}{3}$

    ○ 1

12. For which of the following expressions would the value be greater if 160 were replaced by 120?

    I. $1,000 - 160$

    II. $\dfrac{160}{1+160}$

    III. $\dfrac{1}{1-\dfrac{1}{160}}$

    ◯ None

    ◯ I only

    ◯ III only

    ◯ I and II

    ◯ I and III

13. What is the positive difference between the largest and smallest of the fractions below?

    $$\frac{5}{9}, \frac{5}{12}, \frac{23}{48}, \frac{11}{24}, \frac{3}{7}$$

    ◯ $\dfrac{1}{12}$

    ◯ $\dfrac{5}{36}$

    ◯ $\dfrac{1}{4}$

    ◯ $\dfrac{1}{3}$

    ◯ $\dfrac{7}{18}$

14. If x, y, and z are all positive and $0.04x = 5y = 2z$, then which of the following is true?

    ◯ $x < y < z$

    ◯ $x < z < y$

    ◯ $y < x < z$

    ◯ $y < z < x$

    ◯ $z < y < x$

15. $\dfrac{59.376 \times 7.094}{31.492 \times 6.429}$ is approximately equal to which of the following?

    ◯ 0.02

    ◯ 0.2

    ◯ 2

    ◯ 20

    ◯ 200

KAPLAN

NUMBER PROPERTIES

Number Line and Absolute Value

A **number line** is a straight line that extends infinitely in either direction, on which real numbers are represented as points.

As you move to the right on a number line, the values increase.

Conversely, as you move to the left, the values decrease.

Zero separates the positive numbers (to the right of zero) and the negative numbers (to the left of zero) along the number line. Zero is neither positive nor negative.

The **absolute value** of a number is just the number without its sign. It is written as two vertical lines.

Example: $|-3| = |+3| = 3$

The absolute value can be thought of as the number's distance from zero on the number line; for instance, both $+3$ and -3 are 3 units from zero, so their absolute values are both 3.

Properties of −1, 0, 1, and Numbers in Between

Properties of zero: Adding or subtracting zero from a number does not change the number.

Example: $0 + x = x$; $2 + 0 = 2$; $4 - 0 = 4$

Any number multiplied by zero equals zero.

Example: $z \times 0 = 0$; $12 \times 0 = 0$

Division by zero is **undefined**. When given an algebraic expression, be sure that the denominator is not zero. $\frac{0}{0}$ is also undefined.

Properties of 1 and −1: Multiplying or dividing a number by 1 does not change the number.

Example: $x \div 1 = x$; $4 \times 1 = 4$; $-3 \times 1 = -3$

Multiplying or dividing a number by -1 changes the sign.

Example: $y \times (-1) = -y; \quad 6 \times (-1) = -6; \quad -2 \div (-1) = -(-2) = 2;$
$(x - y) \times (-1) = -x + y = y - x$

Note: The sum of a number and -1 times that number is equal to zero. Zero times -1 is zero.

Example: $a + (-a) = 0; \quad 8 + (-8) = 0; \quad 0 \times (-1) = 0; \quad \dfrac{2}{3} \div \left(-\dfrac{2}{3}\right) = -1$

The **reciprocal** of a number is 1 divided by the number. For a fraction, as we've already seen, the reciprocal can be found by just interchanging the denominator and the numerator. The product of a number and its reciprocal is 1. Zero has no reciprocal, since $\dfrac{1}{0}$ is undefined.

Properties of numbers between -1 and 1: The reciprocal of a number between 0 and 1 is greater than the number.

Example: The reciprocal of $\dfrac{2}{3} = \dfrac{1}{\frac{2}{3}} = \dfrac{3}{2} = 1\dfrac{1}{2}$, which is greater than $\dfrac{2}{3}$.

The reciprocal of a number between -1 and 0 is less than the number.

Example: The reciprocal of $-\dfrac{2}{3} = \dfrac{1}{\left(-\frac{2}{3}\right)} = -\dfrac{3}{2} = -1\dfrac{1}{2}$, which is less than $-\dfrac{2}{3}$.

The square of a number between 0 and 1 is less than the number.

Example: $\left(\dfrac{1}{2}\right)^2 = \dfrac{1}{2} \times \dfrac{1}{2} = \dfrac{1}{4}$, which is less than $\dfrac{1}{2}$.

Multiplying any positive number by a fraction between 0 and 1 gives a product smaller than the original number.

Example: $6 \times \dfrac{1}{4} = 1\dfrac{1}{2}$, which is less than 6.

Multiplying any negative number by a fraction between 0 and 1 gives a product greater than the original number.

Example: $-3 \times \dfrac{1}{6} = -\dfrac{1}{2}$, which is greater than -3.

All of these properties can best be seen by observation rather than by memorization.

Operations with Signed Numbers

The ability to add and subtract signed numbers is best learned by practice and common sense.

Addition: Like signs: Add the absolute values and keep the same sign.

> **Example:** $(-6) + (-3) = -9$

Unlike signs: Take the difference of the absolute values and keep the sign of the number with the larger absolute value.

> **Example:** $(-7) + (+3) = -4$

Subtraction: Subtraction is the inverse operation of addition; subtracting a number is the same as adding its inverse. Subtraction is often easier if you change to addition, by changing the sign of the number being subtracted. Then use the rules for addition of signed numbers.

> **Example:** $(-5) - (-10) = (-5) + (+10) = +5$

Multiplication and division: The product or the quotient of two numbers with the same sign is positive.

> **Example:** $(-2) \times (-5) = +10; \quad \dfrac{-50}{-5} = +10$

The product or the quotient of two numbers with opposite signs is negative.

> **Example:** $(-2)(+3) = -6; \quad \dfrac{-6}{2} = -3$

Odd and Even

Odd and even apply only to integers. There are no odd or even noninteger numbers. Put simply, even numbers are integers that are divisible by 2, and odd numbers are integers that are not divisible by 2. If an integer's last digit is either 0, 2, 4, 6, or 8, it is even; if its last digit is 1, 3, 5, 7, or 9, it is odd. Odd and even numbers may be negative; 0 is even.

A number needs just a single factor of 2 to be even, so the product of an even number and **any** integer will always be even.

Rules for Odds and Evens:

Odd + Odd = Even	Odd × Odd = Odd
Even + Even = Even	Even × Even = Even
Odd + Even = Odd	Odd × Even = Even

You can easily establish these rules when you need them by picking sample numbers.

Example: $3 + 5 = 8$, so the sum of any two odd numbers is even.

Example: $\frac{4}{2} = 2$, but $\frac{6}{2} = 3$, so the quotient of two even numbers could be odd or even (or a fraction!).

Factors, Primes, and Divisibility

Multiples: An integer that is divisible by another integer is a **multiple** of that integer.

Example: 12 is multiple of 3, since 12 is divisible by 3; $3 \times 4 = 12$.

Remainders: The remainder is what is left over in a division problem. A remainder is always smaller than the number we are dividing by.

Example: 17 divided by 3 is 5, with a remainder of 2.

Factors: The **factors**, or **divisors**, of a number are the positive integers that evenly divide into that number.

Example: 36 has nine factors: 1, 2, 3, 4, 6, 9, 12, 18, and 36.
We can group these factors in pairs:
$1 \times 36 = 2 \times 18 = 3 \times 12 = 4 \times 9 = 6 \times 6$

The **greatest common factor**, or **greatest common divisor**, of a pair of numbers is the largest factor shared by the two numbers.

Divisibility tests: There are several tests to determine whether a number is divisible by 2, 3, 4, 5, 6, 7, 8, 9, 10, and 11.

A number is divisible by 2 if its last digit is divisible by 2.

Example: 138 is divisible by 2 because 8 is divisible by 2.

A number is divisible by 3 if the **sum** of its digits is divisible by 3.

Example: 4,317 is divisible by 3 because $4 + 3 + 1 + 7 = 15$, and 15 is divisible by 3.
239 is **not** divisible by 3 because $2 + 3 + 9 = 14$, and 14 is not divisible by 3.

A number is divisible by 4 if its last two digits are divisible by 4.

Example: 1,748 is divisible by 4 because 48 is divisible by 4.

A number is divisible by 5 if its last digit is 0 or 5.

Example: 2,635 is divisible by 5. 5,052 is **not** divisible by 5.

A number is divisible by 6 if it is divisible by both 2 and 3.

Example: 4,326 is divisible by 6 because it is divisible by 2 (last digit is 6) and by 3 ($4 + 3 + 2 + 6 = 15$).

A number is divisible by 7 if the difference between the unit digit multiplied by 2 and the rest of the number is a multiple of 7.

Example: 287 is divisible by 7 because $28 - 7(2) = 28 - 14 = 14$, which is a multiple of 7.

783 is **not** divisible by 7 because $78 - 3(2) = 78 - 6 = 72$, which is not a multiple of 7.

A number is divisible by 8 if the last three digits are divisible by 8.

Example: 76,848 is divisible by 8 because 848 is divisible by 8.

65,102 is **not** divisible by 8 because 102 is not divisible by 8.

A number is divisible by 9 if the sum of its digits is divisible by 9.

Example: 22,428 is divisible by 9 because $2 + 2 + 4 + 2 + 8 = 18$, and 18 is divisible by 9.

A number is divisible by 10 if the unit digit is zero.

Example: 67,890 is divisible by 10. 56,432 is **not** divisible by 10.

A number is divisible by 11 if the difference between the sum of the odd-placed digits and the sum of the even-placed digits is a multiple of 11.

Example: 7,293 is divisible by 11 because $(7 + 9) - (2 + 3) = 16 - 5 = 11$, which is divisible by 11.

25,684 is **not** divisible by 11 because $(5 + 8) - (2 + 6 + 4) = 13 - 12 = 1$, which is not divisible by 11.

Prime number: A **prime** number is an integer greater than 1 that has no factors other than 1 and itself. The number 1 is not considered a prime. The number 2 is the first prime number and the only even prime. (Do you see why? Any other even number has 2 as a factor, and therefore is not prime.) The first ten prime numbers are 2, 3, 5, 7, 11, 13, 17, 19, 23, 29.

Prime factorization: The **prime factorization** of a number is the expression of the number as the product of its prime factors. No matter how you factor a number, its prime factors will always be the same.

Example: $36 = 6 \times 6 = 2 \times 3 \times 2 \times 3$ or $2 \times 2 \times 3 \times 3$ or $2^2 \times 3^2$

Example: $480 = 48 \times 10 = 8 \times 6 \times 2 \times 5$
$= 2 \times 4 \times 2 \times 3 \times 2 \times 5$
$= 2 \times 2 \times 2 \times 2 \times 3 \times 2 \times 5$
$= 2^5 \times 3 \times 5$

The easiest way to determine a number's prime factorization is to figure out a pair of factors of the number, and then determine their factors, continuing the process until you're left with only prime numbers. Those primes will be the prime factorization.

> **Example:** Find the prime factorization of 1,050.

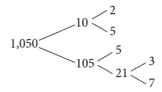

So the prime factorization of 1,050 is $2 \times 3 \times 5^2 \times 7$.

Consecutive Numbers

A list of numbers is **consecutive** if the numbers either occur at a fixed interval, or exhibit a fixed pattern. All the consecutive numbers you will encounter on the exam are integers. Consecutive numbers could be in ascending **or** descending order.

> **Example:** 1, 2, 3, 4, 5, 6 . . . is a series of consecutive positive integers.

> **Example:** −6, −4, −2, 0, 2, 4 . . . is a series of consecutive even numbers.

> **Example:** 5, 7, 11, 13, 17, 19 . . . is a series of consecutive prime numbers.

NUMBER PROPERTIES EXERCISE

Solve the following problems. (Answers are on the following page.)

1. $(-3) \times 4 \times \left(-\dfrac{1}{6}\right) \times \left(-\dfrac{1}{12}\right) \times 16 =$

2. $|6 + (-3)| - |-3 + 6| =$

3. $\left|-\left(\dfrac{1}{4}\right)^2\right| =$

4. Which of the following numbers is divisible by 3: 241; 1,662; 4,915; 3,131?

5. Which of the following numbers is divisible by 4: 126; 324; 442; 598?

6. Which of the following numbers is divisible by 6: 124; 252; 412; 633?

7. What are the first five prime numbers greater than 50?

Find the prime factorization of each of the following:

8. 36

9. 48

10. 162

11. 208

Decide whether each of the following is odd or even. (Don't calculate! Use logic.)

12. $42 \times 21 \times 69$

13. $24 + 32 + 49 + 151$

14. $\left(\dfrac{90}{45} + \dfrac{25}{5}\right) \times 4$

15. $(2,610 + 4,987)(6,321 - 4,106)$

ANSWER KEY—NUMBER PROPERTIES EXERCISE

1. $-\dfrac{8}{3}$

2. 0

3. $\dfrac{1}{16}$

4. 1,662

5. 324

6. 252

7. 53, 59, 61, 67, 71

8. $2 \times 2 \times 3 \times 3$

9. $2 \times 2 \times 2 \times 2 \times 3$

10. $2 \times 3 \times 3 \times 3 \times 3$

11. $2 \times 2 \times 2 \times 2 \times 13$

12. Even

13. Even

14. Even

15. Odd

NUMBER PROPERTIES TEST

Solve the following problems and choose the best answer. (Answers and explanations are at the end of the chapter.)

Basic

1. How many odd integers are between $\frac{10}{3}$ and $\frac{62}{3}$?

   ◯ 19
   ◯ 18
   ◯ 10
   ◯ 9
   ◯ 8

2. What is the greatest integer that will divide evenly into both 36 and 54?

   ◯ 6
   ◯ 9
   ◯ 12
   ◯ 18
   ◯ 27

3. Which of the following is not a factor of 168?

   ◯ 21
   ◯ 24
   ◯ 28
   ◯ 32
   ◯ 42

4. Which of the following is a multiple of all three integers 2, 3, and 5?

   ◯ 525
   ◯ 560
   ◯ 615
   ◯ 620
   ◯ 660

5. What is the smallest positive integer that is evenly divisible by both 21 and 9?

   ◯ 189
   ◯ 126
   ◯ 63
   ◯ 42
   ◯ 21

6. If the sum of three different prime numbers is an even number, what is the smallest of the three?

   ◯ 2
   ◯ 3
   ◯ 5
   ◯ 7
   ◯ It cannot be determined from the information given.

7. The integers A, B, and C are consecutive and $A < B < C$. If $A^2 = C$, which of the following could be the value of A?

   I. -1
   II. 0
   III. 2

   ◯ I only
   ◯ III only
   ◯ I and II only
   ◯ I and III only
   ◯ I, II, and III

Intermediate

8. If *n* is an odd number, which of the following must be even?

   ○ $\dfrac{n-1}{2}$

   ○ $\dfrac{n+1}{2}$

   ○ $n^2 + 2n$

   ○ $2n + 2$

   ○ $3n^2 - 2n$

9. What is the smallest integer greater than 1 that leaves a remainder of 1 when divided by any of the integers 6, 8, and 10?

   ○ 21
   ○ 41
   ○ 121
   ○ 241
   ○ 481

10. If the product of two integers is odd, which of the following must be true?

    ○ The sum of the two integers is an odd number.
    ○ The difference between the two integers is an odd number.
    ○ The square of either integer is an odd number.
    ○ The sum of the squares of the two integers is an odd number.
    ○ The difference between the squares of the two integers is an odd number.

11. For how many positive integers *x* is $\dfrac{130}{x}$ an integer?

    ○ 8
    ○ 7
    ○ 6
    ○ 5
    ○ 3

12. In the repeating decimal 0.097531097531 ..., what is the 44th digit to the right of the decimal point?

    ○ 0
    ○ 1
    ○ 3
    ○ 7
    ○ 9

13. What is the greatest integer that will always evenly divide the sum of three consecutive even integers?

    ○ 2
    ○ 3
    ○ 4
    ○ 6
    ○ 12

14. The sum of three consecutive integers is 312. What is the sum of the next three consecutive integers?

    ○ 315
    ○ 321
    ○ 330
    ○ 415
    ○ 424

15. The integer *P* is greater than 7. If the integer *P* leaves a remainder of 4 when divided by 9, all of the following must be true EXCEPT

    ○ The number that is 4 less than *P* is a multiple of 9.
    ○ The number that is 5 more than *P* is a multiple of 9.
    ○ The number that is 2 more than *P* is a multiple of 3.
    ○ When divided by 3, *P* will leave a remainder of 1.
    ○ When divided by 2, *P* will leave a remainder of 1.

Advanced

16. If the product of two integers is an even number and the sum of the same two integers is an odd number, which of the following must be true?

   ○ The two integers are both odd.
   ○ The two integers are both even.
   ○ One of the two integers is odd and the other is even.
   ○ One of the integers is 1.
   ○ The two integers are consecutive.

17. If both the product and sum of four integers are even, which of the following could be the number of even integers in the group?

   I. 0
   II. 2
   III. 4

   ○ I only
   ○ II only
   ○ III only
   ○ II and III only
   ○ I, II, and III

18. A wire is cut into three equal parts. The resulting segments are then cut into 4, 6, and 8 equal parts respectively. If each of the resulting segments has an integer length, what is the minimum length of the wire?

   ○ 24
   ○ 36
   ○ 48
   ○ 54
   ○ 72

19. How many positive integers less than 60 are equal to the product of a positive multiple of 5 and an even number?

   ○ 4
   ○ 5
   ○ 9
   ○ 10
   ○ 11

AVERAGES

The average (arithmetic mean) of a group of numbers is defined as the sum of the values divided by the number of values.

$$\text{Average value} = \frac{\text{Sum of values}}{\text{Number of values}}$$

Example: Henry buys three items costing $2.00, $0.75, and $0.25. What is the average price?

$$\text{Average price} = \frac{\text{Sum of prices}}{\text{Number of prices}} = \frac{\text{Total price}}{\text{Total items}} = \frac{\$2.00 + \$0.75 + \$0.25}{3}$$
$$= \frac{\$3.00}{3} = \$1.00$$

Rarely on the GMAT might you see a reference to the **median**. If a group of numbers is arranged in numerical order the median is the middle value, or the average of the two middle values . For instance, the median of the numbers 4, 5, 100, 1, and 6 is 5. The median can be quite different from the average. For instance, in the above example, the average is $1.00, while the median is simply the middle of the three prices given, or $0.75.

If we know the average of a group of numbers, and the number of numbers in the group, we can find the **sum** of the numbers. It's as if all the numbers in the group have the average value.

$$\boxed{\text{Sum of values} = \text{Average value} \times \text{Number of values}}$$

Example: The average daily temperature for the first week in January was 31 degrees. If the average temperature for the first six days was 30 degrees, what was the temperature on the seventh day?

The sum for all 7 days = 31 × 7 = 217 degrees.
The sum of the first six days = 30 × 6 = 180 degrees.
The temperature on the seventh day = 217 − 180 = 37 degrees.

For evenly spaced numbers, the average is the middle value. The average of consecutive integers 6, 7, and 8 is 7. The average of 5, 10, 15, and 20 is $12\frac{1}{2}$ (midway between the middle values 10 and 15).

It might be useful to try and think of the average as the "balanced" value. That is, all the numbers below the average are less than the average by an amount that will "balance out" the amount by which the numbers above the average are greater than the average. For example, the average of 3, 5 and 10 is 6. 3 is 3 less than 6 and 5 is 1 less than 6. This in total is 4, which is the same as the amount by which 10 is greater than 6.

Example: The average of 3, 4, 5, and x is 5. What is the value of x?
Think of each value in terms of its position relative to the average, 5.

> 3 is 2 less than the average.
> 4 is 1 less than the average.
> 5 is at the average.

So these 3 terms together are $1 + 2 + 0$, or 3, **less** than the average. Therefore, x must be 3 **more** than the average, to restore the balance at 5. So x is $3 + 5$ or 8.

Average Rate (Average A per B)

$$\text{Average } A \text{ per } B = \frac{\text{Total } A}{\text{Total } B}$$

Example: John travels 30 miles in 2 hours and then 60 miles in 3 hours. What is his average speed in miles per hour?

$$\text{Average miles per hour} = \frac{\text{Total miles}}{\text{Total hours}}$$

$$= \frac{(30 + 60) \text{ miles}}{(2 + 3) \text{ hours}} = \frac{90 \text{ miles}}{5 \text{ hours}} = 18 \text{ miles/hour}$$

STATISTICS AND PROBABILITY

You'll also have to know some basic statistics and probability for the test. **Standard deviation** describes sets of numbers. It is a measure of how spread out a set of numbers is (how much the numbers deviate from the mean). The greater the spread, the higher the standard deviation. You'll never actually have to calculate the standard deviation on test day, but here's how it's calculated:

- Find the average (arithmetic mean) of the set.
- Find the differences between the mean and each value in the set.
- Square each of the differences.
- Find the average of the squared differences.
- Take the positive square root of the average.

Example: For the 5-day listing that follows, which city had the greater standard deviation in high temperatures?
High temperatures, in degrees Fahrenheit, in 2 cities over 5 days:

September	1	2	3	4	5
City *A*	54	61	70	49	56
City *B*	62	56	60	67	65

Even without calculating them out, you can see that City *A* has the greater spread in temperatures, and therefore the greater standard deviation in high temperatures. If you were to go ahead and calculate the standard deviations following the steps described above, you would find that the standard deviation in high temperatures for City $A = \sqrt{\dfrac{254}{5}} \approx 7.1$, while the same for City $B = \sqrt{\dfrac{74}{5}} \approx 3.8$.

On the GMAT, **probability** revolves around situations that have a finite number of outcomes.

$$\text{Probability} = \frac{\text{Number of desired outcomes}}{\text{Number of total possible outcomes}}$$

Example: If you have 12 shirts in a drawer and 9 of them are white, the probability of picking a white shirt at random is $\dfrac{9}{12} = \dfrac{3}{4}$. The probability can also be expressed as 0.75 or 75%.

Many hard probability questions involve finding the probability of a certain outcome after multiple repetitions of the same experiment or different experiments (a coin being tossed several times, etc.). These questions come in two forms: those in which each individual event must occur a certain way, and those in which individual events can have different outcomes.

To determine multiple-event probability where each individual event must occur a certain way:

- Figure out the probability for each individual event.
- Multiply the individual probabilities together.

Example: If 2 students are chosen at random from a class with 5 girls and 5 boys, what's the probability that both students chosen will be girls? The probability that the first student chosen will be a girl is $\dfrac{5}{10} = \dfrac{1}{2}$, and since there would be 4 girls left out of 9 students, the probability that the second student chosen will be a girl is $\dfrac{4}{9}$. So the probability that both students chosen will be girls is $\dfrac{1}{2} \times \dfrac{4}{9} = \dfrac{2}{9}$.

To determine multiple-event probability where individual events can have different types of outcomes, find the *total number of possible outcomes*. Do that by determining the number of possible outcomes for each individual event and multiplying these numbers together. Find the *number of desired outcomes* by listing out the possibilities.

Example: If a fair coin is tossed 4 times, what's the probability that at least 3 of the 4 tosses will come up heads?

There are 2 possible outcomes for each toss, so after 4 tosses there are a total of $2 \times 2 \times 2 \times 2 = 16$ possible outcomes. List out all the possibilities where "at least 3 of the 4 tosses" come up heads:

H, H, H, T   H, T, H, H   H, H, H, H
H, H, T, H   T, H, H, H

There's a total of 5 possible desired outcomes. So the probability that at least 3 of the 4 tosses will come up heads is $\dfrac{\text{Number of desired outcomes}}{\text{Number of possible outcomes}} = \dfrac{5}{16}$.

AVERAGES EXERCISE

In #1–7, find the average. Answer 8–10 as directed. (Answers are on the following page).

1. 10, 12, 16, 17, 20

2. 0, 3, 6, 9

3. 12, 24, 36, 48, 60

4. −0.01, 0.06, 1.9, 1.8, 2.1

5. −4, −2, 4, 0, 2

6. $\dfrac{1}{2}, \dfrac{1}{3}, \dfrac{1}{6}, \dfrac{1}{12}$

7. 100, 100, 100, 0

8. What is the value of x if the average of 2, 4, 6, and x is 3?

9. What is the value of x if the average of −4, 0, 6, and x is 8?

10. If the average of 8, 3, 12, 11, and x is 0, then $x = ?$

ANSWER KEY—AVERAGES EXERCISE

1. 15

2. 4.5, or $\dfrac{9}{2}$

3. 36

4. 1.17

5. 0

6. $\dfrac{13}{48}$

7. 75

8. 0

9. 30

10. -34

AVERAGES TEST

Solve the following problems and choose the best answer. (Answers and explanations are at the end of this chapter.)

Basic

1. If the average (arithmetic mean) of a and -5 is 10, then $a =$

    ○ 25
    ○ 15
    ○ 5
    ○ -10
    ○ -15

2. What is the average (arithmetic mean) of $\frac{1}{2}$ and $\frac{1}{4}$?

    ○ $\frac{1}{6}$
    ○ $\frac{1}{3}$
    ○ $\frac{3}{8}$
    ○ $\frac{5}{9}$
    ○ $\frac{3}{4}$

3. If the average (arithmetic mean) of 8, 11, 25, and p is 15, then $8 + 11 + 25 + p =$

    ○ 16
    ○ 44
    ○ 56
    ○ 60
    ○ 64

4. The average (arithmetic mean) of 6 consecutive integers is $18\frac{1}{2}$. What is the average of the first 5 of these integers?

    ○ $12\frac{1}{2}$
    ○ 15
    ○ 16
    ○ $17\frac{1}{2}$
    ○ 18

5. A violinist practices one hour a day from Monday through Friday. How many hours must she practice on Saturday in order to have an average (arithmetic mean) of two hours a day for the six-day period?

    ○ 5
    ○ 6
    ○ 7
    ○ 8
    ○ 12

6. The average (arithmetic mean) of six numbers is 6. If 3 is subtracted from each of four of the numbers, what is the new average?

    ○ $1\frac{1}{2}$
    ○ 2
    ○ 3
    ○ 4
    ○ $4\frac{1}{2}$

Intermediate

7. What is the sum of the five consecutive even numbers whose average (arithmetic mean) is 12?

   - ○ 30
   - ○ 60
   - ○ 90
   - ○ 120
   - ○ 150

8. If the temperature readings at noon for three consecutive days are $+9°$, $-6°$, and $+8°$, what must the reading be at noon on the fourth day for the average (arithmetic mean) noon temperature of all four days to be $+4°$?

   - ○ $-11°$
   - ○ $-7°$
   - ○ $+2°$
   - ○ $+4°$
   - ○ $+5°$

9. The average (arithmetic mean) weight of the four members of a crew team is 168 pounds. In order to compete in a six-person race, they have recruited a fifth member who weighs 165 pounds. If they must maintain an average weight of at most 170 pounds per team member, what is the maximum allowable weight, in pounds, of their sixth recruit?

   - ○ 165
   - ○ 170
   - ○ 178
   - ○ 183
   - ○ 195

10. What is the average (arithmetic mean) of n, $n + 1$, $n + 2$, and $n + 3$?

    - ○ $n + 1$
    - ○ $n + 1\frac{1}{2}$
    - ○ $n + 2$
    - ○ $n + 2\frac{1}{2}$
    - ○ $n + 6$

11. If the average (arithmetic mean) of $x + 2$, $x + 4$, and $x + 6$ is 0, then $x =$

    - ○ -4
    - ○ -3
    - ○ -2
    - ○ -1
    - ○ 0

12. Fifteen movie theaters average 600 customers per theater per day. If six of the theaters close down but the total theater attendance stays the same, what is the average daily attendance per theater among the remaining theaters?

    - ○ 500
    - ○ 750
    - ○ 1,000
    - ○ 1,200
    - ○ 1,500

KAPLAN

Advanced

13. If the average (arithmetic mean) of 18 consecutive odd integers is 534, then the least of these integers is

    ◯ 517
    ◯ 518
    ◯ 519
    ◯ 521
    ◯ 525

Monday	$75.58
Tuesday	$75.63
Wednesday	$75.42
Thursday	$75.52
Friday	

14. The table above shows the closing price of a stock during a week. If the average (arithmetic mean) closing price for the five days was $75.50, what was the closing price on Friday?

    ◯ $75.35
    ◯ $75.40
    ◯ $75.42
    ◯ $75.45
    ◯ $75.48

15. The average (arithmetic mean) of 6 positive numbers is 5. If the average of the least and greatest of these numbers is 7, what is the average of the other four numbers?

    ◯ 3
    ◯ 4
    ◯ 5
    ◯ 6
    ◯ 7

16. If the average (arithmetic mean) of a, b, and 7 is 13, what is the average of $a + 3$, $b - 5$, and 6?

    ◯ 7
    ◯ 9
    ◯ 10
    ◯ 12
    ◯ 16

RATIOS

A ratio is a comparison of two quantities by division.

Ratios may be written either with a fraction bar $\left(\dfrac{x}{y}\right)$ or with a colon ($x : y$) or with English terms (ratio of x to y). We recommend the first way, since ratios can be treated as fractions for the purposes of computation. Ratios can (and in most cases, should) be reduced to lowest terms just as fractions are reduced.

> **Example:** Joe is 16 years old and Mary is 12.
>
> The ratio of Joe's age to Mary's age is $\dfrac{16}{12}$. (Read "16 to 12.")
>
> $$\frac{16}{12} = \frac{4}{3} \ \text{ or } \ 4 : 3$$

In a ratio of two numbers, the numerator is often associated with the word *of;* the denominator with the word *to.*

The ratio **of** 3 **to** 4 is $\dfrac{\text{of } 3}{\text{to } 4} = \dfrac{3}{4}$.

$$\boxed{\text{Ratio} = \frac{\text{of}\ldots}{\text{to}\ldots}}$$

> **Example:** In a box of doughnuts, 12 are sugar and 18 are chocolate. What is the ratio of sugar doughnuts to chocolate doughnuts?
>
> $$\text{Ratio} = \frac{\text{of sugar}}{\text{to chocolate}} = \frac{12}{18} = \frac{2}{3}$$

We frequently deal with ratios by working with a **proportion**. A proportion is simply an equation in which two ratios are set equal to one another.

Ratios typically deal with "parts" and "wholes." The whole is the entire set; for instance, all the workers in a factory. The part is a certain section of the whole; for instance, the female workers in the factory.

The ratio of a part to a whole is usually called a fraction. "What fraction of the workers are female?" means the same thing as "What is the ratio of the number of female workers to the total number of workers?"

A fraction can represent the ratio of a part to a whole:

$$\frac{\text{Part}}{\text{Whole}} \ \text{ or } \ \text{Part : Whole.}$$

Example: There are 15 men and 20 women in a class. What fraction of the students are female?

$$Fraction = \frac{Part}{Whole}$$

$$= \frac{\# \text{ of female students}}{\text{Total \# of students}}$$

$$= \frac{20}{15 + 20}$$

$$= \frac{^{4}20}{35_{7}}$$

$$= \frac{4}{7}$$

This means that $\frac{4}{7}$ of the students are female, or 4 out of every 7 students are female, or the ratio of female students to total students is $4:7$.

Part : Part Ratios and Part : Whole Ratios

A ratio can compare either a part to another part or a part to a whole. One type of ratio can readily be converted to the other **if** all the parts together equal the whole and there is no overlap among the parts (that is, if the whole is equal to the sum of its parts).

Example: The ratio of domestic sales to foreign sales of a certain product is $3:5$. What fraction of the total sales are domestic sales? (Note: This is the same as asking for the ratio of domestic sales to total sales.)

In this case the whole (total sales) is equal to the sum of the parts (domestic and foreign sales). We **can** convert from a **part:part** ratio to a **part:whole** ratio.

Of every 8 sales of the product, 3 are domestic and 5 are foreign. The ratio of domestic sales to total sales is $\frac{3}{8}$ or $3:8$.

Example: The ratio of domestic to foreign sales of a certain product is $3:5$. What is the ratio of domestic sales to European sales?

Here we cannot convert from a **part:whole** ratio (domestic sales:total sales) to a **part:part** ratio (domestic sales:European sales) because we don't know if there are any other sales besides domestic and European sales. The question doesn't say that the product is sold only domestically and in Europe, so we cannot assume there are no African, Australian, Asian, etc., sales, and so the ratio asked for here cannot be determined.

Ratios with more than two terms: Ratios involving more than two terms are governed by the same principles. These ratios contain more relationships, so they convey more information than two-term ratios. Ratios involving more than two terms are usually ratios of various parts, and it is usually the case that the sum of these parts does equal the whole, which makes it possible to find **part:whole** ratios as well.

Example: Given that the ratio of men to women to children in a room is $4:3:2$, what other ratios can be determined?

Quite a few. The **whole** here is the number of people in the room, and since every person is either a man, a woman, or a child, we can determine **part:whole** ratios for each of these parts. Of every nine $(4 + 3 + 2)$ people in the room, 4 are men, 3 are women, and 2 are children. This gives us three **part:whole** ratios:

$$\text{Ratio of men : total people} = 4:9 \ \text{ or } \ \frac{4}{9}$$

$$\text{Ratio of women : total people} = 3:9 = 1:3 \ \text{ or } \ \frac{1}{3}$$

$$\text{Ratio of children : total people} = 2:9 \ \text{ or } \ \frac{2}{9}$$

In addition, from any ratio of more than two terms, we can determine various two-term ratios among the parts.

$$\text{Ratio of women : men} = 3 : 4$$

$$\text{Ratio of men : children} = 4 : 2, \text{ or } 2 : 1$$

And finally if we were asked to establish a relationship between the number of adults in the room and the number of children, we would find that this would be possible as well. For every 2 children there are 4 men and 3 women, which is $4 + 3$ or 7 adults. So:

$$\text{Ratio of children : adults} = 2 : 7, \text{ or}$$

$$\text{Ratio of adults : children} = 7 : 2$$

Naturally, a test question will require you to determine only one or at most two of these ratios, but knowing how much information is contained in a given ratio will help you to determine quickly which questions are solvable and which, if any, are not.

Ratio versus Actual Number

Ratios are always reduced to simplest form. If a team's ratio of wins to losses is $5:3$, this does not necessarily mean that the team has won 5 games and lost 3. For instance, if a team has won 30 games and lost 18, the ratio is still $5:3$. Unless we know the **actual number** of games played (or the actual number won or lost), we don't know the actual values of the parts in the ratio.

Example: In a classroom of 30 students, the ratio of the boys in the class to students in the class is 2 : 5. How many are boys?

We are given a part to whole ratio (boys : students). This ratio is a fraction. Multiplying this fraction by the actual whole gives the value of the corresponding part. There are 30 students; $\frac{2}{5}$ of them are boys, so the number of boys must be $\frac{2}{5} \times 30$.

$$\frac{2 \text{ boys}}{_1 \cancel{5} \text{ students}} \times \cancel{30}^{\,6} \text{ students} = 2 \times 6 = 12 \text{ boys}$$

PICKING NUMBERS

Ratio problems that do not contain any actual values, just ratios, are ideal for solving by picking numbers. Just make sure that the numbers you pick are divisible by both the numerator and denominator of the ratio.

Example: A building has $\frac{2}{5}$ of its floors below ground. What is the ratio of the number of floors above ground to the number of floors below ground?

  ⬭ 5 : 2
  ⬭ 3 : 2
  ⬭ 4 : 3
  ⬭ 3 : 5
  ⬭ 2 : 5

Pick a value for the total number of floors, one that is divisible by both the numerator and denominator of $\frac{2}{5}$. Let's say 10. Then, since $\frac{2}{5}$ of the floors are below ground, $\frac{2}{5} \times 10$, or 4 floors are below ground. This leaves 6 floors above ground. Therefore, the ratio of the number of floors above ground to the number of floors below ground is 6 : 4, or 3 : 2, choice (2).

We'll see more on ratios, and how we can pick numbers to simplify things, in the Problem Solving chapter.

Rates

A rate is a ratio that relates two different kinds of quantities. Speed, which is the ratio of distance traveled to time elapsed, is an example of a rate.

When we talk about rates, we usually use the word *per,* as in "miles per hour," "cost per item," etc. Since *per* means "for one," or "for each," we express the rates as ratios reduced to a denominator of 1.

Example: John travels 50 miles in two hours. His average rate is:

$$\frac{50 \text{ miles}}{2 \text{ hours}} \text{ or 25 miles per hour}$$

Note: We frequently speak in terms of "average rate," since it may be improbable (as in the case of speed) that the rate has been constant over the period in question. See the Average section for more details.

RATIOS EXERCISE

Reduce each of the following ratios to lowest terms. (Answers are on the following page.)

1. $8 : 128$

2. $72 : 20$

3. $14.2 : 71$

4. $6.9 : 2.1$

5. $1.6 : 0.4 : 0.16$

6. $0.75 : 1.85$

7. $81 : \dfrac{1}{3}$

8. $\dfrac{1}{3} : \dfrac{1}{4}$

9. $\dfrac{5}{12} : \dfrac{1}{12}$

10. $\dfrac{3}{16} : \dfrac{5}{8}$

ANSWER KEY—RATIOS EXERCISE

1. 1 : 16
2. 18 : 5
3. 1 : 5
4. 23 : 7
5. 20 : 5 : 2
6. 15 : 37
7. 243 : 1
8. 4 : 3
9. 5 : 1
10. 3 : 10

RATIOS TEST

Solve the following problems and choose the best answer. (Answers and explanations are at the end of the chapter.)

Basic

1. In a certain pet show there are 24 hamsters and 9 cats. What is the ratio of cats to hamsters at this pet show?

   - ⃝ 1 : 4
   - ⃝ 1 : 3
   - ⃝ 3 : 8
   - ⃝ 2 : 3
   - ⃝ 3 : 4

2. If the ratio of boys to girls in a class is 5 : 3, and there are 65 boys, how many girls must there be in the class?

   - ⃝ 13
   - ⃝ 18
   - ⃝ 26
   - ⃝ 36
   - ⃝ 39

3. On a certain street map, $\frac{3}{4}$ inch represents one mile. What distance, in miles, is represented by $1\frac{3}{4}$ inches?

   - ⃝ $1\frac{1}{2}$
   - ⃝ $1\frac{3}{4}$
   - ⃝ $2\frac{1}{3}$
   - ⃝ $2\frac{1}{2}$
   - ⃝ $5\frac{1}{4}$

4. After spending $\frac{5}{12}$ of his salary, a man has $140 left. What is his salary?

   - ⃝ $200
   - ⃝ $240
   - ⃝ $300
   - ⃝ $420
   - ⃝ $583

5. In a local election, votes were cast for Mr. Dyer, Ms. Frau, and Mr. Borak in the ratio of 4 : 3 : 2. If there were no other candidates and none of the 1,800 voters cast more than one vote, how many votes did Ms. Frau receive?

   - ⃝ 200
   - ⃝ 300
   - ⃝ 400
   - ⃝ 600
   - ⃝ 900

6. The ratio of men to women at a party is exactly 3 : 2. If there are a total of 120 people at the party, how many of them are women?

   - ⃝ 36
   - ⃝ 40
   - ⃝ 48
   - ⃝ 72
   - ⃝ 80

7. The weights of two ships are in the ratio of 5 : 9. If together they weigh 5,600 tons, how many tons does the larger ship weigh?

   - ⃝ 2,000
   - ⃝ 2,400
   - ⃝ 3,000
   - ⃝ 3,200
   - ⃝ 3,600

KAPLAN

8. A laboratory has 55 rabbits, some white and the rest brown. Which of the following could be the ratio of white rabbits to brown rabbits in the lab?

   ○ 1 : 3
   ○ 3 : 8
   ○ 5 : 11
   ○ 3 : 4
   ○ 5 : 1

9. The Greenpoint factory produced two-fifths of the Consolidated Brick Company's bricks in 2008. If the Greenpoint factory produced 1,400 tons of bricks in 2008, what was the Consolidated Brick Company's total output that year, in tons?

   ○ 700
   ○ 2,100
   ○ 2,800
   ○ 3,500
   ○ 7,000

10. A ratio of $3\frac{1}{4}$ to $5\frac{1}{4}$ is equivalent to a ratio of

    ○ 3 to 5
    ○ 13 to 21
    ○ 5 to 7
    ○ 7 to 5
    ○ 5 to 3

11. A certain ship floats with $\frac{3}{5}$ of its weight above the water. What is the ratio of the ship's submerged weight to its exposed weight?

    ○ 3 : 8
    ○ 2 : 5
    ○ 3 : 5
    ○ 2 : 3
    ○ 5 : 3

12. One-twentieth of the entrants in a contest won prizes. If 30 prizes were won, and no entrant won more than one prize, how many entrants did NOT win prizes?

    ○ 30
    ○ 300
    ○ 540
    ○ 570
    ○ 600

13. If a kilogram is equal to approximately 2.2 pounds, which of the following is the best approximation of the number of kilograms in one pound?

    ○ $\frac{11}{5}$
    ○ $\frac{5}{8}$
    ○ $\frac{5}{11}$
    ○ $\frac{1}{3}$
    ○ $\frac{1}{5}$

Intermediate

14. A recipe for eggnog calls for 2 eggs for every 3 cups of milk. If there are 4 cups in a quart, how many eggs will be needed to mix with 6 quarts of milk?

    ○ 12
    ○ 16
    ○ 24
    ○ 36
    ○ 48

15. If the ratio of boys to girls in a class is 5 to 3, which of the following could not be the number of students in the class?

    ○ 32
    ○ 36
    ○ 40
    ○ 48
    ○ 56

16. A student's grade in a course is determined by 4 quizzes and 1 exam. If the exam counts twice as much as each of the quizzes, what fraction of the final grade is determined by the exam?

    ○ $\frac{1}{6}$
    ○ $\frac{1}{5}$
    ○ $\frac{1}{3}$
    ○ $\frac{1}{4}$
    ○ $\frac{1}{2}$

17. If cement, gravel, and sand are to be mixed in the ratio 3 : 5 : 7 respectively, and 5 tons of cement are available, how many tons of the mixture can be made? (Assume there is enough gravel and sand available to use all the cement.)

    ○ 15
    ○ 20
    ○ 25
    ○ 30
    ○ 75

18. Bob finishes the first half of an exam in two-thirds the time it takes him to finish the second half. If the whole exam takes him an hour, how many minutes does he spend on the first half of the exam?

    ○ 20
    ○ 24
    ○ 27
    ○ 36
    ○ 40

19. In a certain factory with 2,700 workers, one-third of the workers are unskilled. If 600 of the unskilled workers are apprentices, what fraction of the unskilled workers are not apprentices?

    ○ $\frac{1}{9}$
    ○ $\frac{1}{7}$
    ○ $\frac{1}{5}$
    ○ $\frac{1}{3}$
    ○ $\frac{1}{2}$

Advanced

20. An alloy of tin and copper has 6 pounds of copper for every 2 pounds of tin. If 200 pounds of this alloy are made, how many pounds of tin are required?

   ⬭ 25
   ⬭ 50
   ⬭ 100
   ⬭ 125
   ⬭ 150

21. A sporting goods store ordered an equal number of white and yellow tennis balls. The tennis ball company delivered 30 extra white balls, making the ratio of white balls to yellow balls 6 : 5. How many tennis balls did the store originally order?

   ⬭ 120
   ⬭ 150
   ⬭ 180
   ⬭ 300
   ⬭ 330

22. If $a = 2b$, $\frac{1}{2}b = c$, and $4c = 3d$, then what is the ratio of d to a ?

   ⬭ $\frac{1}{3}$
   ⬭ $\frac{3}{4}$
   ⬭ 1
   ⬭ $\frac{4}{3}$
   ⬭ 3

23. An oculist charges $30.00 for an eye examination, frames, and glass lenses, but $42.00 for an eye examination, frames, and plastic lenses. If the plastic lenses cost four times as much as the glass lenses, how much do the glass lenses cost?

   ⬭ $2
   ⬭ $4
   ⬭ $5
   ⬭ $6
   ⬭ $8

24. If $\frac{1}{2}$ of the number of white mice in a certain laboratory is $\frac{1}{8}$ of the total number of mice, and $\frac{1}{3}$ of the number of gray mice is $\frac{1}{9}$ of the total number of mice, then what is the ratio of white mice to gray mice?

   ⬭ 16 : 27
   ⬭ 2 : 3
   ⬭ 3 : 4
   ⬭ 4 : 5
   ⬭ 8 : 9

PERCENTS

Percents are one of the most commonly used math relationships. Percents are also a popular topic on the GRE and GMAT. *Percent* is just another word for *hundredth*. Therefore, 19% (19 percent) means 19 hundredths

$$\text{or } \frac{19}{100}$$

or 0.19

or 19 out of every 100 things

or 19 parts out of a whole of 100 parts.

They're all just different names for the same thing.

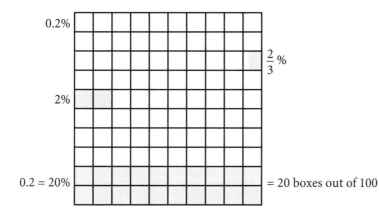

Each box at the left represents 1%. 100 boxes = (100)(1%) = 100% = 1 whole. Note that we have, in increasing order, 0.2%, $\frac{2}{3}$%, 2%, and 20%.

Making and Dropping Percents

To change a decimal or fraction to a percent, multiply by 100%. Since 100% means 100 hundredths or 1, multiplying by 100% will not change the value.

> **Example:** $0.17 = 0.17 \times 100\% = 17\%$

> **Example:** $\frac{1}{4} = \frac{1}{4} \times 100\% = 25\%$

To change a percent to a fraction, divide by 100%. Once again, dividing by 100% will not change the value.

> **Example:** $32\% = \frac{32\%}{100\%} = \frac{32}{100} = \frac{8}{25}$

> **Example:** $\frac{1}{2}\% = \frac{\frac{1}{2}\%}{100\%} = \frac{1}{200}$

To change a percent to a decimal, just drop the percent and move the decimal point two places to the left. (This is the same as dividing by 100%.)

Example: $0.8\% = 0.00.8 = 0.008$

Example: $2\frac{1}{4}\% = 2.25\% = 0.02.25 = 0.0225$

Common Percent and Fractional Equivalents

$\frac{1}{20} = 5\%$	$\frac{1}{10} = 10\%$	$\frac{1}{8} = 12\frac{1}{2}\%$	$\frac{1}{6} = 16\frac{2}{3}\%$
$\frac{1}{5} = 20\%$	$\frac{1}{4} = 25\%$	$\frac{1}{3} = 33\frac{1}{3}\%$	$\frac{1}{2} = 50\%$

$10\% = \frac{1}{10}$

$20\% = \frac{2}{10} = \frac{1}{5}$

$30\% = \frac{3}{10}$

$40\% = \frac{4}{10} = \frac{2}{5}$

$50\% = \frac{5}{10} = \frac{1}{2}$

$60\% = \frac{6}{10} = \frac{3}{5}$

$70\% = \frac{7}{10}$

$80\% = \frac{8}{10} = \frac{4}{5}$

$90\% = \frac{9}{10}$

$100\% = \frac{10}{10} = 1$

$12\frac{1}{2}\% = \frac{1}{8}$

$25\% = \frac{2}{8} = \frac{1}{4}$

$37\frac{1}{2}\% = \frac{3}{8}$

$50\% = \frac{4}{8} = \frac{2}{4} = \frac{1}{2}$

$62\frac{1}{2}\% = \frac{5}{8}$

$75\% = \frac{6}{8} = \frac{3}{4}$

$87\frac{1}{2}\% = \frac{7}{8}$

$16\frac{2}{3}\% = \frac{1}{6}$

$33\frac{1}{3}\% = \frac{2}{6} = \frac{1}{3}$

$50\% = \frac{3}{6} = \frac{1}{2}$

$66\frac{2}{3}\% = \frac{4}{6} = \frac{2}{3}$

$83\frac{1}{3}\% = \frac{5}{6}$

Being familiar with these equivalents can save you a lot of time!

Percent Problems

Most percent problems can be solved by plugging into one formula:

$$\boxed{\text{Percent} \times \text{Whole} = \text{Part}}$$

This formula has three variables: percent, whole, and part. In percent problems, generally, the **whole** will be associated with the word *of;* the **part** will be associated with the word *is.* The percent can be represented as the ratio of the part to the whole, or the *is* to the *of.*

Percent problems will usually give you two of the variables and ask for the third. See the examples of the three types of problems below. On the GMAT, it is usually easiest to change the percent to a common fraction and work it out from there.

Example: What is 25% of 36?

Here we are given the percent and the whole. To find the part, change the percent to a fraction, then multiply. Use the formula above.

$$\text{Percent} \times \text{Whole} = \text{Part}$$

Since $25\% = \dfrac{1}{4}$, we are really asking what one-fourth of 36 is.

$$\frac{1}{4} \times 36 = 9.$$

Example: 13 is $33\dfrac{1}{3}\%$ of what number?

Here we are given the percent and the part and asked for the whole.
If Percent × Whole = Part, then

$$\text{Whole} = \frac{\text{Part}}{\text{Percent}}. \quad \text{Recall that } 33\frac{1}{3}\% = \frac{1}{3}.$$

$$= \frac{13}{\frac{1}{3}}$$

$$= 13 \times \frac{3}{1} = 39$$

We can avoid all this algebra: All we are asked is "13 is one-third of what number?" 13 is one-third of 3 × 13 or 39.

Example: 18 is what percent of 3?

Here we are given the whole (3) and the part (18) and asked for the percent.
If % × Whole = Part, then

$$\% = \frac{\text{Part}}{\text{Whole}}$$

Since the part and the whole are both integers, and we're looking for a percent, we're going to have to make our result into a percent by multiplying it by 100%.

$$\% = \frac{18}{3}(100\%) = 6(100\%) = 600\%$$

Note here that we can find the percent as the "is" part divided by the "of" part:

What percent is 18 of 3?

$$\% = \frac{\text{is}}{\text{of}} = \frac{18}{3} = 6 = 600\%$$

Alternative method: The base 3 represents 100%. Since 18 is 6 times as large, the percent equals $6 \times 100\% = 600\%$.

Percent increase and decrease:

$$\% \text{ increase} = \frac{\text{Amount of increase}}{\text{Original whole}}(100\%)$$

$$\% \text{ decrease} = \frac{\text{Amount of decrease}}{\text{Original whole}}(100\%)$$

New whole = Original whole $\pm$ Amount of change

When dealing with percent increase and percent decrease always be careful to put the amount of increase or decrease over the **original** whole, not the new whole.

Example: If a $120 dress is increased in price by 25 percent, what is the new selling price? Our original whole here is $120, and the percent increase is 25%. Change 25% to a fraction, $\frac{1}{4}$, and use the formula.

Amount of increase = % increase $\times$ Original whole

$$= 25\% \times \$120$$

$$= \frac{1}{4} \times \$120$$

$$= \$30$$

To find the **new whole** (the new selling price):

New whole = Original whole + Amount of increase

$$= \$120 + \$30 = \mathbf{\$150}$$

Combining percents: On some problems, you'll need to find more than one percent, or a percent of a percent. Be careful. You can't just add percents, unless you're taking the percents of the same whole. Let's look at an example.

Example: The price of an antique is reduced by 20 percent and then this price is reduced by 10 percent. If the antique originally cost $200, what is its final price?

First, we know that the price is reduced by 20%. That's the same thing as saying that the price becomes (100% − 20%), or 80% of what it originally was. 80% of $200 is equal to $\frac{8}{10} \times \$200$, or $160. Then, **this** price is reduced by 10%. 10% × $160 = $16, so the final price of the antique is $160 − $16 = $144.

A common error in this kind of problem is to assume that the final price is simply a 30 percent reduction of the original price. That would mean that the final price is 70 percent of the original, or 70% × $200 = $140. But, as we've just seen, this is NOT correct. Adding or subtracting percents directly only works if those percents are being taken of the same whole. In this example, since we took 20% of the original price, and then 10% of that reduced price, we can't just add the percents together.

More practice with percent word problems can be found in the word problems chapter.

PERCENTS EXERCISE

Solve the following problems as directed. (Answers are on the following page.)

Convert to a percent:

1. $0.002 =$

2. $\dfrac{7}{25} =$

3. $1.31 =$

4. $\dfrac{12}{5} =$

5. $\dfrac{1}{400} =$

6. $0.025 =$

7. $\dfrac{1}{80} =$

8. $\dfrac{3}{20} =$

9. $0.675 =$

10. $\dfrac{5}{2} =$

Convert to a fraction:

11. $16\% =$

12. $24\% =$

13. $0.036\% =$

14. $125\% =$

15. $\dfrac{1}{4}\% =$

16. $0.8\% =$

17. $\dfrac{3}{2}\% =$

18. $95\% =$

19. $65\dfrac{1}{2}\% =$

20. $12.6\% =$

Calculate:

21. 50% of $12 =$

22. 75% of $16 =$

23. 150% of $4 =$

24. 24% of $2 =$

25. 10% of $50 =$

**ANSWER KEY
BEGINS ON NEXT PAGE**

ANSWER KEY—PERCENTS EXERCISE

1. 0.2%

2. 28%

3. 131%

4. 240%

5. 0.25%

6. 2.5%

7. 1.25%

8. 15%

9. 67.5%

10. 250%

11. $\dfrac{4}{25}$

12. $\dfrac{6}{25}$

13. $\dfrac{9}{25,000}$

14. $1\dfrac{1}{4}$ or $\dfrac{5}{4}$

15. $\dfrac{1}{400}$

16. $\dfrac{1}{125}$

17. $\dfrac{3}{200}$

18. $\dfrac{19}{20}$

19. $\dfrac{131}{200}$

20. $\dfrac{63}{500}$

21. 6

22. 12

23. 6

24. 0.48

25. 5

PERCENT TEST

Solve the following problems and choose the best answer. (Answers and explanations are at the end of this chapter.)

Basic

1. 200 percent more than 30 is

   ○ 36
   ○ 60
   ○ 90
   ○ 120
   ○ 360

2. What percent of 1,600 is 2?

   ○ $\frac{1}{8}\%$
   ○ 0.8%
   ○ $1\frac{1}{4}\%$
   ○ 8%
   ○ $12\frac{1}{2}\%$

3. What is 0.25 percent of $\frac{4}{3}$?

   ○ $\frac{1}{3,000}$
   ○ $\frac{1}{300}$
   ○ $\frac{1}{30}$
   ○ $\frac{1}{20}$
   ○ $\frac{1}{3}$

4. What percent of 4 is $\frac{2}{3}$ of 8?

   ○ 25%
   ○ $66\frac{2}{3}\%$
   ○ 120%
   ○ $133\frac{1}{3}\%$
   ○ 150%

5. 10 percent of 20 percent of 30 is

   ○ 0.3
   ○ 0.6
   ○ 1.5
   ○ 3
   ○ 6

6. If 60 percent of W equals 20 percent of T, what percent is W of T?

   ○ 12%
   ○ $33\frac{1}{3}\%$
   ○ 60%
   ○ 120%
   ○ $133\frac{1}{3}\%$

7. 36 percent of 18 is 18 percent of what number?

   ○ 9
   ○ 24
   ○ 36
   ○ 40
   ○ 48

KAPLAN

8. The price of a newspaper rises from 5 cents to 15 cents. What is the percent increase in price?

   ○ 2%
   ○ 50%
   ○ 150%
   ○ 200%
   ○ 300%

9. Joseph bought a house for $80,000. If he sells it for a profit of 12.5 percent of the original cost, what is the selling price of the house?

   ○ $92,500
   ○ $90,000
   ○ $89,000
   ○ $88,000
   ○ $80,900

10. A closet contains 24 pairs of shoes. If 25 percent of those pairs of shoes are black, how many pairs are NOT black?

    ○ 4
    ○ 6
    ○ 12
    ○ 18
    ○ 20

11. Bob took 20 math tests last year. If he failed six of them, what percent of the math tests did he pass?

    ○ 37.5%
    ○ 60%
    ○ 62.5%
    ○ $66\frac{2}{3}\%$
    ○ 70%

12. An item is priced 20 percent more than its wholesale cost. If the wholesale cost was $800, what is the price of the item?

    ○ $900
    ○ $960
    ○ $1,000
    ○ $1,040
    ○ $1,200

13. Over a ten-year period Pat's income rose from $15,000 to $35,000. What was the percent increase in her income?

    ○ $33\frac{1}{3}\%$
    ○ 42.8%
    ○ $133\frac{1}{3}\%$
    ○ 142.8%
    ○ $233\frac{1}{3}\%$

14. Of the 20 people who won prize money, 7 have come forward to claim their winnings. What percent of the people have not yet appeared?

    ○ 20%
    ○ 35%
    ○ 42%
    ○ 65%
    ○ 70%

15. A $100 chair is increased in price by 50 percent. If the chair is then discounted by 50 percent of the new price, at what price will it be offered for sale?

    ○ $150
    ○ $125
    ○ $100
    ○ $75
    ○ $50

Intermediate

16. If 65 percent of x is 195, what is 75 percent of x?

   ◯ 215
   ◯ 225
   ◯ 235
   ◯ 250
   ◯ 260

17. During October, a store had sales of $30,000. If this was a 20 percent increase over the September sales, what were the September sales?

   ◯ $22,500
   ◯ $24,000
   ◯ $25,000
   ◯ $27,000
   ◯ $28,000

18. In a state lottery, 40 percent of the money collected goes towards education. If during a certain week 6.4 million dollars were obtained for education, how much money was collected in the lottery during that week, in millions of dollars?

   ◯ 25.6
   ◯ 16.0
   ◯ 8.96
   ◯ 8.0
   ◯ 2.56

19. A 25-ounce solution is 20 percent alcohol. If 50 ounces of water are added to it, what percent of the new solution is alcohol?

   ◯ 5%
   ◯ $6\frac{2}{3}\%$
   ◯ 8%
   ◯ $10\frac{1}{2}\%$
   ◯ 20%

20. After getting a 20 percent discount, Jerry paid $100 for a bicycle. How much did the bicycle originally cost?

   ◯ $80
   ◯ $82
   ◯ $116
   ◯ $120
   ◯ $125

21. A stock decreases in value by 20 percent. By what percent must the stock price increase to reach its former value?

   ◯ 15%
   ◯ 20%
   ◯ 25%
   ◯ 30%
   ◯ 40%

Advanced

22. The population of a certain town increases by 50 percent every 50 years. If the population in 1950 was 810, in what year was the population 160?

    ○ 1650
    ○ 1700
    ○ 1750
    ○ 1800
    ○ 1850

23. Five percent of a certain grass seed is timothy. If the amount of the mixture needed to plant one acre contains 2 pounds of timothy, how many acres can be planted with 240 pounds of the seed mixture?

    ○ 6
    ○ 12
    ○ 20
    ○ 24
    ○ 120

24. A brush salesman earns $50 salary each month plus 10 percent commission on the value of his sales. If he earned $200 last month, what was the total value of his sales?

    ○ $1,000
    ○ $1,200
    ○ $1,500
    ○ $2,000
    ○ $2,500

25. A man bought 10 crates of oranges for $80 total. If he lost 2 of the crates, at what price would he have to sell each of the remaining crates in order to earn a total profit of 25 percent of the total cost?

    ○ $10.00
    ○ $12.50
    ○ $15.00
    ○ $100.00
    ○ $120.00

POWERS AND ROOTS

Rules of Operation with Powers

In the term $3x^2$, 3 is the **coefficient**, x is the **base**, and 2 is the **exponent**. The exponent refers to the number of times the base is multiplied by itself, or how many times the base is a factor. For instance, in 4^3, there are 3 factors of $4: 4^3 = 4 \cdot 4 \cdot 4 = 64$.

A number multiplied by itself twice is called the **square** of that number, e.g., x^2 is x squared.
A number multiplied by itself three times is called the **cube** of that number, e.g., 4^3 is 4 cubed.

To multiply two terms with the same base, keep the base and add the exponents.

Example: $2^2 \cdot 2^3 = (2 \cdot 2)(2 \cdot 2 \cdot 2)$ or $2^2 \cdot 2^3 = 2^{2+3}$

$\qquad\qquad\quad = (2 \cdot 2 \cdot 2 \cdot 2 \cdot 2)$ $\qquad\qquad = 2^5$

$\qquad\qquad\quad = 2^5$

Example: $x^4 \cdot x^7 = x^{4+7} = x^{11}$

To divide two terms with the same base, keep the base and subtract the exponent of the denominator from the exponent of the numerator.

Example: $4^4 \div 4^2 = \dfrac{4 \cdot 4 \cdot 4 \cdot 4}{4 \cdot 4}$ or $4^4 \div 4^2 = 4^{4-2}$

$\qquad\qquad\quad = \dfrac{4 \cdot 4}{1}$ $\qquad\qquad\qquad = 4^2$

$\qquad\qquad\quad = 4^2$

To raise a power to another power, multiply the exponents.

Example: $(3^2)^4 = (3 \cdot 3)^4$ or $(3^2)^4 = 3^{2 \times 4}$

$\qquad\qquad\quad = (3 \cdot 3)(3 \cdot 3)(3 \cdot 3)(3 \cdot 3)$ $\qquad\qquad = 3^8$

$\qquad\qquad\quad = 3^8$

Any nonzero number raised to the zero power is equal to 1. If $a \neq 0$, $a^\circ = 1$. 0° is undefined.

A negative exponent indicates a reciprocal. To arrive at an equivalent expression, take the reciprocal of the base and change the sign of the exponent.

$$a^{-n} = \frac{1}{a^n} \text{ or } \left(\frac{1}{a}\right)^n$$

Example: $2^{-3} = \left(\dfrac{1}{2}\right)^3 = \dfrac{1}{2^3} = \dfrac{1}{8}$

A fractional exponent indicates a **root**.

$(a)^{\frac{1}{n}} = \sqrt[n]{a}$ (read "the nth root of a." If no "n" is present, the radical sign means a square root.)

Example: $8^{\frac{1}{3}} = \sqrt[3]{8} = 2$

On the GMAT you will probably only see the square root. The square root of a nonnegative number x is equal to the number which when multiplied by itself gives you x. Every positive number has two square roots, one positive and one negative. The positive square root of 25 is 5, since $5^2 = 25$; the negative square root of 25 is -5, since $(-5)^2 = 25$ also. Other types of roots have appeared on the tests (cube root, or $\sqrt[3]{\ }$, is an example), but they tend to be extremely rare.

Note: In the expression $3x^2$, only the x is being squared, not the 3. In other words, $3x^2 = 3(x^2)$. If we wanted to square the 3 as well, we would write $(3x)^2$. (Remember that in the order of operations we raise to a power **before** we multiply, so in $3x^2$ we square x and **then** multiply by 3.)

Rules of Operations with Roots

By convention, the symbol $\sqrt{\ }$ (radical) means the **positive** square root only.

Example: $\sqrt{9} = +3; \quad -\sqrt{9} = -3$

Even though there are two different numbers whose square is 9 (both 3 and -3), we say that $\sqrt{9}$ is the positive number 3 only.

When it comes to the four basic arithmetic operations, we treat radicals in much the same way we would treat variables.

Addition and Subtraction: Only like radicals can be added to or subtracted from one another.

Example: $2\sqrt{3} + 4\sqrt{2} - \sqrt{2} - 3\sqrt{3} = (4\sqrt{2} - \sqrt{2}) + (2\sqrt{3} - 3\sqrt{3})$ [Note: $\sqrt{2} = 1\sqrt{2}$]
$$= 3\sqrt{2} + (-\sqrt{3})$$
$$= 3\sqrt{2} - \sqrt{3}$$

Multiplication and Division: To multiply or divide one radical by another, multiply or divide the numbers outside the radical signs, then the numbers inside the radical signs.

Example: $(6\sqrt{3}) \times (2\sqrt{5}) = (6 \times 2) \cdot (\sqrt{3} \times \sqrt{5}) = 12\sqrt{3 \times 5} = 12\sqrt{15}$

Example: $12\sqrt{15} \div 2\sqrt{5} = (12 \div 2) \cdot (\sqrt{15} \div \sqrt{5}) = 6\left(\sqrt{\dfrac{15}{5}}\right) = 6\sqrt{3}$

Example: $\dfrac{4\sqrt{18}}{2\sqrt{6}} = \left(\dfrac{4}{2}\right)\left(\dfrac{\sqrt{18}}{\sqrt{6}}\right) = 2\left(\sqrt{\dfrac{18}{6}}\right) = 2\sqrt{3}$

If the number inside the radical is a multiple of a perfect square, the expression can be simplified by factoring out the perfect square.

Example: $\sqrt{72} = \sqrt{36 \times 2} = \sqrt{36} \times \sqrt{2} = 6\sqrt{2}$

Powers of 10

The exponent of a power of 10 tells us how many zeros the number would contain if written out.

Example: $10^6 = 1,000,000$ (6 zeros) since 10 multiplied by itself six times is equal to 1,000,000.

When multiplying a number by a power of 10, move the decimal point to the right the same number of places as the number of zeros in that power of 10.

Example: $0.029 \times 10^3 = 0.029 \times 1,000 = 0.029. = 29$

3 places

When dividing by a power of 10, move the decimal point the corresponding number of places to the left. (Note that dividing by 10^4 is the same as multiplying by 10^{-4}.)

Example: $416.03 \times 10^{-4} = 416.03 \div 10^4 = 0.0416.03 = 0.041603$

4 places

Large numbers or small decimal fractions can be expressed more conveniently using scientific notation. Scientific notation means expressing a number as the product of a decimal between 1 and 10, and a power of 10.

Example: $5,600,000 = 5.6 \times 10^6$ (5.6 million)

Example: $0.00000079 = 7.9 \times 10^{-7}$

Example: $0.00765 \times 10^7 = 7.65 \times 10^4$

POWERS AND ROOTS EXERCISE

Solve the following problems. (Answers are on the following page.)

1. $5^4 =$

2. $2^5 =$

3. $4 \cdot 3^3 =$

4. $(4 \cdot 3)^2 =$

5. $(4+3)^2 =$

6. $1.016 \times 10^2 =$

7. $(2^2)^4 =$

8. $(\sqrt{2})(\sqrt{8}) =$

9. $(\sqrt{6})(\sqrt{21}) =$

10. $\dfrac{\sqrt{48}}{\sqrt{3}} =$

11. $(2^5)\left(\dfrac{1}{2^6}\right) =$

12. $\sqrt{5} + \sqrt{125} =$

ANSWER KEY
BEGINS ON NEXT PAGE

ANSWER KEY—POWERS AND ROOTS EXERCISE

1. 625

2. 32

3. 108

4. 144

5. 49

6. 101.6

7. $2^8(=256)$

8. 4

9. $(\sqrt{6})(\sqrt{21}) = (\sqrt{3})(\sqrt{2})(\sqrt{3})(\sqrt{7})$
$= (\sqrt{3})(\sqrt{3})(\sqrt{2})(\sqrt{7})$
$= 3\sqrt{14}$

10. $\dfrac{\sqrt{48}}{\sqrt{3}} = \sqrt{\dfrac{48}{3}} = \sqrt{16} = 4$

11. $\dfrac{1}{2}$

12. $\sqrt{5} + \sqrt{125} = \sqrt{5} + \sqrt{25 \cdot 5}$
$= \sqrt{5} + (\sqrt{25})(\sqrt{5})$
$= 1\sqrt{5} + 5\sqrt{5}$
$= 6\sqrt{5}$

POWERS AND ROOTS TEST

Solve the following problems and choose the best answer. (Answers are at the end of this chapter.)

Basic

1. $(7-3)^2 =$

   ○ 4
   ○ 9
   ○ 16
   ○ 40
   ○ 49

2. If $a = 3$, then $(3a)^2 - 3a^2 =$

   ○ 0
   ○ 9
   ○ 27
   ○ 54
   ○ 72

3. $2^4 \times 4^3 =$

   ○ 8^{12}
   ○ 8^7
   ○ 6^7
   ○ 2^{10}
   ○ 2^7

4. If $x = 9a^2$ and $a > 0$, then $\sqrt{x} =$

   ○ $-3a$
   ○ $3a$
   ○ $9a$
   ○ $3a^2$
   ○ $81a^4$

5. $\dfrac{4^3 - 4^2}{2^2} =$

   ○ 1
   ○ 2
   ○ 4
   ○ 12
   ○ 16

6. If $3^x = 81$, then $x^3 =$

   ○ 12
   ○ 16
   ○ 64
   ○ 81
   ○ 128

7. If $x = 2$, then $3^x + (x^3)^2 =$

   ○ 18
   ○ 42
   ○ 45
   ○ 70
   ○ 73

KAPLAN

Intermediate

8. Which of the following is NOT equal to 0.0675?

   ○ 67.5×10^{-3}

   ○ 6.75×10^{-2}

   ○ 0.675×10^{-1}

   ○ 0.00675×10^2

   ○ 0.0000675×10^3

9. If q is an odd integer greater than 1, what is the value of $(-1)^q + 1$?

   ○ -2

   ○ -1

   ○ 0

   ○ 2

   ○ It cannot be determined from the information given.

10. If $x > 0$, then $4^x 8^x =$

    ○ 2^{9x}

    ○ 2^{8x}

    ○ 2^{6x}

    ○ 2^{5x}

    ○ 2^{4x}

11. If $5^n > 10{,}000$ and n is an integer, the smallest possible value of n is

    ○ 4

    ○ 5

    ○ 6

    ○ 7

    ○ 8

12. The cube root of what positive number is equal to the square root of the square root of 81?

    ○ 3

    ○ 9

    ○ 27

    ○ 81

    ○ 243

Advanced

13. Which of the following is (are) equal to 8^5 ?

    I. $2^5 \cdot 4^5$
    II. 2^{15}
    III. $2^5 \cdot 2^{10}$

    ◯ II only

    ◯ I and II only

    ◯ I and III only

    ◯ II and III only

    ◯ I, II, and III

14. If $27^n = 9^4$, then $n =$

    ◯ $\dfrac{4}{3}$

    ◯ 2

    ◯ $\dfrac{8}{3}$

    ◯ 3

    ◯ 8

15. If $xyz \neq 0$, then $\dfrac{x^3 yz^4}{xy^{-2}z^3} =$

    ◯ $x^2 y^3 z$

    ◯ $x^4 y^{-1} z^7$

    ◯ $x^2 y^{-1} z$

    ◯ $x^2 y^3 z^2$

    ◯ $x^2 yz$

16. If line segments AB and CD have lengths of $10 + \sqrt{7}$ and $5 - \sqrt{7}$ respectively, AB is greater than CD by how much?

    ◯ $5 - 2\sqrt{7}$

    ◯ $5 + 2\sqrt{7}$

    ◯ $15 + 2\sqrt{7}$

    ◯ 5

    ◯ 15

17. If $x^a \cdot x^b = 1$ and $x \neq \pm 1$, then $a + b =$

    ◯ x

    ◯ -1

    ◯ 0

    ◯ 1

    ◯ It cannot be determined from the information given.

NUMBER OPERATIONS TEST
ANSWERS AND EXPLANATIONS

1. $3\frac{11}{25}$

We are asked to find the fractional equivalent of 3.44. Since there are two digits to the right of the decimal point, the denominator of the fractional part is 100.

$$3.44 = 3\frac{44}{100} = 3\frac{11}{25}$$

2. 0.43

The first thing to do in this problem is to put both numbers into the same form. If we convert the $6\frac{3}{4}$ into decimal form, then we can easily subtract, since both numbers would be in decimal form. And, since our answer choices are all in decimal form, we'd need to do no further work. First, let's convert $\frac{3}{4}$ into a fraction with a denominator that is a power of 10 (e.g., 10, 100, 1000, etc.). If we multiply both the numerator and denominator of $\frac{3}{4}$ by 25, then our fraction becomes $\frac{75}{100}$, which is 0.75. So, $6\frac{3}{4}$ is equal to 6.75. Now we can subtract.

$$\begin{array}{r} 6.75 \\ -6.32 \\ \hline 0.43 \end{array}$$

3. $1\frac{1}{2}$

We are asked for the sum of several decimals. Note that all answer choices are in fractional form. Line up the decimal points and add:

$$\begin{array}{r} 0.125 \\ 0.25 \\ 0.375 \\ +\ 0.75 \\ \hline 1.500 = 1.5 = 1\frac{1}{2} \end{array}$$

Or, we could have converted all the decimals to fraction form first. It helps to know these basic conversions by heart.

$$0.125 = \frac{1}{8}, 0.25 = \frac{1}{4}, 0.375 = \frac{3}{8}, 0.75 = \frac{3}{4}.$$

So we add:

$$\frac{1}{8} + \frac{1}{4} + \frac{3}{8} + \frac{3}{4} = \frac{1}{4} + \frac{3}{4} + \frac{1}{8} + \frac{3}{8}$$
$$= 1 + \frac{4}{8}$$
$$= 1\frac{1}{2}$$

4. **0.1666**

We are asked which of the five values is less than $\frac{1}{6}$. Since $\frac{1}{6} = 0.166\overline{6}$ (the bar indicates that the six repeats),

$0.1667 > 0.166\overline{6}$, because the "7" in the fourth decimal place of 0.1667 is greater than the "6" in the fourth decimal

place of $0.166\overline{6}$. No good.

$\frac{3}{18} = \frac{1 \times 3}{6 \times 3} = \frac{1}{6}$. No good.

$0.167 > 0.16\overline{6}$ because the "7" in the third decimal place of 0.167 is greater than the "6" in the third decimal place of $0.16\overline{6}$. No good.

0.1666 is less than $0.1666\overline{6}$. Therefore, it is less than $\frac{1}{6}$, so this is the correct answer.

Just for practice:

$$\frac{1}{6} = \frac{8}{48} \text{ and } \frac{8}{47} > \frac{8}{48}; \text{ therefore}$$
$$\frac{8}{47} > \frac{1}{6}. \text{ No good.}$$

5. **0.003**

Let's start with the numerator. When we multiply decimals, the first step is to simply ignore the decimals and multiply the numbers as if they were whole numbers. The second step is to count the total number of places to the right of the decimal point in both numbers and then move the decimal point this many places to the **left** in our result.

$(0.02) \times (0.0003)$

$2 \times 3 = 6$

0.02   0.0003

2 places + 4 places = 6 places

so $(0.02) \times (0.0003) = 0.000006$

To divide 2 decimals, move the decimal point in both numbers as many places to the right as necessary to make the divisor
(the number you're dividing by) a whole number. Then divide:

$$\frac{0.000006}{0.002} = \frac{0.006}{2} = 0.003$$

A better way of doing this is to cancel a factor of 0.002 from numerator and denominator. Since 0.02 is simply 10 times 0.002, we can simply rewrite our problem as 10 times 0.0003. Multiplying a decimal by 10 is the same as moving the decimal point 1 place to the right. So our result is 0.003. This method certainly requires much less calculating, and so it can lead you to the answer more quickly. Look for ways to avoid extensive calculation.

6. $\dfrac{49}{24}$

There are 2 ways of doing this. One is to estimate the answer and the other is to actually add the fractions. Using the first approach, if the problem had us add $\dfrac{1}{8}$ instead of the $\dfrac{1}{6}$, then our problem would read $1 + \dfrac{1}{2} + \dfrac{1}{4} + \dfrac{1}{8} + \dfrac{1}{8}$.

If you're comfortable using these fractions you might see, with little effort, that this is simply 2. Since $\dfrac{1}{6}$ is actually slightly larger than $\dfrac{1}{8}$, our actual result must be slightly larger than 2. Looking at the answer choices, the only fraction in which the numerator is more than twice the denominator (in other words, the only value larger than 2) is $\dfrac{49}{24}$. Alternatively, we can simply find a common denominator for the fractions, convert them, and then add them. A quick glance at the answer choices suggests 24 as a common denominator. Converting the fractions we get:

$$\frac{24}{24} + \frac{12}{24} + \frac{6}{24} + \frac{4}{24} + \frac{3}{24} = \frac{49}{24}$$

7. 48

Turn this division problem into multiplication by applying the "invert and multiply" rule:

$$12 \text{ divided by } \frac{1}{4} = 12 \text{ times } \frac{4}{1} = 48$$

8. $\dfrac{1}{4}, \dfrac{3}{10}, \dfrac{9}{26}$

We need to arrange three fractions in ascending order. (Note that the same three fractions appear in each answer choice.)

Method I:

Convert to decimals: $\dfrac{1}{4} = 0.25$

$\dfrac{3}{10} = 0.3$. This is a little less than $\dfrac{1}{3}$, but more than $\dfrac{1}{4}$. $\dfrac{9}{26}$ is harder to express as a decimal, but

$\dfrac{9}{26} > \dfrac{9}{27}$, and $\dfrac{9}{27}$ or $\dfrac{1}{3} > \dfrac{3}{10}$. Therefore, $\dfrac{9}{26} > \dfrac{3}{10}$. The correct ascending order is $\dfrac{1}{4}, \dfrac{3}{10}, \dfrac{9}{26}$.

Method II:

If you have trouble comparing fractions directly, try cross-multiplying. Here, we find that

$\dfrac{1}{4} < \dfrac{3}{10}$ since $1 \times 10 < 3 \times 4$, and $\dfrac{3}{10} < \dfrac{9}{26}$ since $3 \times 26 < 9 \times 10$ (that is, $78 < 90$).

Method III:

You can also set the numerators equal to each other and compare the denominators. The LCM of the numerators is 9. Thus, convert $\frac{1}{4} = \frac{9}{36}$ and $\frac{3}{10} = \frac{9}{30}$ while $\frac{9}{26}$ already has a numerator of 9. The smaller the denominator, the bigger the number making the correct order: $\frac{9}{36} < \frac{9}{30} < \frac{9}{26}$.

9. $\frac{1}{25}$

We could perform the subtraction within the parentheses and then multiply, but it's simpler to use the distributive law.

$$\frac{7}{5} \cdot \left(\frac{3}{7} - \frac{2}{5} \right) = \frac{7}{5} \cdot \frac{3}{7} - \frac{7}{5} \cdot \frac{2}{5}$$
$$= \frac{3}{5} - \frac{14}{25}$$
$$= \frac{3}{5} \cdot \frac{5}{5} - \frac{14}{25}$$
$$= \frac{15}{25} - \frac{14}{25} = \frac{1}{25}$$

10. $\frac{3}{8}$

The easiest approach here is to find (quickly) which **two** choices are closest to 0.40—one larger, one smaller, and then find which of **those** is closer. Since $0.4 < \frac{1}{2}$, we can eliminate both $\frac{5}{9}$ and $\frac{4}{7}$ —since they are each greater than $\frac{1}{2}$, they are further from 0.4 than $\frac{1}{2}$ is.

On the other hand, $\frac{3}{8} < 0.4$ (the decimal equivalent of $\frac{3}{8}$ is 0.375), and since $\frac{1}{3} = \frac{3}{9} < \frac{3}{8}$, we can eliminate $\frac{1}{3}$.

So it comes down to $\frac{3}{8}$ or $\frac{1}{2}$. Since $\frac{3}{8} = 0.375$, it is 0.025 away from 0.4, which is much closer than $\frac{1}{2}$ (or 0.5, which is 0.1 away). So $\frac{3}{8}$ is the closest.

11. $\frac{1}{2}$

Method I:

$$\frac{\frac{1}{6} + \frac{1}{3} + 2}{\frac{3}{4} + \frac{5}{4} + 3} = \frac{\frac{1}{2} + 2}{\frac{8}{4} + 3} = \frac{2\frac{1}{2}}{5} = \frac{\frac{5}{2}}{5} = \frac{5}{2} \div 5 = \frac{5}{2} \cdot \frac{1}{5} = \frac{1}{2}$$

Method II:

Multiply numerator and denominator by the least common multiple of all the denominators. Here, the LCM is 12:

$$\frac{12\left(\frac{1}{6}+\frac{1}{3}+2\right)}{12\left(\frac{3}{4}+\frac{5}{4}+3\right)}=\frac{2+4+24}{9+15+36}=\frac{30}{60}=\frac{1}{2}$$

12. I and III

In statement I, if we were to subtract a smaller number from 1,000, then our result will be a larger number. In general, the smaller the number you subtract, the larger the result will be. So, if we substitute 120 for 160 in this expression, our result would be greater. We can eliminate choices that do not include statement I.

Statement II is a little more tricky. Our expression is equivalent to $\frac{160}{161}$. If we were to replace each 160 with 120, our result would be $\frac{120}{1+120}$, which is $\frac{120}{121}$. Which is greater? Think of each fraction's distance from 1. Both fractions are a tiny bit less than 1. Imagine a number line. $\frac{160}{161}$ is $\frac{1}{161}$ away from 1, while $\frac{120}{121}$ is $\frac{1}{121}$ away from 1. Since $\frac{1}{161}$ is less than $\frac{1}{121}$, that means that $\frac{160}{161}$ must be *closer* to 1 than $\frac{120}{121}$. And that means $\frac{160}{161}$ is a little larger than $\frac{120}{121}$. So if we did replace 160 with 120, we would get a smaller result. Eliminate the fourth choice.

Statement III is even tougher. We're dividing 1 by a fraction. So we'll have to multiply 1 by the reciprocal of the fraction. In order to get a *larger* reciprocal, we need to start with a *smaller* fraction. So, which is smaller, $1-\frac{1}{160}$ or $1-\frac{1}{120}$? $1-\frac{1}{120}$ is smaller since it is further to the left from 1 on the number line. So by replacing 160 with 120 we get a smaller fraction in the denominator of our expression and, therefore, a *larger* reciprocal. That will give the expression a larger value. So III is part of the correct answer.

13. $\frac{5}{36}$

Obviously, we have to start by picking out the largest and smallest fractions. $\frac{5}{9}>\frac{1}{2}$ and all the others are less than $\frac{1}{2}$, so $\frac{5}{9}$ is the greatest. The other four are close together, but it's easy to find a common denominator for $\frac{5}{12},\frac{11}{24}$, and $\frac{23}{48}$.

Convert everything to 48ths: $\frac{5}{12} = \frac{20}{48}$ and $\frac{11}{24} = \frac{22}{48}$, so $\frac{5}{12} < \frac{11}{24} < \frac{23}{48}$. Is $\frac{5}{12} < \frac{3}{7}$? Using the cross-multiplication method, $7 \times 5 = 35$, and $12 \times 3 = 36$, so $\frac{5}{12} < \frac{3}{7}$.

Now we have to find the difference between $\frac{5}{9}$ and $\frac{5}{12}$. Let's use the least common denominator, 36.

$$\frac{5}{9} \cdot \frac{4}{4} = \frac{20}{36} \text{ and } \frac{5}{12} \cdot \frac{3}{3} = \frac{15}{36}$$

$$\frac{20}{36} - \frac{15}{36} = \frac{5}{36}$$

14. $y < z < x$

We're given $0.04x = 5y = 2z$. Let's change the decimal to a fraction and work from there:

$$0.04 = \frac{4}{100} \text{ or } \frac{1}{25}.$$

Therefore, $\frac{1}{25}x = 5y = 2z$. Multiply all the terms by 25 to eliminate the fraction in front of x.

$$x = 125y = 50z$$

Since all the terms are positive, we know that it takes more y's than z's to equal one x. Therefore, x is the biggest, followed by z, and y is the smallest.

15. 2

The answer choices are pretty far apart, so we can estimate with impunity.

$\frac{59.376 \times 7.094}{31.492 \times 6.429}$ is about $\frac{60 \times 7}{30 \times 6} = \frac{420}{180}$, or roughly 2.

NUMBER PROPERTIES TEST
ANSWERS AND EXPLANATIONS

1. 8

Here we're asked for the odd integers between $\frac{10}{3}$ and $\frac{62}{3}$. First let's be clearer about this range. $\frac{10}{3}$ is the same as $3\frac{1}{3}$, and $\frac{62}{3}$ is the same as $20\frac{2}{3}$. So we need to count the odd integers between $3\frac{1}{3}$ and $20\frac{2}{3}$. Well, we can't include 3 since 3 is less than $3\frac{1}{3}$. Similarly, we can't include 21 since it's larger than $20\frac{2}{3}$. So the odd integers in the appropriate range are 5, 7, 9, 11, 13, 15, 17, and 19. That's a total of 8.

2. 18

To answer this question, it is most efficient just to try each answer choice. When asked to choose the "greatest" number that fulfills the given conditions, start with the biggest answer choice. (When asked to choose the "least" number, start with the smallest answer choice.) 27 is indeed a factor of 54—it is exactly half of 54—but it is not among the factors of 36, and so choice (5) is not the correct answer. The next largest choice, 18, divides into 54 exactly three times and into 36 exactly two times, and so this is the correct answer.

3. 32

One way to do this problem is to find the prime factorization of 168:

$$168 = 2 \cdot 84$$
$$= 2 \cdot 2 \cdot 42$$
$$= 2 \cdot 2 \cdot 6 \cdot 7$$
$$= 2 \cdot 2 \cdot 2 \cdot 3 \cdot 7$$

Now we can go through the answer choices. We've already seen that 42 is a factor of 168, and 21 is a factor of 42, so 21 is also factor of 168. This eliminates choices (1) and (5). Choice (2), 24, is 8 · 3 or 2 · 2 · 2 · 3, so it's also a factor of 168. Choice (3), 28, is 4 · 7, or 2 · 2 · 7, so 28 is a factor of 168. That leaves only choice (4). Indeed, 32 has five factors of 2, which is more factors of 2 than 168 has.

4. 660

We know from our divisibility rules that multiples of 2, 3, and 5 all have certain easily recognizable characteristics. All multiples of 5 end with the digits 5 or 0. All multiples of 2 have an even number in the units place. Therefore, any number that is divisible by both 2 and 5 must end with the digit 0. If a number is a multiple of 3, the sum of its digits is a multiple of 3. Of our five choices, we can eliminate (1) and (3) because their last digits are not 0. Now add up the digits in each of the remaining answer choices to see whether they are multiples of 3. For (2), 5 + 6 + 0 = 11, so 560 is not a multiple of 3. For (4), 6 + 2 + 0 = 8, so 620 is not a multiple of 3 either. For (5), 6 + 6 + 0 = 12, so 660 is a multiple of 3. That is the correct answer.

5. 63

In this question, we need to find the smallest integer divisible by both 9 and 21. The fastest method is to start with the smallest answer choice and test each one for divisibility. Choice (5) is clearly divisible by 21, but not by 9. Similarly, choice (4) is just 2 × 21, but it is not divisible by 9. Choice (3), 63, is divisible by both 21 (21 × 3 = 63) and 9 (9 × 7 = 63).

A more mathematical approach is to find the prime factors of 9 and 21, and, by eliminating shared factors, find the **least common multiple.** Breaking each into prime factors:

$$21 = 3 \times 7$$
$$9 = 3 \times 3$$

We can drop one factor of 3 from the 9, since it is already present in the factors of 21. The least common multiple is $3 \times 3 \times 7$, or 63.

6. 2

If the sum of three numbers is even, how many of the three are even? Either all three or exactly one of the three must be even. The sum of three odd numbers can **never** be even, nor can the sum of one odd and two evens. Remember though—we're dealing with three different **prime** numbers. There's only one even prime, 2; all the rest are odd. Therefore, only one of our group can be even, and that must be 2. Since 2 is the smallest prime, it must also be the smallest of the three.

7. I and III only

Let's try each possibility to see in which case(s) $A^2 = C$.

    I: If $A = -1$, then $B = 0$ and $C = 1$. $(-1)^2 = 1$. This works.

    II: If $A = 0$, then $B = 1$, and $C = 2$. $(0)^2 \neq 2$. No good.

    III: If $A = 2$, then $B = 3$, and $C = 4$. $(2)^2 = 4$. This works.

Only I and III satisfy the conditions.

8. $2n + 2$

The simplest approach here is to pick a sample odd value for n, such as 3. If we plug 3 into an expression and get an odd result, then we know that answer choice cannot be right. (We want the one that is even for **any** odd value.)

$\dfrac{n-1}{2} = \dfrac{3-1}{2} = \dfrac{2}{2} = 1$. Not even.

$\dfrac{n+1}{2} = \dfrac{3+1}{2} = \dfrac{4}{2} = 2$. Even.

Try another value, such as 1.

$\dfrac{1+1}{2} = \dfrac{2}{2} = 1$. So this doesn't **have** to be even.

$n^2 + 2n = (3)^2 + 2(3) = 9 + 6 = 15$. No.

$2n + 2 = 2(3) + 2 = 6 + 2 = 8$. Even. We could try some more values for n here or just use logic: If we double an odd number we get an even result, and if we then add 2, we still have an even number. So this will always be even, and it is our answer.

Just for practice:

$3n^2 - 2n = 3(3)^2 - 2(3) = 3(9) - 2(3) = 27 - 6 = 21$. No.

9. 121

We are asked for the smallest positive integer that leaves a remainder of 1 when divided by 6, 8, or 10. In other words, if we find the smallest integer that is a common multiple of these three numbers, we can add 1 to that number to get our answer. Subtracting 1 from each of our choices gives us 20, 40, 120, 240, and 480. Our best tactic is to work from the smallest up until we get our answer. All are multiples of 10, but 20 is not a multiple of 6 or 8, and 40 is not a multiple of 6; 120 is a multiple of 6 (6×20), 8 (8×15), and 10 (10×12). One more than 120 is 121. Answer choice (3), 121, is thus the smallest number to leave a remainder of 1.

An alternative approach to finding the least common multiple is to look at their prime factors:

$$6 = 2 \times 3$$

$$8 = 2 \times 2 \times 2$$

$$10 = 2 \times 5$$

So a common multiple must have three factors of 2 (6 and 10 only need one factor, but 8 needs all three), one factor of 3, and one factor of 5.

$$2 \times 2 \times 2 \times 3 \times 5 = 120; 120 + 1 = 121$$

10. **The square of either integer is an odd number.**

If the product of two integers is odd, then both of the integers must themselves be odd, since just one even factor would make a product even. If we add two odd numbers, we get an even number, and if we subtract an odd number from an odd number, we again get an even number. (For instance, $5 + 3 = 8; 5 - 3 = 2$.) Choices (1) and (2) are therefore wrong. The square of any odd number is odd (since the square is an odd times an odd), so choice (3) is correct. Since these squares are always odd, if we add them together or subtract one from the other, we get an even number.

11. **8**

Since $\dfrac{130}{x}$ will be an integer whenever x evenly divides into 130, we want to find all the positive integer divisors (or factors) of 130.

Method I: *Factor pairs*

Let's start by looking for factor pairs. This is easy at first:

$$130 = 1 \cdot 130 = 2 \cdot 65 = 5 \cdot 26 = 10 \cdot 13$$

Are there any more? Do we have to check all the integers from 1 to 130? No. We only have to try integers less than the square root of 130. For any integer x, you can find the smaller integer of its factor pairs by checking the integers up to the square root of x. The square root of 130 is a little less than 12, and it turns out that we've already found all four factor pairs: 1 and 130, 2 and 65, 5 and 26, 10 and 13. There are 8 positive factors of 130.

Method II: *Prime Factoring*

Factor 130 into primes. $130 = 2 \cdot 65 = 2 \cdot 5 \cdot 13$. These three numbers obviously divide 130 evenly, but they are not the only ones. All combinations of these primes will also divide 130 evenly. The combinations are 2, 5, 13, $2 \cdot 5$, $2 \cdot 13$, $5 \cdot 13$, and $2 \cdot 5 \cdot 13$. Don't forget 1—it's also a factor (although **not** a prime). It is not necessary to multiply these products out—we know they are all different. There are a total of 8 factors.

12. 9

First we have to identify the pattern. It consists of the same 6 numerals, 0, 9, 7, 5, 3, and 1, in that order, repeating infinitely. Our job is to identify the 44th digit to the right of the decimal point. Since the patter of 6 numerals will continually repeat, every 6th digit of the digits to the right of the decimal point will be the same, namely the numeral 1. So 1 will be the 6th, 12th, 18th, 24th (and so on) digit. Since 44 is just 2 more than 42, which is a multiple of 6, the 44th digit will be the digit 2 places to the right of 1. Well, that's 9.

13. 6

The easiest approach is to work with actual numbers. Let's take 0 and the first two positive even numbers. (Remember: 0 is even.) Their sum is $0 + 2 + 4 = 6$. Of the answer choices, only (1), (2), and (4) divide evenly into 6. Try another group of three: $2 + 4 + 6 = 12$. Again, 2, 3, and 6 divide evenly into 12. The next group is $4 + 6 + 8 = 18$. By now you should notice that the sums are all multiples of 6. Six will always divide evenly into the sum of three consecutive even integers.

14. 321

The hard way to do this problem is to find the exact values of the three consecutive integers, then find the next three, and then add. There's a shorter way, though. Suppose we call the three original integers $x, x + 1$, and $x + 2$. Their sum is 312, so $x + (x + 1) + (x + 2) = 312$ or $3x + 3 = 312$. The **next** three integers are $x + 3, x + 4$, and $x + 5$. What is the value of $(x + 3) + (x + 4) + (x + 5)$? It's $3x + 12$. $3x + 12$ is 9 greater than $3x + 3$. $3x + 3 = 312$, so $3x + 12 = 312 + 9$, or 321.

15. When divided by 2, *P* will leave a remainder of 1.

We need to find the one choice that isn't **always** true. To find it, let's test each choice. Choice (1) is always true: since $P \div 9$ has a remainder of 4, P is 4 greater than some multiple of 9. And if $P - 4$ is a multiple of 9, then the next multiple of 9 would be $(P - 4) + 9$, or $P + 5$; thus choice (2) is also true. With choice (3), we know that since $P - 4$ is a multiple of 9, it is also a multiple of 3. By adding 3s, we know that $(P - 4) + 3$, or $P - 1$, and $(P - 4) + 3 + 3$, or $P + 2$, are also multiples of 3. Choice (3) must be true. And since $P - 1$ is a multiple of 3, when P is divided by 3, it will have a remainder of 1, and choice (4) is always true.

This only leaves choice (5). In simpler terms, choice (5) states that P is always odd. Since multiples of 9 are alternately odd and even (9, 18, 27, 36 . . .), $P - 4$ could either be even or odd, so P also could be either even or odd. Choice (5) is not always true, so it is the correct answer choice.

16. One of the two integers is odd and the other is even.

If two numbers have an even product, at least one of the numbers is even, so we can eliminate choice (1). If both numbers were even, their sum would be even, but we know the sum of these numbers is odd, so we can eliminate choice (2). If one number is odd and the other is even, their product is even and their sum is odd. Choice (3) gives us what we're looking for. Choices (4) and (5) both can be true, but they're not necessarily true.

17. II and III only

Since these four integers have an even product, at least one of them must be even, so choice I, 0, is impossible. Is it possible for exactly 2 of the 4 to be even? If there are 2 odds and 2 evens, the sum is even, since odd + odd = even and even + even = even. Also, if there's at least one even among the integers, the product is even, so choice II **is** possible. Similarly, choice III gives an even product and an even sum, so our answer is II and III only.

18. 72

The wire can be divided into three equal parts, each with an integer length, so the minimum length must be a multiple of 3. Unfortunately, all of the answer choices are multiples of 3. One of those 3 pieces is cut into 8 pieces, again all with integer lengths, so the length of the wire must be at least 3 · 8, or 24. Another of those three segments is cut into 6 pieces. Now, what does that mean? Each third can be divided into either 6 or 8 segments with integer lengths. In other words, the thirds have an integer length evenly divisible by both 6 and 8. The smallest common multiple of 6 and 8 is 24, so the minimum length of the wire is 3 · 24, or 72.

19. 5

Here we want to determine, basically, how many numbers between 0 and 60 are even multiples of 5. Well, all even multiples of 5 must be multiples of 10. So, the multiples of 10 between 0 and 60 are 10, 20, 30, 40, and 50. That's 5 altogether.

AVERAGES TEST
ANSWERS AND EXPLANATIONS

1. 25

We can plug everything we are given into the standard formula for an average of two numbers and then solve for a. Since we know the average of -5 and a is 10:

$$\frac{\text{Sum of numbers}}{\text{Number of numbers}} = \text{Average of numbers}$$

$$\frac{-5 + a}{2} = 10$$

$$-5 + a = 20 \text{ (multiply both sides by 2)}$$

$$a = 20 + 5 \text{ (add 5 to both sides)}$$

$$a = 25$$

A much faster method is to think in terms of balance: Since -5 is 15 less than the average, a must be 15 **more** than the average, or $10 + 15 = 25$.

2. $\frac{3}{8}$

Our formula's no different just because we are working with fractions. The average is still the sum divided by the number of values.

$$\text{Average} = \frac{\frac{1}{2} + \frac{1}{4}}{2} = \frac{\frac{2}{4} + \frac{1}{4}}{2} = \frac{\frac{3}{4}}{2} = \frac{3}{4} \cdot \frac{1}{2} = \frac{3}{8}$$

Notice that the average of $\frac{1}{2}$ and $\frac{1}{4}$ is **not** $\frac{1}{3}$.

3. 60

This problem is easier than it may appear. Here we're told the average of four numbers and asked for the sum of these four numbers. Well, we can rearrange the average formula so that it reads:

$$\text{Sum} = \text{Number of terms} \times \text{Average}$$

$$\text{Sum} = 4 \times 15 = 60$$

The whole business of p and the value of three of the numbers was unnecessary to solving the problem.

4. 18

The average of evenly spaced numbers is the middle number. The average of six such numbers lies halfway between the third and fourth numbers.

Since $18\frac{1}{2}$ is the average, the third number must be 18 and the fourth number 19. The six numbers are:

$$16 \quad 17 \quad 18 \quad 19 \quad 20 \quad 21$$

Since the first five numbers are also evenly spaced, their average will be the middle, or third number: 18.

5. 7

To average 2 hours a day over 6 days, the violinist must practice 2×6, or 12 hours. From Monday through Friday, the violinist practices 5 hours, 1 hour each day. To total 12 hours, she must practice $12 - 5$, or 7 hours, on Saturday.

6. 4

If six numbers have an average of 6, their sum is 6·6 or 36. When we subtract 3 from four of the numbers, we subtract $4 \cdot 3$ or 12 from the sum. The new sum is $36 - 12$ or 24, so the new average is $24 \div 6$ or 4.

7. 60

The average of any five numbers is $\frac{1}{5}$ of the sum, so if these five numbers have an average of 12, their sum is $5 \cdot 12$ or 60.

Note that the information about consecutive even numbers is irrelevant to solving the problem. **Any** group of five numbers whose average is 12 will have a sum of 60.

8. +5°

If the average temperature over four days is $+4°$, the sum of the daily noon temperatures must be $4 \cdot (+4°)$ or $+ 16°$. Over the first three days, the sum is $(+9°) + (−6°) + (+8°)$ or $+ 11°$. On the fourth day, the temperature at noon must be $+ 5°$ to bring the sum up to $+16°$ and the average, in turn, up to $+ 4°$.

9. 183

Because the numbers in this problem are rather large, it's easiest to visualize the weights of the team members "balancing" around the average. Initially, the average for the team is 2 pounds below the maximum average of 170. There are four team members, so their total weight is $4 \times 2 = 8$ pounds below the maximum total allowed weight. Since the fifth team member is 5 pounds below the target average, the team is a total of $8 + 5 = 13$ pounds below what they are allowed. So, their sixth member can be up to 13 pounds above 170, for a maximum weight of $170 + 13 = 183$.

10. $n + 1\frac{1}{2}$

Don't let the n's in the numbers bother you; the arithmetic we perform is the same.

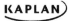

Method I:

Add the terms and divide by the number of terms. Since each term contains n, we can ignore the n and add it back at the end. Without the n's, we get

$$\frac{0+1+2+3}{4} = \frac{6}{4} = 1\frac{1}{2}$$

The average is $n + 1\frac{1}{2}$.

Method II:

These are just evenly spaced numbers (regardless of what n is). Since there are four of them, the average is between the second and third terms: midway between $n + 1$ and $n + 2$, or $n + 1\frac{1}{2}$.

11. −4

The fastest way to solve this problem is to recognize that $x + 2$, $x + 4$, and $x + 6$ are evenly spaced numbers, so the average equals the middle value, $x + 4$. We're told that the average of these values is zero, so:

$$x + 4 = 0$$

$$x = -4$$

12. 1,000

The key to this problem is that the total theater attendance stays the same after six theaters close. No matter how many theaters there are:

$$\text{Total attendance} = (\text{number of theaters}) \times (\text{Average attendance})$$

We know that originally there are 15 theaters, and they average 600 customers per day. Plug these values into the formula above to find the total theater attendance:

$$\text{Total attendance} = (15)(600) = 9{,}000$$

Even after the six theaters close, the total attendance remains the same. Now, though, the number of theaters is only nine:

$$\text{New average attendance} = \frac{\text{Total attendance}}{\text{New number of theaters}}$$
$$= \frac{9{,}000}{9}$$
$$= 1{,}000$$

13. 517

The average of a group of evenly spaced numbers is equal to the middle number. Here there is an even number of terms (18), so the average is between the two middle numbers, the 9th and 10th terms. This tells us that the **9th** consecutive odd integer here will be the first odd integer less than 534, which is **533**. Once we have the **9th** term, we can count backward to find the first.

10th	Average	9th	8th	7th
535	534	533	531	529

6th	5th	4th	3rd	2nd	1st
527	525	523	521	519	517

14. $75.35

This is a good opportunity to use the "balance" method. We're told the average closing price for all five days: $75.50. We're also given the closing prices for the first 4 days. Using the "balance" method we make the fifth day "balance out" the first four:

Monday	$75.58	average + $0.08
Tuesday	$75.63	average + $0.13
Wednesday	$75.42	average − $0.08
Thursday	$75.52	average + $0.02
after 4 days		average + $0.15

To make the values "balance out" the fifth day must be (average − $0.15) or $75.35.

15. 4

We can't find individual values for any of these six numbers. However, with the given information we can find the sum of the six numbers, and the sum of just the largest and smallest. Subtracting the sum of the smallest and largest from the sum of all six will leave us with the sum of the four others, from which we can find *their* average.

The sum of all six numbers is (average of all 6 numbers) × (number of values) = 5 × 6, or 30.

The sum of the greatest and smallest can be found in the same way: 2 × average = 2 × 7 = 14.

The sum of the other 4 numbers is (the sum of all six) − (the sum of the greatest and smallest) = (30 − 14) = 16.

The sum of the other four numbers is 16. Their average is $\frac{16}{4}$ or 4.

16. 12

The key to doing this problem is to link what we're given to what we need to find. We need to solve for the average of $a + 3, b − 5$, and 6. If we could determine their sum, then all we'd need to do is divide this sum by 3 to find their average. Well, we don't know a and b, but we can determine their sum. We are given the average of a, b and 7. Clearly we can figure out the sum of these 3 values by multiplying the average by the number of terms: 13 × 3 = 39. That allows us to determine the sum of a and b. If $a + b + 7 = 39$, then $a + b = 39 − 7$, or 32. Now, remember we're asked for the average of $a + 3, b − 5$, and 6. The sum of these expressions can be rewritten as $a + b + 3 − 5 + 6$, or $a + b + 4$. If $a + b = 32$, then $a + b + 4 = 32 + 4$, or 36. Therefore, the sum is 36 and the number of terms is 3, so the average is $\frac{36}{3}$, or 12.

RATIOS TEST
ANSWERS AND EXPLANATIONS

1. 3 : 8

We are asked for the ratio of cats to hamsters. Cats : hamsters $= 9 : 24 = \dfrac{9}{24}$. Reduce the numerator and denominator by a factor of 3. Thus, $\dfrac{9}{24} = \dfrac{3}{8} = 3 : 8$. For every 3 cats there are 8 hamsters.

2. 39

Since the ratio of boys to girls is 5 : 3, we know that the number of boys divided by the number of girls must equal five-thirds. And we know that the number of boys is 65. This is enough information to set up a **proportion**. We know that:

$$\frac{65}{\text{\# of girls}} = \frac{5}{3}$$

In place of "# of girls," let's put "G":

$$\frac{65}{G} = \frac{5}{3}$$

At this point, you might realize that since $65 = 13 \times 5$, and the two fractions are equivalent, G must equal 13×3, or 39. Or you can simply cross-multiply $\dfrac{65}{G} = \dfrac{5}{3}$, which gives you:

$$65 \times 3 = 5 \times G$$
$$\text{Divide by 5: } \frac{65 \times 3}{5} = G$$
$$\text{Cancel: } 13 \times 3 = G$$
$$G = 39$$

3. $2\dfrac{1}{3}$

In this question, the ratio is implied: for every $\dfrac{3}{4}$ inch of map there is one real mile, so the ratio of inches to the miles they represent is always $\dfrac{3}{4}$ to 1.

Therefore, we can set up the proportion:

$$\frac{\text{\# of inches}}{\text{\# of miles}} = \frac{\frac{3}{4}}{1} = \frac{3}{4}$$

Now $1\frac{3}{4}$ inches $= \frac{7}{4}$ inches.

Set up a proportion: $\dfrac{\frac{7}{4}\text{ inches}}{\#\text{ of miles}} = \dfrac{3}{4}$

Cross-multiply:

$$\frac{7}{4} \times 4 = 3 \times \#\text{ of miles}$$

$$7 = 3 \times \#\text{ of miles}$$

$$\frac{7}{3} = \#\text{ of miles}$$

or

$$2\frac{1}{3} = \#\text{ of miles}$$

4. **$240**

If the man has spent $\frac{5}{12}$ of his salary, then he has left $1 - \frac{5}{12}$, or $\frac{7}{12}$ of his salary. So $140 represents $\frac{7}{12}$ of his

salary. Set up a proportion, using S to represent his salary:

$$\frac{7}{12} = \frac{140}{S}$$

Cross-multiply:

$$7S = 12 \times 140$$

$$S = \frac{12 \times 140}{7}$$

$$= 240$$

5. **600**

The ratio of parts is 4 : 3 : 2, making a total of 9 parts. Since 9 parts are equal to 1,800 votes, each part represents 1,800 ÷ 9, or 200 votes. Since Ms. Frau represents 3 parts, she received a total of 3 × 200, or 600 votes.

Another way to think about it: Out of every 9 votes, Ms. Frau gets 3, which is $\frac{3}{9}$, or $\frac{1}{3}$, of the total number of votes. $\frac{1}{3}$ of 1,800 is 600. We could also have solved it algebraically, by setting up a proportion, with F as Ms. Frau's votes

$$\frac{3}{9} = \frac{F}{1,800}$$

$$\frac{3}{9} \times 1,800 = F$$

$$600 = F$$

6. **48**

We are given the ratio of men to women at a party, and the total number of people. To find the number of women, we need the ratio of the number of women to the total number of people. If the ratio of men to women is 3 : 2, then for every 5 people, 3 are men and 2 are women. So the ratio of women to total people is 2 : 5. Since 120 people are at the party, $\frac{2}{5} \times 120$, or 48 of them are women.

7. **3,600**

We are given a part-to-part ratio and total; we need to convert the ratio to a part-to-whole ratio. If the weights are in the ratio of 5 : 9, then the larger ship represents $\frac{9}{5+9}$, or $\frac{9}{14}$ of the total weight. We're told this total weight is 5,600 tons, so the larger ship must weigh:

$$\frac{9}{14} \times 5,600 = 9 \times 400 = 3,600 \text{ tons.}$$

8. **3 : 8**

Before we deal with the laboratory rabbits, think about this: Suppose the ratio of men to women in a room is 2 : 1. The number of women in the room is $\frac{1}{2+1}$, or $\frac{1}{3}$ of the total.

Therefore, the total number of people must be a multiple of 3—otherwise we'll end up with fractional people. (Note that this is only true because the ratio was expressed in lowest terms. We could also express a 2 : 1 ratio as 6 : 3, but that doesn't imply that the total must be some multiple of 9. Ratios on the GRE and GMAT will usually be expressed in lowest terms, so you need not worry about that too much.)

Returning to our problem, we see that we have 55 rabbits, and presumably want to avoid partial rabbits. The sum of the terms in the ratio must be a factor of 55. There are only four factors of 55 : 1, 5, 11, and 55. The only answer choice that fits this condition is choice (2): the sum of the terms in a 3 : 8 ratio is 11. We can quickly see why the other answer choices wouldn't work. In choice (1), for example, the ratio of white to brown rabbits is 1 : 3. If this were true, the total number of rabbits would be a multiple of 4, (that is, of 1 + 3). Since 55 isn't a multiple of 4, this can't possibly be the ratio we need. Similarly, the ratios in the other wrong choices are impossible.

9. **3,500**

If **two**-fifths of Consolidated's output (the bricks produced by the Greenpoint factory) was 1,400 tons, **one**-fifth must have been half as much, or 700 tons. The entire output for 2008 was **five**-fifths or five times as much: 5 × 700, or 3,500 tons.

10. 13 to 21

We are asked which of five ratios is equivalent to the ratio of $3\frac{1}{4}$ to $5\frac{1}{4}$. Since the ratios in the answer choices are expressed in whole numbers, turn this ratio into whole numbers:

$$3\frac{1}{4} : 5\frac{1}{4} = \frac{13}{4} : \frac{21}{4} = \frac{\frac{13}{4}}{\frac{21}{4}} = \frac{13}{4} \times \frac{4}{21}$$

$$= \frac{13}{21}, \text{ or } 13 : 21$$

11. 2 : 3

If $\frac{3}{5}$ of the ship is above water, then the rest of the ship, or $\frac{5}{5} - \frac{3}{5} = \frac{2}{5}$ of the ship, must be below water. Then the ratio of the submerged weight to the exposed weight is $\frac{2}{5} : \frac{3}{5} = 2 : 3$.

12. 570

If **one**-twentieth of the entrants were prize winners, the number of entrants was **twenty**-twentieths or 20 times the number of prize winners: $20 \times 30 = 600$. This is the **total** number of entrants. All but 30 of these entrants went away empty-handed: $600 - 30 = 570$.

13. $\frac{5}{11}$

Here we can set up a direct proportion:

$$\frac{1 \text{ kilogram}}{2.2 \text{ pounds}} = \frac{x \text{ kilograms}}{1 \text{ pound}}$$

Cross-multiply (the units drop out):

$$1 \times 1 = 2.2(x)$$
$$x = \frac{1}{2.2} = \frac{10}{22} = \frac{5}{11}$$

If you have trouble setting up the proportion, you could use the answer choices to your advantage and take an educated guess. Since 2.2 pounds equals a kilogram, a pound must be a little less than $\frac{1}{2}$ a kilogram. Of the possible answers, $\frac{11}{5}$ is over 2; $\frac{5}{8}$ is over $\frac{1}{2}$; $\frac{1}{3}$ and $\frac{1}{5}$ seem too small. But $\frac{5}{11}$ is just under $\frac{1}{2}$, and so it should be the correct answer.

14. 16

Start by putting everything in the same units:

$$6 \text{ quarts} = 6 \text{ quarts} \times \frac{4 \text{ cups}}{1 \text{ quart}} = 24 \text{ cups}$$

Now set up the ratios: the ratio of eggs to milk stays the same, so

$$\frac{2 \text{ eggs}}{3 \text{ cups}} = \frac{x \text{ eggs}}{24 \text{ cups}}$$

Cross-multiply:

$$2 \cdot 24 = 3x$$
$$2 \cdot 8 = x$$
$$x = 16$$

15. 36

The ratio 5 boys to 3 girls tells you that for every 5 boys in the class there must be 3 girls in the class. If there happen to be 5 boys in the class, then there must be 3 girls in the class. If there are 10 boys, then there will be 6 girls; 15 boys means 9 girls, and so on. The total number of students in the class would be 8, 16, or 24 in these three cases. Notice that all these sums are multiples of 8, since the smallest possible total is 5 + 3, or 8. Any other total must be a multiple of 8. Since 36 is not divisible by 8 (it's the only answer choice that isn't), 36 cannot be the total number of students.

16. $\frac{1}{3}$

The grade is decided by 4 quizzes and 1 exam. Since the exam counts twice as much as each quiz, the exam equals two quizzes, so we can say the grade is decided by the equivalent of 4 quizzes and 2 quizzes, or 6 quizzes. The exam equals two quizzes, so it represents $\frac{2}{6}$, or $\frac{1}{3}$, of the grade.

17. 25

Since the ratio of cement to gravel to sand is 3 : 5 : 7, for every 3 portions of cement we put in, we get 3 + 5 + 7, or 15 portions of the mixture. Therefore, the recipe gives us $\frac{15}{3}$ or 5 times as much mixture as cement. We have 5 tons of cement available, so we can make 5 × 5, or 25 tons of the mixture.

18. 24

The time it takes to complete the entire exam is the sum of the time spent on the first half of the exam and the time spent on the second half. We know the time spent on the first half is $\frac{2}{3}$ of the time spent on the second half. If we let S represent the time spent on the second half, then the total time spent is $\frac{2}{3}S + S$, or $\frac{5}{3}S$. We know this total time is one hour or 60 minutes. So set up a simple equation and solve for S.

$$\frac{5}{3}S = 60$$

$$\frac{3}{5} \cdot \frac{5}{3}S = 60 \cdot \frac{3}{5}$$

$$S = 36$$

So the second half takes 36 minutes. The first half takes $\frac{2}{3}$ of this, or 24 minutes. (You could also find the first half by subtracting 36 minutes from the total time, 60 minutes.)

19. $\frac{1}{3}$

This problem might seem confusing at first, but it is not too bad if you work methodically. What we need is the fraction of the unskilled workers who are not apprentices; to find this we need the number of unskilled workers and the number of non-apprentice unskilled workers. There are 2,700 workers total; one-third of them are unskilled, giving us $2{,}700 \times \frac{1}{3} = 900$ unskilled workers. 600 of **them** are apprentices, so the remaining $900 - 600$, or 300 are not apprentices.

Then the fraction of unskilled workers who are not apprentices to total workers is $\frac{300}{900} = \frac{1}{3}$.

20. 50

Every 8 pounds of the alloy has 6 pounds of copper and 2 pounds of tin. Therefore, $\frac{2}{8}$ or $\frac{1}{4}$ of the alloy is tin. To make 200 pounds of the alloy, we need $\frac{1}{4} \times 200$, or 50 pounds of tin.

21. 300

We can solve this algebraically. Let the number of yellow balls received be x. Then the number of white balls received is 30 more than this, or $x + 30$.

$$\text{So } \frac{\text{\# of white balls}}{\text{\# of yellow balls}} = \frac{6}{5} = \frac{x + 30}{x}$$

$$\text{Cross-multiply: } 6x = 5(x + 30)$$

$$\text{Solve for } x : 6x = 5x + 150$$

$$x = 150$$

Since the number of white balls ordered equals the number of yellow balls ordered, the total number of balls ordered is $2x$, which is 2×150, or 300.

We could also solve this more intuitively.

The store originally ordered an equal number of white and yellow balls; they ended up with a white to yellow ratio of 6 : 5. This means for every 5 yellow balls, they got 6 white balls, or they got $\frac{1}{5}$ more white balls than yellow balls. The difference between the number of white balls and the number of yellow balls is just the 30 extra white balls they got. So 30 balls represents $\frac{1}{5}$ of the number of yellow balls. Then the number of yellow balls is 5×30, or 150. Since they ordered the same number of white balls as yellow balls, they also ordered 150 white balls, for a total order of $150 + 150$, or 300 balls.

22. $\dfrac{1}{3}$

Method I:

We want to eliminate the b's and c's. We start with $a = 2b$. Since $\dfrac{1}{2}b = c$, we see that by multiplying both sides of the equation by 4, $2b = 4c$. Therefore, $a = 4c$.

But $4c = 3d$, which means that $a = 3d$. If a is 3 times d, then $\dfrac{a}{d} = \dfrac{3}{1}$, or $\dfrac{d}{a} = \dfrac{1}{3}$.

Method II:

We're looking for the ratio of d to a, or in other words, the value of the fraction $\dfrac{d}{a}$. Notice that we can

use successive cancellations and write:

$$\frac{d}{a} = \frac{\cancel{b}^{1}}{a} \times \frac{\cancel{c}^{1}}{\cancel{b}_{1}} \times \frac{d}{\cancel{c}}$$

Find values for each of the fractions $\dfrac{b}{a}, \dfrac{c}{b}$, and $\dfrac{d}{c}$.

$$a = 2b, \text{ so } \frac{b}{a} = \frac{1}{2}$$
$$\frac{1}{2}b = c, \text{ so } \frac{c}{b} = \frac{1}{2}$$
$$4c = 3d, \text{ so } \frac{d}{c} = \frac{4}{3}$$

Now substitute these values into the equation above.

$$\frac{d}{a} = \frac{b}{a} \times \frac{c}{b} \times \frac{d}{c}$$
$$= \frac{1}{2} \times \frac{1}{2} \times \frac{4}{3}$$
$$= \frac{4}{12} = \frac{1}{3}$$

Method III:

And, if all of this algebra confuses you, you can also solve this problem by picking a value for a. Then, by using the relationships given, determine what value d must have and hence the value of $\dfrac{d}{a}$.

Since terms have coefficients of 2, 3, and 4, it's best to pick a number that's a multiple of 2, 3, and 4. Then we're less likely to have to deal with calculations involving fractions. Say a is 12. Since $a = 2b$, then $b = 6$. Since $\dfrac{1}{2}b = c$, $c = 3$. Finally, if $4c = 3d$, we get $4 \times 3 = 3d$, or $d = 4$. Then the ratio of d to a is $\dfrac{4}{12}$, or $\dfrac{1}{3}$.

23. $4

In each case, the examination and the frames are the **same**; the difference in cost must be due to a difference in the costs of the lenses. Since plastic lenses cost four times as much as glass lenses, the **difference** in cost must be **three** times the cost of the glass lenses.

$$\text{Difference in cost} = \text{Cost of plastic} - \text{Cost of glass}$$
$$= 4(\text{cost of glass}) - 1(\text{cost of glass})$$
$$= 3(\text{cost of glass})$$

The difference in cost is $42 − $30, or $12. Since this is 3 times the cost of the glass lenses, the glass lenses must cost $\frac{\$12}{3}$, or $4.

24. 3 : 4

In this question we cannot determine the **number** of white mice or gray mice, but we can still determine their ratio.

Since $\frac{1}{2}$ of the white mice make up $\frac{1}{8}$ of the total mice, the **total** number of white mice must be double $\frac{1}{8}$ of the total number of mice, or $\frac{1}{4}$ of the total number of mice. Algebraically, if $\frac{1}{2} \times W = \frac{1}{8} \times T$, then $W = \frac{1}{4} \times T$. So $\frac{1}{4}$ of the total mice are white. Similarly, since $\frac{1}{3}$ of the number of gray mice is $\frac{1}{9}$ of the total number of mice, $3 \times \frac{1}{9}$ of all the mice, or $\frac{1}{3}$ of all the mice are gray mice. Therefore, the ratio of white mice to gray mice is $\frac{1}{4} : \frac{1}{3}$, which is the same as $\frac{3}{12} : \frac{4}{12}$, or 3 : 4.

PERCENTS TEST
ANSWERS AND EXPLANATIONS

1. 90

Method I:

We want 200% more than 30; 200% more than 30 is 30 + (200% of 30):

$$30 + 200\%(30) = 30 + 2(30)$$
$$= 30 + 60$$
$$= 90$$

Method II:

200% **more** than a number means 200% plus the 100% that the original number represents. This means 200% + 100%, or 300% **of** the number. 300% means three times as much, and $3 \times 30 = 90$.

2. $\frac{1}{8}$%

We are asked what percent of 1,600 is 2.

Remember: a percent is a ratio. Compare the part to the whole:

$$\% = \frac{\text{part}}{\text{whole}} \times 100\%$$
$$= \frac{2}{1,600} \times 100\% = \frac{2}{16}\% = \frac{1}{8}\%$$

Note: $\frac{1}{8}\%$ means $\frac{1}{8}$ of 1%, or $\frac{1}{800}$.

3. $\frac{1}{300}$

Let's start by converting 0.25% to a fraction (since our answer choices are expressed as fractions). 0.25 is $\frac{1}{4}$, but this is 0.25 percent, or $\frac{1}{4}$ of 1%, which is $\frac{1}{4} \times \frac{1}{100}$, or $\frac{1}{400}$.

$$0.25\% \text{ of } \frac{4}{3} = \left(\frac{1}{400}\right) \times \left(\frac{4}{3}\right)$$
$$= \frac{1}{300}$$

4. $133\frac{1}{3}\%$

Translate: **of** means "times," **is** means "equals." $\frac{2}{3}$ of 8 becomes $\frac{2}{3} \times 8$, and let's call the percent we're looking for p.

$$\frac{2}{3} \times 8 = p \times 4$$

$$\frac{\frac{2}{3} \times 8}{4} = p$$

$$\frac{4}{3} = p$$

We convert $\frac{4}{3}$ to a percent by multiplying by 100%.

$$\frac{4}{3} = \frac{4}{3} \times 100\% = \frac{400}{3}\% = 133\frac{1}{3}\%$$

5. **0.6**

We are asked for 10% of 20% of 30. We change our percents to fractions, then multiply:

$$10\% = \frac{1}{10};\ 20\% = \frac{1}{5}.$$

So 10% of 20% of 30 becomes

$$\frac{1}{10} \times \frac{1}{5} \times 30 = \frac{3}{5} = 0.6$$

6. $33\frac{1}{3}\%$

The question asks us to find W as a percent of T. First, let's change the percents into fractions:

$$60\% \text{ of } W = 20\% \text{ of } T$$

$$\frac{3}{5}W = \frac{1}{5}T$$

Now solve for W:

$$\frac{5}{3} \cdot \frac{3}{5}W = \frac{5}{3} \cdot \frac{1}{5}T$$

$$W = \frac{1}{3}T$$

$\frac{1}{3}$ is $33\frac{1}{3}\%$, so W is $33\frac{1}{3}\%$ of T.

7. 36

This question involves a principle that appears frequently on the GRE and GMAT: $a\%$ of $b = b\%$ of a. We can show that with this example:

$$36\% \text{ of } 18 = \frac{36}{100} \times 18$$
$$= \frac{18}{100} \times 36$$
$$= 18\% \text{ of } 36$$

So the answer here is 36.

8. 200%

$$\text{Percent increasee} = \frac{\text{Amount of increase}}{\text{ORIGINAL whole}} \times 100\%$$

The original whole is the price **before** the increase. The amount of increase is the difference between the increased price and the original price. So the amount of increase is $15¢ - 5¢ = 10¢$.

$$\% \text{ increase} = \frac{10¢}{5¢} \times 100\% = 2 \times 100\% = 200\%$$

9. $90,000

Start by converting the percent to a fraction. 12.5 percent is the same as $\frac{1}{8}$. The profit is $\frac{1}{8} \times \$80,000$, or $10,000.

This gives us a total selling price of $80,000 + $10,000, or $90,000.

10. 18

If 25% of the shoes are black, then $100\% - 25\%$, or 75% of the shoes are not black.

$$75\% \text{ of } 24 = \frac{3}{4} \times 24 = 18.$$

11. 70%

We can assume Bob either passed or failed each test; there's no third possibility. This means he passed each test he didn't fail. If he failed 6 tests out of 20, he passed the other 14. Bob passed $\frac{14}{20}$ of the tests. To convert $\frac{14}{20}$ to a percent, multiply the numerator and denominator by 5; this will give us a fraction with a denominator of 100. $\frac{14}{20} \times \frac{5}{5} = \frac{70}{100}$, or 70%. (Or realize that since $\frac{1}{20} = 5\%$, $\frac{14}{20}$ must be 14 times as big, or $14 \times 5\%$, or 70%.) Bob passed 70% of his tests.

12. $960

20% is the same as $\frac{1}{5}$, so 20% of $800 = \frac{1}{5} \cdot 800 = 160$. The selling price of the item is $800 + $160, or $960.

13. $133\frac{1}{3}\%$

The **amount of increase** in Pat's income was $35,000 − $15,000, or $20,000. The formula for percent increase is

$$\frac{\text{Amount of increase}}{\text{Original whole}} \times 100\% = \text{Percent increase}$$

Plugging in the figures for Pat, $\frac{\$20,000}{\$15,000} \times 100\% = \frac{4}{3} \times 100\% = 133\frac{1}{3}\%$.

14. **65%**

If 7 of the 20 winners have come forward, the other 13 have not. $\frac{13}{20}$ of the winners have not claimed their prizes.

$\frac{13}{20}$ as a percent is $\frac{13}{20} \times 100\% = 13 \times 5\% = 65\%$.

15. **$75**

Convert percents to fractions: $50\% = \frac{1}{2}$. A 50% increase on $100 is one-half of 100 or $50. So the increased price is $100 + $50, or $150. Now the 50% **decrease** is a decrease from $150, *not* $100. Thus, the amount of decrease from $150 is 50% of $150, or one-half of $150, or $75. Therefore, the final price is $150 − $75, or $75.

16. **225**

We first need to find what x is. If 65% of $x = 195$,

$$\frac{65}{100} \times x = 195$$

$$x = 195 \times \frac{100}{65}$$

$$= 3 \times \frac{100}{1}$$

$$= 300$$

$$75\% \text{ of } 300 = \frac{3}{4} \times 300 = 225.$$

In fact, it's not necessary to calculate the value of x, only the value of 75% of x. So we have:

$$x = 195 \times \frac{100}{65}$$

Rather than do the arithmetic now, we can get an expression for 75% of x, and then simplify.

$$75\% \text{ of } x = \frac{3}{4}x$$

$$= \frac{3}{4} \times 195 \times \frac{100}{65}$$

$$= \frac{3}{\cancel{4}_{1}} \times \cancel{195}^{3} \times \frac{\cancel{100}^{25}}{\cancel{65}_{1}}$$

$$= 225$$

17. $25,000

This is a percent increase problem. We need to identify the different items in our equations:

$$\text{New whole} = \text{Original whole} + \text{Amount of increase}$$

and

$$\text{Percent increase} = \frac{\text{Amount of increase}}{\text{Original whole}} (100\%)$$

Our new whole is the October sales, the original whole was the September sales. The percent increase, we're told, was 20%. So we can fill in for the first equation:

$$(\text{October}) = (\text{September}) + (\text{Amount of increase})$$

and rewrite the second equation as

$$(\text{Amount of increase}) = (20\%)(\text{September})$$

Putting the equations together we get

$$(\text{October}) = (\text{September}) + (20\%)(\text{September})$$

Now the important thing to realize is that the September sales are equal to 100% of September sales (anything is equal to 100% of itself), so October's sales are actually 100% + 20%, or 120% of the September sales. Therefore,

$$\text{October sales} = (120\%)(\text{September})$$

$$\$30,000 = \frac{6}{5}(\text{September})$$

$$\text{September} = \frac{5}{6} \times \$30,000$$

$$= \$25,000$$

18. 16.0

We're told that 40% of the total equals 6.4 million dollars, and we're asked to find the total. We can write this as an equation:

$$40\% \times w = 6.4$$

$$\frac{4}{10}w = 6.4$$

$$\left(\frac{10}{4}\right)\left(\frac{4}{10}\right)w = \left(\frac{10}{4}\right)(6.4)$$

$$w = \frac{64}{4} = 16$$

We could also have used the answer choices, either multiplying each answer choice by 40% to see which equals 6.4, or realizing that 40% is a little less than $\frac{1}{2}$ and picking the answer choice a bit more than double 6.4, or 12.8. The closest choice is 16.

19. $6\frac{2}{3}\%$

We're asked what percent of the new solution is alcohol. The part is the number of ounces of alcohol; the whole is the total number of ounces of the new solution. There were 25 ounces originally. Then 50 ounces were added, so there are 75 ounces of new solution. How many ounces are alcohol? 20% of the original 25-ounce solution was alcohol. 20% is $\frac{1}{5}$, so $\frac{1}{5}$ of 25, or 5 ounces are alcohol. Now we can find the percent of alcohol in the new solution:

$$\% \text{ alcohol} = \frac{\text{alcohol}}{\text{total solution}} \times 100\%$$
$$= \frac{5}{75} \times 100\%$$
$$= \frac{20}{3}\% = 6\frac{2}{3}\%$$

20. $125

The bicycle was discounted by 20%; this means that Jerry paid 100% − 20%, or 80% of the original price. Jerry paid $100, so we have the percent and the part and need to find the whole. Now substitute into the formula:

$$80\% \times \text{Whole} = \$100$$
$$\frac{4}{5} \times \text{Whole} = \$100$$
$$\frac{5}{4}\left(\frac{4}{5} \times \text{Whole}\right) = \$100 \times \frac{5}{4}$$
$$\text{Whole} = \$125$$

The bicycle originally sold for $125.

21. 25%

The key to this problem is that while the value of the stock must decrease and increase by the same **amount**, it doesn't decrease and increase by the same **percent**. When the stock first decreases, that amount of change is part of a larger whole. If the stock were to increase to its former value, that same amount of change would be a larger percent of a smaller whole. Pick a number for the original value of the stock, $100. (Since it's very easy to take percents of 100, it's usually best to choose 100.) The 20% decrease represents $20, so the stock decreases to a value of $80. Now in order for the stock to reach the value of $100 again, there must be a $20 increase. What percent of $80 is $20?

It's $\frac{\$20}{\$80} \times 100\%$, or $\frac{1}{4} \times 100\%$, or 25%.

22. 1750

Since the population increases by 50% every 50 years, the population in 1950 was 150%, or $\frac{3}{2}$ of the 1900 population. This means the 1900 population was $\frac{2}{3}$ of the 1950 population. Similarly, the 1850 population was $\frac{2}{3}$ of the 1900 population, and so on. We can just keep multiplying by $\frac{2}{3}$ until we get to a population of 160.

$$1950 : 810 \times \frac{2}{3} = 540 \text{ in } 1900$$

$$1900 : 540 \times \frac{2}{3} = 360 \text{ in } 1850$$

$$1850 : 360 \times \frac{2}{3} = 240 \text{ in } 1800$$

$$1800 : 240 \times \frac{2}{3} = 160 \text{ in } 1750$$

The population was 160 in 1750.

23. 6

5% of the total mixture is timothy (a type of grass) so, to find the **amount** of timothy, we use

% timothy × whole = amount of timothy.

Thus, the amount of timothy in 240 pounds of mixture is 5% × 240 pounds, or 12 pounds. If 12 pounds of timothy are available and each acre requires 2 pounds, then $\frac{12}{2}$ or 6 acres can be planted.

Alternately, you could find the weight of the entire mixture per acre. If 5%, or $\frac{1}{20}$, of the mixture is 2 pounds, then the total mixture is 2 × 20 or 40 pounds per acre. Since 240 pounds of mixture are available, $\frac{240}{40}$, or 6 acres, can be planted.

24. $1,500

The commission earned was $200 minus the $50 salary, or $150. This represents 10% of his total sales, or $\frac{1}{10}$ of his total. Since this is $\frac{1}{10}$ of the total, the total must be 10 times as much, or 10 × $150 = $1,500.

25. $12.50

The man paid $80 for 10 crates of oranges, and then lost 2 crates. That leaves him with 8 crates. We want to find the price per crate that will give him an overall profit of 25%. First, what is 25% or $\frac{1}{4}$ of $80? It's $20. So to make a 25% profit, he must bring in $80 + $20, or $100 in sales receipts. If he has 8 crates, that means that each crate must sell for $100 ÷ 8, or $12.50.

POWERS AND ROOTS TEST
ANSWERS AND EXPLANATIONS

1. 16

Remember the order of operations. We do what's within the parentheses first, and then square.

$$(7 - 3)^2 = 4^2 = 16$$

2. 54

Plug in 3 for a. We get

$$
\begin{aligned}
(3a)^2 - 3a^2 &= [3(3)]^2 - 3(3)^2 \\
&= 9^2 - 3(9) \\
&= 81 - 27 \\
&= 54
\end{aligned}
$$

3. 2^{10}

To multiply two numbers with the same base, **add** the two exponents. Here, we have two different bases, 2 and 4. We must rewrite one of the numbers such that the bases are the same. Since $4 = 2^2$, we can easily rewrite 4^3 as a power of $2 : 4^3 = (2^2)^3$. To raise a power to an exponent, **multiply** the exponents, so $(2^2)^3 = 2^6$.

$$
\begin{aligned}
\text{Therefore, } 2^4 \times 4^3 &= 2^4 \times 2^6 \\
&= 2^{4+6} \\
&= 2^{10}
\end{aligned}
$$

4. $3a$

We can find the value of $\sqrt{x}$ by substituting $9a^2$ for x.

$$
\begin{aligned}
\sqrt{x} &= \sqrt{9a^2} \\
&= \sqrt{9} \cdot \sqrt{a^2} \\
&= 3a
\end{aligned}
$$

Note: we could do this only because we know that $a > 0$. The radical sign ($\sqrt{}$) refers to the positive square root of a number.

5. 12

To divide powers with the same base, keep the base and subtract the exponent of the denominator from the exponent of the numerator. First get everything in the same base, since $2^2 = 4 = 4^1$, then:

$$
\begin{aligned}
\frac{4^3 - 4^2}{2^2} &= \frac{4^3 - 4^2}{4^1} \\
&= \frac{4^3}{4^1} - \frac{4^2}{4^1} \\
&= 4^{3-1} - 4^{2-1} \\
&= 4^2 - 4^1 \\
&= 16 - 4 \\
&= 12
\end{aligned}
$$

Or, since the calculations required aren't too tricky, just simplify following the order of operations.

$$\frac{4^3 - 4^2}{2^2} = \frac{64 - 16}{4} = \frac{48}{4} = 12$$

6. 64

First we need to find the value of x using the equation $3^x = 81$. Then we can find the value of x^3.

We need to express 81 as a power with a base of 3.

$$81 = 9^2 = (3^2)^2 = 3^{2 \times 2} = 3^4$$
$$x = 4$$
$$x^3 = 4^3$$
$$= 4 \times 4 \times 4 = 64$$

7. 73

Substitute 2 for x. Then $3^x + (x^3)^2 = 3^2 + (2^3)^2$

$$= 3^2 + 8^2$$
$$= 9 + 64$$
$$= 73$$

8. 0.00675×10^2

To multiply or divide a number by a power of 10, we move the decimal point to the right or left, respectively, the same number of places as the number of zeros in the power of 10. Multiplying by a negative power of 10 is the same as dividing by a positive power. For instance: $3 \times 10^{-2} = \frac{3}{10^2}$. Keeping this in mind, let's go over the choices one by one. Remember: we are looking for the choice that is NOT equal to 0.0675.

$67.5 \times 10^{-3} = 0.0675$ No good.

$6.75 \times 10^{-2} = 0.0675$ No good.

$0.675 \times 10^{-1} = 0.0675$ No good.

$0.00675 \times 10^2 = 0.675$

$0.675 \neq 0.0675$ This is the correct answer.

9. 0

The product of two negatives is positive, and the product of three negatives is negative. In fact, if we have any odd number of negative terms in a product, the result will be negative; any even number of negative terms gives a positive product. Since q is odd, we have an odd number of factors of -1. The product is -1. Adding 1 to -1, we get 0.

10. 2^{5x}

Remember the rules for operations with exponents. First you have to get both powers in terms of the same base so you can combine the exponents. Note that the answer choices all have base 2. Start by expressing 4 and 8 as powers of 2.

$$(4^x)(8^x) = (2^2)^x \cdot (2^3)^x$$

To raise a power to an exponent, multiply the exponents:

$$(2^2)^x = 2^{2x}$$

$$(2^3)^x = 2^{3x}$$

To multiply powers with the same base, add the exponents:

$$2^{2x} \cdot 2^{3x} = 2^{(2x + 3x)}$$

$$= 2^{5x}$$

11. 6

Try approximating to find n. Well, $5^2 = 25$, $5^3 = 125$, so $5^3 > 100$.

Then
$$5^4 > 100 \times 5, \text{ or } 5^4 > 500$$

$$5^5 > 500 \times 5, \text{ or } 5^5 > 2{,}500$$

$$5^6 > 2{,}500 \times 5, \text{ or } 5^6 > 12{,}500$$

5^6 must be greater than 10,000, but 5^5 clearly is a lot less than 10,000. So in order for 5^n to be greater than 10,000, n must be at least 6.

12. 27

This problem rewards careful translation. The square root of 81 is 9, and the square root *of the square root* of 81 is $\sqrt{9} = 3$. The question asks for the positive number whose cube root is 3. That's $3^3 = 27$.

13. I, II, and III

This question is a good review of the rules for the product of exponential expressions. In order to make the comparison easier, try to transform 8^5 and each of the three options so that they have a common base. Since 2 is the smallest base among the expressions to be compared, let it be our common base. Since $8^5 = (2^3)^5 = 2^{3 \cdot 5} = 2^{15}$, we will look for options equivalent to 2^{15}.

I: $2^5 \cdot 4^5 = 2^5 \cdot (2^2)^5 = 2^5 \cdot 2^{2 \cdot 5} = 2^5 \cdot 2^{10} = 2^{5+10} = 2^{15}$ OK
II: 2^{15} OK
III: $2^5 \cdot 2^{10} = 2^{5+10} = 2^{15}$ OK

It turns out that all three are equivalent to 2^{15} or 8^5.

14. $\dfrac{8}{3}$

The simplest approach is to express both 9 and 27 as an exponent with a common base. The most convenient base is 3, since $3^2 = 9$ and $3^3 = 27$. Then the equation becomes:

$$27^n = 9^4$$
$$(3^3)^n = (3^2)^4$$
$$3^{3 \cdot n} = 3^{2 \cdot 4}$$
$$3^{3n} = 3^8$$

If two terms with the same base are equal, the exponents must be equal.

$$3n = 8$$

$$n = \frac{8}{3}$$

15. x^2y^3z

First let's break up the expression to separate the variables, transforming the fraction into a product of three simpler fractions:

$$\frac{x^3yz^4}{xy^{-2}z^3} = \left(\frac{x^3}{x}\right)\left(\frac{y}{y^{-2}}\right)\left(\frac{z^4}{z^3}\right)$$

Now carry out each division by keeping the base and subtracting the exponents.

$$\frac{x^3}{x} = x^{3-1} = x^2$$

$$\frac{y}{y^{-2}} = y^{1-(-2)} = y^{1+2} = y^3$$

$$\frac{z^4}{z^3} = z^{4-3} = z^1 = z$$

The answer is the product of these three expressions, or x^2y^3z.

16. $5 + 2\sqrt{7}$

Subtract the length of CD from the length of AB to find out how much greater AB is than CD.

$$AB - CD = (10 + \sqrt{7}) - (5 - \sqrt{7})$$
$$= 10 + \sqrt{7} - 5 - (-\sqrt{7})$$
$$= 10 - 5 + \sqrt{7} + \sqrt{7}$$
$$= 5 + 2\sqrt{7}$$

17. 0

We are told that $x^a \cdot x^b = 1$. Since $x^a \cdot x^b = x^{a+b}$, we know that $x^{a+b} = 1$. If a number raised to a power is equal to 1, either the base is 1 or -1, or the exponent is zero. Since we are told $x \neq 1$ or -1 here, the exponent must be zero; therefore, $a + b = 0$.

Chapter 3:
Algebra

Algebra is the least frequently tested of the major math topics on the GMAT—sort of. What we mean is that there won't be that many problems that involve only algebra—maybe 20 percent of your exam. But a lot of the questions on the test will involve algebra to some degree or another, whether they are word problems, geometry, or even arithmetic problems. This makes algebra a necessary skill—you have to understand basic equations and how to solve them.

ALGEBRA LEVEL ONE

Terminology

Terms: A **term** is a numerical constant or the product (or quotient) of a numerical constant and one or more variables. Examples of terms are $3x$, $4x^2yz$, and $\dfrac{2a}{c}$.

Expressions: An **algebraic expression** is a combination of one or more terms. Terms in an expression can be separated by either + or − signs. Examples of expressions are $3xy$, $4ab + 5cd$, and $x^2 - 1$.

In the term $3xy$, the numerical constant 3 is called a **coefficient**. In a simple term such as z, 1 is the coefficient. A number without any variables is called a **constant term**. An expression with one term, such as $3xy$, is called a **monomial**; one with two terms, such as $4a + 2d$, is a **binomial**; one with three terms, such as $xy + z - a$, is a **trinomial**. The general name for expressions with more than one term is **polynomial**.

Substitution

Substitution is a method that we employ to evaluate an algebraic expression or to express an algebraic expression in terms of other variables.

Example: Evaluate $3x^2 - 4x$ when $x = 2$.
Replace every x in the expression with 2 and then carry out the designated operations.
Remember to follow the order of operations (PEMDAS).
$3x^2 - 4x = 3(2)^2 - 4(2) = 3 \times 4 - 4 \times 2 = 12 - 8 = 4$

Example: Express $\dfrac{a}{b-a}$ in terms of x and y if $a = 2x$ and $b = 3y$.

Here, we replace every "a" with $2x$ and every "b" with $3y$:

$$\frac{a}{b-a} = \frac{2x}{3y-2x}$$

Symbolism

Symbols such as $+$, $-$, $\times$, and $\div$ should be familiar. However, you may see strange symbols such as $\check{\mathrm{S}}$, $\diamond$, and $\blacklozenge$ on a math problem. These symbols may confuse you but the question stem in each of these problems always tells you what a strange symbol does to numbers. This type of problem may seem weird, but it is typically nothing more than an exercise in substitution.

Example: Let x^* be defined by the equation: $x^* = \dfrac{x^2}{1 - x^2}$. Evaluate $\left(\dfrac{1}{2}\right)^*$.

$$\left(\frac{1}{2}\right)^* = \frac{\left(\frac{1}{2}\right)^2}{1 - \left(\frac{1}{2}\right)^2} = \frac{\frac{1}{4}}{1 - \frac{1}{4}} = \frac{\frac{1}{4}}{\frac{3}{4}} = \frac{1}{3}$$

Operations with Polynomials

All of the laws of arithmetic operations, such as the associative, distributive, and commutative laws, are also applicable to polynomials.

Commutative law: $2x + 5y = 5y + 2x$

$5a \times 3b = 3b \times 5a = 15ab$

Associative law: $2x - 3x + 5y + 2y = (2x - 3x) + (5y + 2y) = -x + 7y$

$(-2x)\left(\dfrac{1}{2}x\right)(3y)(-2y) = (-x^2)(-6y^2) = 6x^2y^2$

Both laws: $2x + 3x^2 - 6x + 4x^2 = 2x - 6x + 3x^2 + 4x^2$ (commutative law)

$= (2x - 6x) + (3x^2 + 4x^2)$ (associative law)

$= -4x + 7x^2$

Note: This process of simplifying an expression by subtracting or adding together those terms with the same variable component is called **combining like terms.**

Distributive law: $3a(2b - 5c) = (3a \times 2b) - (3a \times 5c) = 6ab - 15ac$

Note: The product of two binomials can be calculated by applying the distributive law twice.

Example:
$$(x + 5)(x - 2) = x \cdot (x - 2) + 5 \cdot (x - 2)$$
$$= x \cdot x - x \cdot 2 + 5 \cdot x - 5 \cdot 2$$
$$= x^2 - 2x + 5x - 10$$
$$= x^2 + 3x - 10$$

A simple mnemonic for this is the word **FOIL**. Using the FOIL method in the above multiplication,

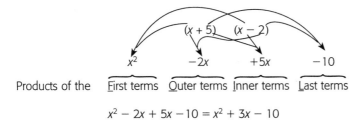

Products of the   First terms   Outer terms   Inner terms   Last terms

$$x^2 - 2x + 5x - 10 = x^2 + 3x - 10$$

Factoring Algebraic Expressions

Factoring a polynomial means expressing it as a product of two or more simpler expressions.

Common monomial factor: When there is a monomial factor common to every term in the polynomial, it can be factored out by using the distributive law.

Example: $2a + 6ac = 2a(1 + 3c)$ (here $2a$ is the greatest common factor of $2a$ and $6ac$).

Difference of two perfect squares: The difference of two squares can be factored into a product: $a^2 - b^2 = (a - b)(a + b)$.

Example: $9x^2 - 1 = (3x)^2 - (1)^2 = (3x + 1)(3x - 1)$

Polynomials of the form $a^2 + 2ab + b^2$: Any polynomial of this form is equivalent to the square of a binomial. Notice that $(a + b)^2 = a^2 + 2ab + b^2$ (try FOIL).

Factoring such a polynomial is just reversing this procedure.

Example: $x^2 + 6x + 9 = (x)^2 + 2(x)(3) + (3)^2 = (x + 3)^2$.

Polynomials of the form $a^2 - 2ab + b^2$: Any polynomial of this form is equivalent to the square of a binomial like the previous example. Here, though, the binomial is the difference of two terms: $(a - b)^2 = a^2 - 2ab + b^2$.

Polynomials of the form $x^2 + bx + c$: The polynomials of this form can nearly always be factored into a product of two binomials. The product of the first terms in each binomial must equal the first term of the polynomial. The product of the last terms of the binomials must equal the third term of the polynomial. The sum of the remaining products must equal the second term of the polynomial. Factoring can be thought of as the FOIL method backwards.

Example: $x^2 - 3x + 2$

We can factor this into two binomials, each containing an x term. Start by writing down what we know.

$x^2 - 3x + 2 = (x\qquad)(x\qquad)$

In each binomial on the right we need to fill in the missing term. The **product** of the two missing terms will be the last term in the polynomial: 2. The **sum** of the two missing terms will be the coefficient of the second term of the polynomial: -3. Try the possible factors of 2 until we get a pair that adds up to -3. There are two possibilities: 1 and 2, or -1 and -2. Since $(-1) + (-2) = -3$, we can fill -1 and -2 into the empty spaces.

Thus, $x^2 - 3x + 2 = (x - 1)(x - 2)$.

Note: Whenever you factor a polynomial, you can check your answer by using FOIL to obtain the original polynomial.

Linear Equations

An **equation** is an algebraic sentence that says that two expressions are equal to each other. The two expressions consist of numbers, variables, and arithmetic operations to be performed on these numbers and variables. To **solve** for some variable we can manipulate the equation until we have isolated that variable on one side of the equal sign, leaving any numbers or other variables on the other side. Of course, we must be careful to manipulate the equation only in accordance with the equality postulate: whenever we perform an operation on one side of the equation we must perform the same operation on the other side. Otherwise, the two sides of the equation will no longer be equal.

A linear or first-degree equation is an equation in which all the variables are raised to the first power (there are no exponents). In order to solve such an equation, we'll perform operations on both sides of the equation in order to get the variable we're solving for all alone on one side. The operations we can perform without upsetting the balance of the equation are addition, subtraction, multiplication, and division by a number other than 0. Typically, at each step in the process, we'll need to use the reverse of the operation that's being applied to the variable in order to isolate the variable. In the equation $n + 6 = 10$, 6 is being added to n on the left side. To isolate the n, we'll need to perform the reverse operation, that is, to subtract 6 from both sides. That gives us:

$$n + 6 - 6 = 10 - 6, \text{ or } n = 4.$$

Let's look at another example.

Example: If $4x - 7 = 2x + 5$, what is x?

1. Get all the terms with the variable on one side of the equation. Combine the terms.	$4x - 7 = 2x + 5$ $4x - 2x - 7 = 2x - 2x + 5$ $2x - 7 = 5$
2. Get all constant terms on the other side of the equation.	$2x - 7 + 7 = 5 + 7$ $2x = 12$
3. Isolate the variable by dividing both sides by its coefficient.	$\dfrac{2x}{2} = \dfrac{12}{2}$ $x = 6$

We can easily check our work when solving this kind of equation. The answer we arrive at represents the value of the variable which makes the equation hold true. Therefore, to check that it's correct, we can just substitute this value for the variable in the original equation. If the equation holds true, we've found the correct answer. In the above example, we got a value of 6 for x. Replacing x with 6 in our original equation gives us $4(6) - 7 = 2(6) + 5$, or $17 = 17$. That's clearly true, so our answer is indeed correct.

Equations with fractional coefficients can be a little more tricky. They can be solved using the same approach, although this often leads to rather involved calculations. Instead, they can be transformed into an equivalent equation that does not involve fractional coefficients. Let's see how to solve such a problem.

Example: Solve: $\dfrac{x-2}{3} + \dfrac{x-4}{10} = \dfrac{x}{2}$

1. Multiply both sides of the equation by the Lowest Common Denominator (LCD). Here the LCD is 30.

$$30\left(\frac{x-2}{3}\right) + 30\left(\frac{x-4}{10}\right) = 30\left(\frac{x}{2}\right)$$

$$10(x-2) + 3(x-4) = 15(x)$$

2. Clear parentheses using the distributive property, and combine like terms.

$$10x - 20 + 3x - 12 = 15x$$
$$13x - 32 = 15x$$

3. Isolate the variable. Again, combine like terms.

$$-32 = 15x - 13x$$
$$-32 = 2x$$

4. Divide both sides by the coefficient of the variable.

$$x = \frac{-32}{2} = -16$$

ALGEBRA LEVEL ONE EXERCISE

Simplify questions 1–10; factor questions 11–20. (Answers are on the following page.)

1. $2x + 4y + 7x - 6y =$

2. $2x(4y + 3x) =$

3. $x(x^2 + x + 1) - x^2 =$

4. $(y^2 + 1)(x^2 + 1) =$

5. $(2a - b)(2a + b) =$

6. $(4x + y)(x + 4y) - 17xy =$

7. $(x^2 - 1)(x^2 + 1) =$

8. $xyz\left(\dfrac{1}{xy} + \dfrac{x}{zy} + \dfrac{yz}{xyz}\right) =$

9. $\left(\dfrac{zxy}{z}\right)\left(\dfrac{z^2y}{x}\right)\left(\dfrac{z}{y^2}\right) =$

10. $\left(\dfrac{x^4}{y^3}\right)\left(\dfrac{y^2}{x^3}\right)\left(\dfrac{x}{y}\right) =$

11. $x^2 + xy + x =$

12. $y^3 + 2y^2 + y =$

13. $5x^2 - 5 =$

14. $x^4 - x^2 =$

15. $x^2 - 6x + 9 =$

16. $x^2 + 10x + 25 =$

17. $x^2 + x + \dfrac{1}{4} =$

18. $x^2 - 4x + 4 =$

19. $x^2 + 7x + 10 =$

20. $x^2 + 10x + 9 =$

ANSWER KEY
BEGINS ON NEXT PAGE

ANSWER KEY—ALGEBRA LEVEL ONE EXERCISE

1. $9x - 2y$

2. $8xy + 6x^2$

3. $x^3 + x$

4. $x^2y^2 + x^2 + y^2 + 1$

5. $4a^2 - b^2$

6. $4x^2 + 4y^2$

7. $x^4 - 1$

8. $z + x^2 + yz$

9. z^3

10. $\dfrac{x^2}{y^2}$

11. $x(x + y + 1)$

12. $y(y + 1)^2$

13. $5(x - 1)(x + 1)$

14. $x^2(x - 1)(x + 1)$

15. $(x - 3)^2$

16. $(x + 5)^2$

17. $\left(x + \dfrac{1}{2}\right)^2$ or $\dfrac{(2x+1)^2}{4}$

18. $(x - 2)^2$

19. $(x + 2)(x + 5)$

20. $(x + 9)(x + 1)$

ALGEBRA LEVEL ONE TEST

Solve the following problems and choose the best answer. (Answers and explanations are at the end of the chapter.)

Basic

1. If $x = -3$, what is the value of the expression $x^2 + 3x + 3$?

   ○ -21

   ○ -15

   ○ -6

   ○ 3

   ○ 21

2. If $3x + 1 = x$, then $x =$

   ○ -2

   ○ -1

   ○ $-\dfrac{1}{2}$

   ○ $\dfrac{1}{3}$

   ○ $\dfrac{1}{2}$

3. If $0.5959 = 59x$, then $x =$

   ○ 0.01

   ○ 0.0101

   ○ 0.11

   ○ 0.111

   ○ 1.01

4. If $5 - 2x = 15$, then $x =$

   ○ -10

   ○ -5

   ○ 1

   ○ 5

   ○ 10

5. $5z^2 - 5z + 4 - z(3z - 4) =$

   ○ $2z^2 - z + 4$

   ○ $2z^2 - 9z + 4$

   ○ $5z^2 - 8z + 8$

   ○ $5z^2 - 8z$

   ○ $2z^2 - 5z$

6. If $a = -1$ and $b = -2$, what is the value of the expression $2a^2 - 2ab + b^2$?

   ○ -6

   ○ -2

   ○ 0

   ○ 2

   ○ 4

7. If $b = -3$, what is the value of the expression $3b^2 - b$?

   ○ -30

   ○ -24

   ○ 0

   ○ 24

   ○ 30

KAPLAN

8. What is the value of the expression
   $x^2 + xy + y^2$ when $x = -2$ and $y = 2$?

   ○ -24

   ○ -4

   ○ 2

   ○ 4

   ○ 6

9. What is the value of a if $ab + ac = 21$ and
   $b + c = 7$?

   ○ -3

   ○ -1

   ○ 0

   ○ 3

   ○ 7

10. If $a = 2$, $b = -1$ and $c = 1$, which of the
    following is (are) true?

    I. $a + b + c = 2$

    II. $2a + bc = 4$

    III. $4a - b + c = 8$

    ○ I only

    ○ III only

    ○ I and II only

    ○ I and III only

    ○ I, II, and III

Intermediate

11. If $y \neq z$, then $\dfrac{xy - zx}{z - y} =$

    ○ x

    ○ 1

    ○ 0

    ○ -1

    ○ $-x$

12. If $q \times 34 \times 36 \times 38 = 17 \times 18 \times 19$, then $q =$

    ○ $\dfrac{1}{8}$

    ○ $\dfrac{1}{6}$

    ○ $\dfrac{1}{2}$

    ○ 2

    ○ 8

13. For all x and y, $(x + 1)(y + 1) - x - y =$

    ○ $xy - x - y + 1$

    ○ $xy + 1$

    ○ $-x - y + 1$

    ○ $x^2 + y^2 - 1$

    ○ 1

14. If the product of 4, 5, and q is equal to the product of 5, p, and 2, and $pq \neq 0$, what is the value of the quotient $\dfrac{p}{q}$?

    ○ $\dfrac{5}{2}$

    ○ 2

    ○ $\dfrac{1}{2}$

    ○ $\dfrac{2}{5}$

    ○ $\dfrac{1}{10}$

15. If $\dfrac{x + 3}{2} + x + 3 = 3$, then $x =$

    ○ -3

    ○ $-\dfrac{3}{2}$

    ○ -1

    ○ 0

    ○ 1

16. Which of the following is equivalent to $3x^2 + 18x + 27$?

    ○ $3(x^2 + 6x + 3)$

    ○ $3(x + 3)(x + 6)$

    ○ $3(x + 3)(x + 3)$

    ○ $3x(x + 6 + 9)$

    ○ $3x^2 + x(18 + 27)$

KAPLAN

17. In the equation $mx + 5 = y$, m is a constant. If $x = 2$ when $y = 1$, then what is the value of x when $y = -1$?

   ○ -1

   ○ 0

   ○ 1

   ○ 2

   ○ 3

18. If $\dfrac{5q + 7}{2} = 8 + q$, then $q =$

   ○ -3

   ○ 0

   ○ 3

   ○ $3\dfrac{1}{4}$

   ○ 9

19. $(a^2 + b)^2 - (a^2 - b)^2 =$

   ○ $-4a^2b$

   ○ 0

   ○ $(2ab)^2$

   ○ $4a^2b$

   ○ b^4

20. If $x = 4$ and $y = 5$, then
   $$\frac{y}{x} + \frac{x}{y} =$$

   ○ 1

   ○ $\dfrac{41}{40}$

   ○ $\dfrac{9}{5}$

   ○ 2

   ○ $\dfrac{41}{40}$

Advanced

21. If $abc \neq 0$, then $\dfrac{a^2bc + ab^2c + abc^2}{abc} =$

    ○ $a + b + c$

    ○ $\dfrac{a+b+c}{abc}$

    ○ $a^3b^3c^3$

    ○ $3abc$

    ○ $2abc$

22. The expression $\dfrac{3}{x-1} - 6$ will equal 0 when x equals which of the following?

    ○ -3

    ○ $-\dfrac{2}{3}$

    ○ $\dfrac{1}{2}$

    ○ $\dfrac{3}{2}$

    ○ 3

23. If $\dfrac{3M}{2N} = 0.125$, what is the value of N in terms of M?

    ○ $\dfrac{M}{8}$

    ○ $\dfrac{8}{M}$

    ○ $4M$

    ○ $8M$

    ○ $12M$

24. If $m \blacktriangle n$ is defined by the equation $m \blacktriangle n = \dfrac{m^2 - n + 1}{mn}$, for all nonzero m and n, then $3 \blacktriangle 1 =$

    ○ $\dfrac{9}{4}$

    ○ 3

    ○ $\dfrac{11}{3}$

    ○ 6

    ○ 9

25. If $y > 0$ and $3y - 2 = \dfrac{-1}{3y+2}$, then $y =$

    ○ $\dfrac{1}{3}$

    ○ $\dfrac{\sqrt{3}}{3}$

    ○ 1

    ○ $\sqrt{3}$

    ○ $\sqrt{3} + 1$

26. For all m and n, $m(m - n) - n(m - n) =$

    ○ $m^2 - 2mn - n^2$

    ○ $m^2 - 2mn + n^2$

    ○ $m^2 + 2mn + n^2$

    ○ $m^2 + 2mn - n^2$

    ○ $m^2 - n^2$

KAPLAN

ALGEBRA LEVEL TWO

Inequalities

Inequality symbols:

> $>$ greater than
>
> $<$ less than
>
> $\geq$ greater than or equal to
>
> $\leq$ less than or equal to

Example: $x > 4$ means x can be any number greater than 4.

Example: $x < 0$ means x can be any number less than zero (the negative numbers).

Example: $x \geq -2$ means x can be -2 or any number greater than -2.

Example: $x \leq \frac{1}{2}$ means x can be $\frac{1}{2}$ or any number less than $\frac{1}{2}$.

A range of values is often expressed on a number line. Two ranges are shown below.

(a)

(b)

(a) represents the set of all numbers between -4 and 0 **excluding** the endpoints -4 and 0, or $-4 < x < 0$.

(b) represents the set of all numbers greater than -1, up to and **including** 3, or $-1 < x \leq 3$.

Solving Inequalities: We use the same methods as used in solving equations with one exception:

If the inequality is multiplied or divided by a negative number, the direction of the inequality is reversed.

If the inequality $-3x < 2$ is multiplied by -1, the resulting inequality is $3x > -2$.

Example: Solve for x and represent the solution set on a number line: $3 - \frac{x}{4} \geq 2$

(1) Multiply both sides by 4. $\qquad\qquad\qquad 12 - x \geq 8$

(2) Subtract 12 from both sides. $\qquad\qquad\qquad -x \geq -4$

(3) Divide both sides by -1 and change the direction of the sign. $\qquad\qquad x \leq 4$

Note: The solution set to an inequality is not a single value but a range of possible values. Here the values include 4 and all numbers below 4.

Literal Equations

If a problem involves more than one variable, we cannot find a specific value for a variable; we can only solve for one variable in terms of the others. To do this, try to get the desired variable alone on one side, and all the other variables on the other side.

Example: In the formula $V = \dfrac{PN}{R + NT}$, solve for N in terms of P, R, T, and V.

(1) Clear denominators by **cross-multiplying**.

$$\frac{V}{1} = \frac{PN}{R + NT}$$
$$V(R + NT) = PN$$

(2) Remove parentheses by distributing.

$$VR + VNT = PN$$

(3) Put all terms containing N on one side and all other terms on the other side.

$$VNT - PN = -VR$$

(4) Factor out the common factor N.

$$N(VT - P) = -VR$$

(5) Divide by $(VT - P)$ to get N alone.

$$N = \frac{-VR}{VT - P}$$

Note: We can reduce the number of negative terms in the answer by multiplying both the numerator and the denominator of the fraction on the right-hand side by -1.

$$N = \frac{VR}{P - VT}$$

Simultaneous Equations

Earlier, we solved one equation for one variable, and were able to find a numerical value for that variable. In the example above we were not able to find a numerical value for N because our equation contained variables other than just N. In general, if you want to find numerical values for all your variables, you will need as many distinct equations as you have variables. Let's say, for example, that we have one equation with two variables: $x - y = 7$. There are an infinite number of solution sets to this equation: e.g., $x = 8$ and $y = 1$ (since $8 - 1 = 7$), or $x = 9$ and $y = 2$ (since $9 - 2 = 7$), etc. If we are given two distinct equations with two variables, we can combine the equations to obtain a unique solution. Isolate the variable in one equation, then plug that expression into the other equation.

Example: Find the values of m and n if $m = 4n + 2$ and $3m + 2n = 16$.

(1) We know that $m = 4n + 2$. Substitute $4n + 2$ for m in the second equation.

$$3(4n + 2) + 2n = 16$$
$$12n + 6 + 2n = 16$$

(2) Solve for n.

$$14n = 10$$
$$n = \frac{10}{14} = \frac{5}{7}$$

(3) To find the value of m, substitute $\frac{5}{7}$ for n in the first equation and solve.

$$m = 4n + 2$$
$$m = 4\left(\frac{5}{7}\right) + 2$$
$$m = \frac{20}{7} + \frac{14}{7} = \frac{34}{7}$$

Quadratic Equations

If we set the polynomial $ax^2 + bx + c$ equal to 0, we have a special name for it. We call it a **quadratic equation**. Since it is an equation, we can find the value(s) for x which make the equation work.

Example: $x^2 - 3x + 2 = 0$

To find the solutions, or roots, let's start by doing what we did earlier in this chapter and factoring. Let's factor $x^2 - 3x + 2$. We can factor $x^2 - 3x + 2$ into $(x - 2)(x - 1)$, making our quadratic equation:

$$(x - 2)(x - 1) = 0$$

Now, we have a product of two binomials which is equal to 0. When is a product of two terms equal to 0? The only time that happens is when at least one of the terms is 0. If the product of $(x - 2)$ and $(x - 1)$ is equal to 0, that means either the first term equals 0 or the second term equals 0. So to find the roots, we just need to set the two binomials equal to 0. That gives us:

$$x - 2 = 0 \quad \text{or} \quad x - 1 = 0$$

Solving for x, we get $x = 2$ or $x = 1$. As a check, we can plug in 1 and 2 into the equation $x^2 - 3x + 2 = 0$, and we'll see that either value makes the equation work.

Functions

Classic function notation problems may appear on the test. An algebraic expression of only one variable may be defined as a function, f or g, of that variable.

Example: What is the minimum value of the function $f(x) = x^2 - 1$?

In the function $f(x) = x^2 - 1$, if x is 1, then $f(1) = 1^2 - 1 = 0$. In other words, by inputting 1 into the function, the output $f(x) = 0$. Every number inputted has one and only one output (though the reverse is not necessarily true). You're asked here to find the minimum value, that is, the smallest possible value of the function. Minimums are usually found using calculus, but there is no need to use anything that complicated on the GMAT.

Any minimum (or maximum) value problem on the test can be solved in one of two simple ways. Either plug the answer choices into the function and find which gives you the lowest value, or use some common sense. In the case of $f(x) = x^2 - 1$, the function will be at a minimum when x^2 is as small as possible. Since x^2 gets larger the farther x is from 0, x^2 is as small as possible when $x = 0$. Consequently, the smallest value of $x^2 - 1$ occurs when $x = 0$. So $f(0) = 0^2 - 1 = -1$, which is the minimum value of the function.

ALGEBRA LEVEL TWO EXERCISE

Solve the following problems as directed. (Answers are on the following page.)

Solve each of the following inequalities for x.

1. $3x + 4 > 64$

2. $2x + 1 < 21$

3. $-x + 1 \leq 63 + x$

4. $21x - 42 \leq 14x$

5. $6 > x + 4 > 4$

6. $2x > x + 10$

Solve each of the following for x in terms of the other variables. (Assume none of the variables equals zero.)

7. $abx = c$

8. $a + bx = c + dx$

9. $ax - x = bx + c$

10. $\dfrac{ax}{b + cx} = 1$

Solve each of the following pairs of equations for x and y.

11. $x + y = 2$
    $x - y = 4$

12. $2x + y = 3$
    $2x + 3y = 6$

13. $2x + 3y = 0$
    $-2x + 3y = 6$

14. $21x + 7y = 3$
    $21x + 10y = 3$

15. $x + 2y = 9$
    $2x - 3y = 4$

ANSWER KEY—ALGEBRA LEVEL TWO EXERCISE

1. $x > 20$

2. $x < 10$

3. $x \geq -31$

4. $x \leq 6$

5. $0 < x < 2$

6. $x > 10$

7. $\dfrac{c}{ab}$

8. $\dfrac{c-a}{b-d}$

9. $\dfrac{c}{a-b-1}$

10. $\dfrac{b}{a-c}$

11. $x = 3, y = -1$

12. $x = \dfrac{3}{4}, y = \dfrac{3}{2}$

13. $x = -\dfrac{3}{2}, y = 1$

14. $x = \dfrac{1}{7}, y = 0$

15. $x = 5, y = 2$

ALGEBRA LEVEL TWO TEST

Solve the following problems and choose the best answer. (Answers and explanations are at the end of this chapter.)

Basic

1. If $3m < 48$ and $2m > 24$, then m could equal which of the following?

   ○ 10

   ○ 12

   ○ 14

   ○ 16

   ○ 18

2. If $a < b$ and $b < c$, then which of the following must be true?

   ○ $b + c < 2a$

   ○ $a + b < c$

   ○ $a - b < b - c$

   ○ $a + b < 2c$

   ○ $a + c < 2b$

3. The inequality $3x - 16 > 4x + 12$ is true if and only if which of the following is true?

   ○ $x < -28$

   ○ $x < -7$

   ○ $x > -7$

   ○ $x > -16$

   ○ $x > -28$

4. For all integers m and n, where $m \neq n$, $m \uparrow n = \left| \dfrac{m^2 - n^2}{m - n} \right|$. What is the value of $-2 \uparrow 4$?

   ○ 10

   ○ 8

   ○ 6

   ○ 2

   ○ 0

5. If $a > b > c$, then all of the following could be true EXCEPT

   ○ $b + c < a$

   ○ $2a > b + c$

   ○ $2c > a + b$

   ○ $ab > bc$

   ○ $a + b > 2b + c$

KAPLAN

6. If $b \neq -2$ and $\dfrac{a+3}{b+2} = \dfrac{3}{5}$, what is b in terms of a?

    ◯ $\dfrac{5}{3}a + 1$

    ◯ $\dfrac{3}{5}a + 3$

    ◯ $\dfrac{5}{3}a + 3$

    ◯ $\dfrac{3}{5}a - 1$

    ◯ $\dfrac{5}{3}a - 3$

7. If $m \neq -1$ and $mn - 3 = 3 - n$, then $n =$

    ◯ 6

    ◯ $\dfrac{6}{m+1}$

    ◯ $\dfrac{6}{m-1}$

    ◯ $\dfrac{6}{m+n}$

    ◯ $\dfrac{6}{m-n}$

Intermediate

8. If $a = \dfrac{c-b}{bd}$, then $b =$

   ⬭ $\dfrac{c}{ad-1}$

   ⬭ $\dfrac{c+1}{ad}$

   ⬭ $ad + c$

   ⬭ $\dfrac{c}{ad+1}$

   ⬭ $adc + 1$

9. If $a < b < c < 0$, which of the following quotients is the greatest?

   ⬭ $\dfrac{a}{b}$

   ⬭ $\dfrac{b}{c}$

   ⬭ $\dfrac{c}{a}$

   ⬭ $\dfrac{a}{c}$

   ⬭ It cannot be determined from the information given.

10. If $2x + y = -8$ and $-4x + 2y = 16$, what is the value of y?

    ⬭ -4

    ⬭ -2

    ⬭ 0

    ⬭ 2

    ⬭ 4

Advanced

11. Which of the following describes all values of x that are solutions to the inequality $|x + 2| > 6$?

    ○ $x > 4$

    ○ $x > 8$

    ○ $x < -8$ or $x > 4$

    ○ $x < 4$ or $x > 8$

    ○ $-8 < x < 4$

12. Let $\&x\& = 5x - 7$ and let $\heartsuit y \heartsuit z \heartsuit = \dfrac{3y}{z}$. If $p = \heartsuit 7 \heartsuit 15 \heartsuit$, then $\&p\& =$

    ○ 0

    ○ 2

    ○ 15

    ○ $\dfrac{176}{7}$

    ○ 28

13. If $x^2 - 9 < 0$, which of the following is true?

    ○ $x < -3$

    ○ $x > 3$

    ○ $x > 9$

    ○ $x < -3$ or $x > 3$

    ○ $-3 < x < 3$

14. If $n > 4$, which of the following is equivalent to $\dfrac{n - 4\sqrt{n} + 4}{\sqrt{n} - 2}$?

    ○ $\sqrt{n}$

    ○ $2\sqrt{n}$

    ○ $\sqrt{n} + 2$

    ○ $\sqrt{n} - 2$

    ○ $n + \sqrt{n}$

15. What is the set of all values of x for which $x^2 - 3x - 18 = 0$?

    ○ $\{-6\}$

    ○ $\{-3\}$

    ○ $\{-3, 6\}$

    ○ $\{3, 6\}$

    ○ $\{2, 6\}$

ALGEBRA LEVEL ONE TEST
ANSWERS AND EXPLANATIONS

1. **3**

We want to find the value of the expression when x is -3. Let's plug in -3 for each x and see what we get:

$$x^2 + 3x + 3 = (-3)^2 + 3(-3) + 3 = 9 + (-9) + 3 = 3$$

2. $-\dfrac{1}{2}$

What we have to do is herd all the x's to one side of the equal sign and all the numerical values to the other side: adding $-x$ to both sides we see that $2x + 1 = 0$. Adding -1 to both sides, we get $2x = -1$. Now we can find out what x must equal by dividing both sides by 2:

$$2x = -1$$
$$\frac{2x}{2} = -\frac{1}{2}$$
$$x = -\frac{1}{2}$$

3. **0.0101**

Divide both sides by 59. (Watch your decimal places!)

$$0.5959 = 59x$$
$$\frac{0.5959}{59} = x$$
$$x = 0.0101$$

4. **−5**

We are given that $5 - 2x = 15$. Solve for x by subtracting 5 from each side of the equation, then dividing each side by -2:

$$5 - 2x = 15$$
$$-2x = 10 \text{ (Subtracting 5 from each side)}$$
$$x = -5 \text{ (Dividing each side by } -2)$$

5. $2z^2 - z + 4$

Before we can carry out any other operations, we have to remove the parentheses (that's what the "P" stands for in PEMDAS). Here we can use the distributive law:

$$z(3z - 4) = z \cdot 3z - z \cdot 4$$
$$= 3z^2 - 4z$$

But this is not all there is to it—we're **subtracting** this whole expression from $5z^2 - 5z + 4$. Since subtraction is the inverse operation of addition, we must change the signs of $3z^2 - 4z$.

$$5z^2 - 5z + 4 - (3z^2 - 4z) = 5z^2 - 5z + 4 - 3z^2 + 4z$$

And finally, combining like terms gives us

$$= (5z^2 - 3z^2) + (-5z + 4z) + 4$$
$$= 2z^2 - z + 4$$

6. 2

Plug in -1 for each a and -2 for each b:

$$2a^2 - 2ab + b^2 = 2(-1)^2 - 2(-1)(-2) + (-2)^2$$
$$= 2 - 4 + 4$$
$$= 2$$

7. 30

Plug in -3 for b wherever it occurs. Remember to square before multiplying:

$$3b^2 - b = 3(-3)^2 - (-3)$$
$$= 3(9) - (-3)$$
$$= 27 + 3$$
$$= 30$$

8. 4

Here we have two values to substitute for two variables. Plug in -2 for x and 2 for y:

$$x^2 + xy + y^2 = (-2)^2 + (-2)(2) + (2)^2$$
$$= 4 + (-4) + 4$$
$$= 4$$

9. **3**

We have to use algebraic factoring to make better use of the first equation. We're given:

$$ab + ac = 21$$
$$a(b + c) = 21$$

We're also told that $b + c = 7$, so substitute 7 for $b + c$:

$$a(b + c) = 21$$
$$a(7) = 21$$

Now solve for a:

$$a = \frac{21}{7} = 3$$

10. **I only**

Substitute $a = 2, b = -1$ and $c = 1$ into the statements.

Statement I: $a + b + c = 2 + (-1) + 1$
$$= 2$$

Statement I is true, so eliminate choice (2).

Statement II: $2a + bc = 2(2) + (-1)(1)$
$$= 4 - 1$$
$$= 3$$

Statement II is false, so eliminate choices (3) and (5).

Statement III: $4a - b + c = 4(2) - (-1) + 1$
$$= 8 + 1 + 1$$
$$= 10$$

Statement III is false, and the correct answer is choice (1).

11. **$-x$**

Whenever you are asked to simplify a fraction involving binomials, your first thought should be: Factor! Since x is in both terms of the numerator, we can factor out x and get

$$xy - zx = x(y - z)$$

Performing this operation on the original fraction, we find that

$$\frac{xy - zx}{z - y} = \frac{x(y - z)}{z - y}$$

Rewriting $(z - y)$ as $-1(y - z)$, we get

$$= \frac{x(y - z)}{-1(y - z)}$$

Now cancel $y - z$ from the top and bottom

$$= \frac{x}{-1} = -x$$

Note: It is important that we are told that $y \neq z$ here; otherwise we could have zero in the denominator, and the expression would be undefined.

12. $\dfrac{1}{8}$

Don't multiply anything out! If you are given such a bizarre-looking expression, there must be a way to simplify. Notice that each of the numbers on the right side is a factor of a number on the left side. So divide each side of the equation by $34 \times 36 \times 38$ to isolate q:

$$q = \frac{17 \times 18 \times 19}{34 \times 36 \times 38}$$

$$= \frac{17}{34} \times \frac{18}{36} \times \frac{19}{38}$$

$$= \frac{1}{2} \times \frac{1}{2} \times \frac{1}{2}$$

$$= \frac{1}{8}$$

13. $xy + 1$

To simplify the expression, first use the FOIL method to multiply the binomials $x + 1$ and $y + 1$, then combine terms.

$$\begin{array}{cccc} \text{F} & \text{O} & \text{I} & \text{L} \end{array}$$
$$(x + 1)(y + 1) = xy + x \cdot 1 + y \cdot 1 + 1 \cdot 1$$
$$= xy + x + y + 1$$

So,

$$(x + 1)(y + 1) - x - y = xy + x + y + 1 - x - y$$
$$= xy + 1$$

14. 2

We're told that $4 \times 5 \times q = 5 \times p \times 2$. The number 5 is a common factor so we can cancel it from each side. We are left with $4q = 2p$ or $2q = p$. Dividing both sides by q in order to get the quotient $\frac{p}{q}$ on one side, we find $\frac{p}{q} = 2$.

15. −1

We start with:

$$\frac{x+3}{2} + x + 3 = 3$$

Multiply both sides of the equation by 2, to get rid of the 2 in the denominator of the first term.

$$\frac{2(x+3)}{2} + 2(x+3) = 2(3)$$

$$(x+3) + 2(x+3) = 6$$

Next multiply out the parentheses and combine like terms. Our equation becomes:

$$x + 3 + 2x + 6 = 6$$

$$3x + 9 = 6$$

Now isolate the variable on one side of the equation:

$$3x + 9 - 9 = 6 - 9$$

$$3x = -3$$

Finally divide both sides by the coefficient of the variable.

$$\frac{3x}{3} = \frac{-3}{3}$$

$$x = -1$$

16. $3(x+3)(x+3)$

First factor out the 3 common to all terms:

$$3x^2 + 18x + 27 = 3(x^2 + 6x + 9)$$

This is not the same as any answer choice, so we factor the polynomial.

$x^2 + 6x + 9$ is of the form $a^2 + 2ab + b^2$, with $a = x$ and $b = 3$.

KAPLAN

So $x^2 + 6x + 9 = (x + 3)^2 = (x + 3)(x + 3)$.

That is, $3x^2 + 18x + 27 = 3(x + 3)(x + 3)$.

An alternate method would be to multiply out the answer choices, and see which matches $3x^2 + 18x + 27$.

Choice 1—reject:

$$3(x^2 + 6x + 3) = 3x^2 + 18x + 9$$

Choice 2—reject:

$$3(x + 3)\,(x + 6) = 3(x^2 + 6x + 3x + 18)$$
$$= 3(x^2 + 9x + 18)$$
$$= 3x^2 + 27x + 3(18)$$

Choice 3—correct:

$$3(x + 3)\,(x + 3) = 3(x^2 + 3x + 3x + 9)$$
$$= 3(x^2 + 6x + 9)$$
$$= 3x^2 + 18x + 27$$

17. 3

First, find the value of m by substituting $x = 2$ and $y = 1$ into $mx + 5 = y$, and solving for m.

$$mx + 5 = y$$
$$m(2) + 5 = 1$$
$$2m + 5 - 5 = 1 - 5$$
$$2m = -4$$
$$m = \frac{-4}{2}$$
$$m = -2$$

Since we're told m is a constant, we know that m is -2 regardless of the values of x and y. We can rewrite $mx + 5 = y$ as $-2x + 5 = y$, or $5 - 2x = y$.

Now if $y = -1$, then $5 - 2x = -1$.

Solve for x: $\quad 5 - 2x - 5 = -1 - 5$
$$-2x = -6$$
$$x = \frac{-6}{-2}$$
$$x = 3$$

18. **3**

First, get rid of the 2 in the denominator of the left hand side by multiplying both sides by 2.

$$\frac{2(5q + 7)}{2} = 2(8 + q)$$

$$5q + 7 = 16 + 2q$$

Now isolate q on one side.

$$5q + 7 = 16 + 2q$$
$$5q + 7 - 2q = 16 + 2q - 2q$$
$$3q + 7 = 16$$
$$3q + 7 - 7 = 16 - 7$$
$$3q = 9$$
$$\frac{3q}{3} = \frac{9}{3}$$
$$q = 3$$

19. **$4a^2 b$**

Multiply out each half of the expression using FOIL.

$$(a^2 + b)^2 = (a^2 + b)(a^2 + b)$$
$$= a^4\textbf{[F]} + a^2b\textbf{[O]} + ba^2\textbf{[I]} + b^2\textbf{[L]}$$
$$= a^4 + 2a^2b + b^2$$

$$(a^2 - b)^2 = (a^2 - b)(a^2 - b)$$
$$= a^4\textbf{[F]} + a^2(-b)\textbf{[O]} + (-b)a^2\textbf{[I]} + (-b)^2\textbf{[L]}$$
$$= a^4 - 2a^2b + b^2$$

Now subtract

$$(a^2 + b)^2 - (a^2 - b)^2 = (a^4 + 2a^2b + b^2) - (a^4 - 2a^2b + b^2)$$
$$= a^4 + 2a^2b + b^2 - a^4 + 2a^2b - b^2$$
$$= 2a^2b + 2a^2b$$
$$= 4a^2b$$

20. $\dfrac{41}{20}$

We begin by substituting the values given for *x* and for *y*. Then we'll find a common denominator and add the numerators to solve:

$$\frac{5}{4} + \frac{4}{5} = \frac{25}{20} + \frac{16}{20} = \frac{41}{20}$$

21. $a + b + c$

In this problem, the expression has three terms in the numerator, and a single term, abc, in the denominator. Since the three terms in the numerator each have abc as a factor, abc can be factored out from both the numerator and the denominator, and the expression can be reduced to a simpler form.

$$\frac{a^2bc + ab^2c + abc^2}{abc} = \frac{a(abc) + b(abc) + c(abc)}{abc}$$
$$= \frac{(a + b + c)(abc)}{abc}$$
$$= (a + b + c)\frac{abc}{abc}$$
$$= a + b + c$$

22. $\dfrac{3}{2}$

We are asked to find *x* when $\dfrac{3}{x-1} - 6 = 0$. Clear the denominator by multiplying both sides by $x - 1$.

$$\frac{3}{x-1}(x-1) - 6(x-1) = 0(x-1)$$

$$3 - 6(x - 1) = 0 \qquad \text{Remove parentheses.}$$
$$3 - 6x + 6 = 0 \qquad \text{Gather like terms.}$$
$$9 - 6x = 0 \qquad \text{Isolate the variable.}$$
$$9 - 6x + 6x = 0 + 6x$$
$$9 = 6x$$
$$\frac{9}{6} = \frac{6x}{6}$$
$$\frac{3}{2} = x$$

Answer choice 4 is correct. You can check your answer by plugging $\dfrac{3}{2}$ into the original equation:

$$\frac{3}{\frac{3}{2} - 1} - 6 = \frac{3}{\frac{1}{2}} - 6 = 6 - 6 = 0$$

23. 12*M*

We want to isolate *N*. Fractions are often easier to deal with than decimals: $0.125 = \dfrac{1}{8}$.

$$\frac{3M}{2N} = \frac{1}{8}$$

Cross multiply: $\quad 8 \times 3M = 1 \times 2N$

$$24M = 2N$$

Divide by 2: $\quad 12M = N$

You also could have picked numbers. Given that one answer is $\dfrac{M}{8}$ and another is $\dfrac{8}{M}$, and the fraction in the equation is $\dfrac{1}{8}$, $M = 8$ would be a good choice.

24. 3

Here we have a symbolism problem, involving a symbol (▲) that doesn't really exist in mathematics. All you need to do is simply follow the directions given in the definition of this symbol. To find the value of 3 ▲ 1, simply plug 3 and 1 into the formula given for *m* ▲ *n*, substituting 3 for *m* and 1 for *n*. Then the equation becomes:

$$3 ▲ 1 = \frac{(3)^2 - (1) + 1}{(3)(1)}$$
$$= \frac{9 - 1 + 1}{3}$$
$$= \frac{9}{3}$$
$$= 3$$

25. $\dfrac{\sqrt{3}}{3}$

First clear the fraction by multiplying both sides of the equation by $3y + 2$.

$$(3y + 2)(3y + 2) = \frac{-1}{(3y + 2)}(3y + 2)$$

$$9y^2 - 6y + 6y - 4 = -1$$

$$9y^2 - 4 = -1$$

$$9y^2 - 4 + 4 = -1 + 4$$

$$9y^2 = 3$$

$$y^2 = \frac{3}{9}$$

$$= \frac{\sqrt{3}}{\sqrt{9}}$$

$$= \frac{\sqrt{3}}{3}$$

(Since $y > 0$, y cannot also equal $-\dfrac{\sqrt{3}}{3}$.)

26. $m^2 - 2mn + n^2$

First, we factor out the common binomial $(m - n)$:

$$m(m - n) - n(m - n) = (m - n)(m - n)$$

We should recognize that this expression would FOIL into the classic quadratic equation

$$m^2 - 2mn + n^2.$$

ALGEBRA LEVEL TWO TEST
ANSWERS AND EXPLANATIONS

1. **14**

If $3m < 48$, then $m < \dfrac{48}{3}$ or $m < 16$. And if $2m > 24$, then $m > \dfrac{24}{2}$ or $m > 12$. Thus, m has any value between 12 and 16, or $12 < m < 16$. Choice 3, 14, is the only answer choice within this range.

2. $a + b < 2c$

We're given two inequalities here: $a < b$ and $b < c$, which we can combine into one, $a < b < c$. We need to go through the answer choices to see which **must** be true.

$b + c < 2a$. Since c is greater than a and b is greater than a, the sum of b and c must be **greater** than twice a. For instance, if $a = 1$, $b = 2$, and $c = 3$, then $b + c = 5$ and $2a = 2$, so $b + c > 2a$. Choice 1 is never true.

$a + b < c$. This may or may not be true, depending on the actual values of a, b, and c. If $a = 1$, $b = 2$, and $c = 4$, then $a + b < c$. However, if $a = 2$, $b = 3$, $c = 4$, then $a + b > c$. So choice 2 is no good either.

$a - b < b - c$. This choice is easier to evaluate if we simplify it by adding $(b + c)$ to both sides.
$a - b + (b + c) < b - c + (b + c)$

$\qquad a + c < 2b$

As in choice 2, this **can** be true, but can also be false, depending on the values of a, b, and c. If $a = -1$, $b = 2$, and $c = 3$, then $a + c < 2b$. But if $a = 1$, $b = 2$, and $c = 4$, then $a + c > 2b$. Choice 3 is no good.

$a + b < 2c$. We know that $a < c$ and $b < c$. If we add these inequalities we'll get $a + b < c + c$, or $a + b < 2c$. This statement is **always** true, so it must be the correct answer.

At this point on the real exam, you should proceed to the next problem. Just for discussion, however:

$a + c < 2b$. This is the same inequality as choice 3. That was no good, and neither is this.

3. $x < -28$

Solve the inequality for x:

$3x - 16 > 4x + 12$	Subtract $3x$ from each side.
$-16 > x + 12$	Subtract 12 from each side.
$-28 > x$	

or

$\qquad x < -28$

4. 2

A fast way to solve this problem is to notice $(m^2 - n^2)$, which is the numerator of the fraction in the equation for $m \uparrow n$, is the difference between two squares. Remember that this can be factored into the product of $(m + n)$ and $(m - n)$. So the equation for $m \uparrow n$ can be simplified:

$$m \uparrow n = \left| \frac{m^2 - n^2}{m - n} \right|$$

$$= \left| \frac{(m + n)(m - n)}{m - n} \right| \qquad \text{Factoring the numerator.}$$

$$= |m + n| \qquad \text{Cancelling out } m - n.$$

So, if we substitute -2 for m and 4 for n in the simplified equation, the arithmetic is much easier, and we get:

$$-2 \uparrow 4 = |-2 + 4|$$

$$= |2|$$

$$= 2$$

5. $2c > a + b$

For this problem, we must examine each of the answer choices. We are told $a > b > c$, and asked which of the answer choices **cannot** be true. If we can find just one set of values a, b, and c, where $a > b > c$, that satisfies an answer choice, then that answer choice is eliminated.

$b + c < a$. This inequality can be true if a is sufficiently large relative to b and c. For example, if $a = 10$, $b = 3$, and $c = 2$, $a > b > c$ still holds, and $b + c < a$. No good.

$2a > b + c$. This is always true because a is greater than either b or c. So $a + a = 2a$ must be greater than $b + c$. For instance, $2(4) > 3 + 2$.

$2c > a + b$. This inequality can never be true. The sum of two smaller numbers (c's) can never be greater than the sum of two larger numbers (a and b). This is the correct answer.

Again on the real exam, you would move on after finding the right answer, but for discussion:

$ab > bc$. This will be true when the numbers are all positive. Try $a = 4$, $b = 3$, and $c = 2$.

$a + b > 2b + c$. Again this can be true if a is large relative to b and c. Try $a = 10$, $b = 2$, and $c = 1$.

6. $\frac{5}{3}a + 3$

First clear the fraction by multiplying both sides by $b + 2$.

$$\frac{a + 3}{b + 2} \cdot (b + 2) = \frac{3}{5} \cdot (b + 2)$$

$$a + 3 = \frac{3b + 6}{5} \qquad \text{Multiply both sides by 5.}$$

$$5(a + 3) = \frac{3b + 6}{5} \cdot 5$$

$$5a + 15 = 3b + 6$$
$$5a + 15 - 6 = 3b + 6 - 6$$
$$5a + 9 = 3b$$
$$\frac{5a + 9}{3} = \frac{3b}{3}$$
$$\frac{5a}{3} + \frac{9}{3} = b$$
$$\frac{5a}{3} + 3 = b$$

7. $\dfrac{6}{m+1}$

We need to isolate n on one side of the equation, and whatever's left on the other side will be an expression for n in terms of m.

$$mn - 3 = 3 - n \qquad\qquad \text{First, get all the } n\text{'s on one side.}$$
$$n + mn - 3 = 3 - n + n$$
$$mn + n - 3 = 3$$
$$mn + n = 6 \qquad\qquad \text{Then isolate } n \text{ by factoring and dividing.}$$
$$n(m + 1) = 6$$
$$\frac{n(m + 1)}{m + 1} = \frac{6}{m + 1}$$
$$n = \frac{6}{m + 1}$$

8. $\dfrac{c}{ad+1}$

When an equation contains a fraction, the first step to isolate a variable is to multiply both sides to eliminate the fraction:

$abd = c - b$

We are solving for b, so we use addition or subtraction to move all terms with b to one side:

$abd + b = c$

Now we can factor out the desired variable, then divide by everything else:

$b(ad + 1) = c$

$b = \dfrac{c}{ad + 1}$

9. $\dfrac{a}{c}$

Since the quotient of two negatives is always positive and all the variables are negative, all these quotients are positive. To maximize the value of this quotient we need a numerator with the largest possible absolute value and a denominator with the smallest possible absolute value. This means the "most" negative numerator and the "least" negative denominator.

10. **0**

To solve for y, make the x terms drop out. The first equation involves $2x$, while the second involves $-4x$, so multiply both sides of the first equation by 2.

$$2\,(2x + y) = 2\,(-8)$$
$$4x + 2y = -16$$

Adding the corresponding sides of this equation and the second equation together gives us

$$4x + 2y = -16$$
$$+\ (-4x + 2y = 16)$$
$$\overline{}$$
$$4x + 2y - 4x + 2y = -16 + 16$$
$$4y = 0$$
$$y = 0$$

11. $x < -8$ or $x > 4$

We can think of the absolute value of a number as the number's distance from zero along the number line. Here, since the absolute value of the expression is greater than 6, it could be either that the expression $x + 2$ is **greater than 6** (more than six units to the right of zero) or that the expression is **less than −6** (more than six units to the left of zero). Therefore either

$x + 2 > 6$	or	$x + 2 < -6$
$x > 4$	or	$x < -8$

12. 0

This is a symbolism problem, so && and ♥♥♥ aren't real mathematical terms we're expected to know. Rather, the definitions for each symbol are given by the question stem, so all we need to do is plug the given values into the correct equations.

Begin with the ♥♥♥ equation:

$$p = ♥7♥15♥ = \frac{3 \times 7}{15} = \frac{7}{5}$$

Now plug this value into the && equation:

$$\&p\& = \&\frac{7}{5}\& = (5 \times \frac{7}{5}) - 7 = 7 - 7 = 0$$

13. $-3 < x < 3$

Rearrange $x^2 - 9 < 0$ to get $x^2 < 9$. We're looking for all the values of x that would fit this inequality.

We need to be very careful and consider both positive **and** negative values of x. Remember that $3^2 = 9$ and also that $(-3)^2 = 9$.

We can consider the case that x is positive. If x is positive, and $x^2 < 9$, then we can simply say that $x < 3$. But what if x is negative? x can only take on values whose square is less than 9. In other words, x cannot be less than or equal to -3. (Think of smaller numbers like -4 or -5; their squares are greater than 9.)

So if x is negative, $x > -3$. Since x can also be 0, we can simply write $-3 < x < 3$.

14. $\sqrt{n} - 2$

We must try to get rid of the denominator by factoring it out of the numerator. $n - 4\sqrt{n} + 4$ is a difficult expression to work with. It may be easier if we let $t = \sqrt{n}$. Keep in mind then that $t^2 = \left(\sqrt{n}\right)\left(\sqrt{n}\right) = n$.

Then $\quad n - 4\sqrt{n} + 4 = t^2 - 4t + 4$

Using FOIL in reverse $\quad = (t-2)(t-2)$

$$= \left(\sqrt{n} - 2\right)\left(\sqrt{n} - 2\right)$$

So $\quad \dfrac{n - 4\sqrt{n} + 4}{\sqrt{n} - 2} = \dfrac{\left(\sqrt{n} - 2\right)\left(\sqrt{n} - 2\right)}{\left(\sqrt{n} - 2\right)}$

$$= \sqrt{n} - 2$$

Or pick a number for n and try each answer choice.

15. {−3,6}

Factor the quadratic

$$x^2 - 3x - 18 = (x + a)(x + b)$$

The product of a and b is $ab = -18$

The sum of a and b is $a + b = -3$

Try the factors of -18 that add to -3:

Try $a = 3,\ b = -6$ $3 \times (-6) = -18$

                                  $3 + (-6) = -3$

So $x^2 - 3x - 18 = (x + 3)(x - 6) = 0$

If this is zero, either $x + 3 = 0$, i.e., $x = -3$

or $x - 6 = 0$, i.e., $x = 6$

The set of values is therefore $\{-3, 6\}$.

Chapter 4:
Geometry

The geometry tested on the GMAT is very basic: lines, triangles, circles etc. There are only a few fundamental definitions and formulas you need to know. The exam emphasizes new ways of applying a couple of elementary rules.

Diagrams

Pay a lot of attention to diagrams. There can be a lot of information "hidden" in a diagram. If a diagram of an equilateral triangle gives you the length of one side, for instance, it actually gives the length of all sides. Similarly, if you are given the measure of one of the angles formed by the intersection of two lines, you can easily find the measure of all four angles. In fact, many geometry questions specifically test your ability to determine what additional information is implied by the information you are given in the diagram.

The diagrams on the GMAT **are** drawn to scale unless otherwise stated. You can estimate distances, angles and such from the diagram. Also note that the diagrams on Data Sufficiency questions can change if one of the statements introduces new information.

Since all diagrams on the problem solving section of the GMAT are drawn to scale, if you are stuck and are going to have to guess anyway, try to eliminate answer choices by eyeballing. By *eyeballing*, we mean estimating lengths or measures by comparing to other lengths or measures given in the diagram. If you are given the length of one line, you can use this line to get a rough idea of how long another, unmarked line might be. If the size of one angle is marked, use this angle to estimate the size of other angles.

For instance, if you are asked to find the degree measure of an angle, and the answers are widely spaced, you may be able to eliminate some answer choices by deciding if the angle in question is less than or greater than, say, 45°. For this reason you should try to get a feel for what the most commonly encountered angles look like. Angles of 30°, 45°, 60°, 90°, 120° and 180° are the most common, and you will find examples of them in the test and questions which follow.

You can also on occasion use the diagram to your advantage by looking at the question logically. For instance:

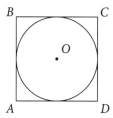

In the figure above, the circle with center O has area 4π. What is the area of square $ABCD$?

   ⭘ 4   ⭘ 2π ⭘ 12   ⭘ 16   ⭘ 8π

We know from the question stem that we have a square and a circle and we can see from the diagram that the circle is inscribed in the square, that is, touches it on all four sides. Whatever the area of the circle, we can see that the square's area must be bigger; otherwise the circle wouldn't fit inside it. So the right answer must be larger than the area of the circle, that is, larger than 4π. Now we can approximate 4π to a little more than 12. Since the correct answer is larger than 12, it must be either the fourth or fifth choice. (The correct answer is 16).

This example highlights an important point: π appears very often on geometry problems, so you should have some idea of its value. It is approximately equal to 3.14, but for most purposes you only need to remember that it is slightly greater than 3. Two other numbers you should know the approximate values of are $\sqrt{2}$, which is about 1.4, and $\sqrt{3}$, which is about 1.7.

Lines and Angles

A line is a one-dimensional geometrical abstraction—infinitely long with no width. It is not physically possible to **draw** a line; any physical line would have a finite length and some width, no matter how long and thin we tried to make it. Two points determine a straight line; given any two points, there is exactly one straight line that passes through them.

Lines: A **line segment** is a section of a straight line, of finite length with two endpoints. A line segment is named for its endpoints, as in segment AB. The **midpoint** is the point that divides a line segment into two equal parts.

$$\overset{\displaystyle 6}{\underset{\displaystyle A \qquad\qquad M \qquad\qquad B}{\bullet\!\!-\!\!-\!\!-\!\!-\!\!-\!\!-\!\!-\!\!-\!\!-\!\!-\!\!-\!\!-\!\!-\!\!-\!\!\bullet}}$$

Example: In the figure above, A and B are the endpoints of the line segment AB and M is the midpoint ($AM = MB$). What is the length of AB?

                   Since AM is 6, MB is also 6, and so AB is 6 + 6, or 12.

Two lines are **parallel** if they lie in the same plane and never intersect each other regardless of how far they are extended. If line ℓ_1 is parallel to line ℓ_2, we write $\ell_1 \parallel \ell_2$.

Angles: An **angle** is formed by two lines or line segments intersecting at a point. The point of intersection is called the **vertex** of the angle. Angles are measured in degrees(°).

Angle x, $\angle ABC$, and $\angle B$ all denote the same angle shown in the diagram above.

An **acute angle** is an angle whose degree measure is between 0° and 90°. A **right angle** is an angle whose degree measure is exactly 90°. An **obtuse angle** is an angle whose degree measure is between 90° and 180°. A **straight angle** is an angle whose degree measure is exactly 180° (half of a circle, which contains 360°).

Acute	Right	Obtuse	Straight
$(x < 90)$	$(y = 90)$	$(90 < z < 180)$	$(w = 180)$

The sum of the measures of the angles on one side of a straight line is 180°.

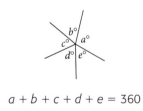

Straight
$$x + y + z = 180$$

The sum of the measures of the angles around a point is 360°.

$$a + b + c + d + e = 360$$

Two lines are **perpendicular** if they intersect at a 90° angle. The shortest distance from a point to a line is the line segment drawn from the point to the line such that it is perpendicular to the line. If line ℓ_1 is perpendicular to line ℓ_2, we write $\ell_1 \perp \ell_2$. If $\ell_1 \perp \ell_2$ and $\ell_2 \perp \ell_3$, then $\ell_1 \parallel \ell_3$, or ℓ_1 and ℓ_3 are **parallel**:

Two angles are **supplementary** if together they make up a straight angle, i.e., if the sum of their measures is 180°. Two angles are **complementary** if together they make up a right angle, i.e., if the sum of their measures is 90°.

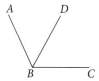

A line or line segment **bisects** an angle if it splits the angle into two smaller, equal angles. Line segment *BD* below bisects ∠*ABC*, and ∠*ABD* has the same measure as ∠*DBC*. The two smaller angles are each half the size of ∠*ABC*.

Vertical angles are a pair of opposite angles formed by two intersecting line segments. At the point of intersection, two pairs of vertical angles are formed. Angles *a* and *c* below are vertical angles, as are *b* and *d*.

The two angles in a pair of vertical angles have the same degree measure. In the diagram above, $a = c$ and $b = d$. In addition, since ℓ_1 and ℓ_2 are straight lines,

$$a + b = c + d = a + d = b + c = 180$$

In other words, each angle is supplementary to each of its two adjacent angles.

If two parallel lines intersect with a third line (called a *transversal*), each of the parallel lines will intersect the third line at the same angle. In the figure below, $a = e$. Since *a* and *e* are equal, and $c = a$ and $e = g$ (vertical angles), we know that $a = c = e = g$. Similarly, $b = d = f = h$.

If $\ell_1 \parallel \ell_2$, then,
$a = c = e = g$ and
$b = d = f = h$

In other words, when two parallel lines intersect with a third line, all acute angles formed are equal, all obtuse angles formed are equal, and any acute angle is supplementary to any obtuse angle.

SLOPE

The slope of a line tells you how steeply that line goes up or down. If a line gets higher as you move to the right, it has a positive slope. If it goes down as you move to the right, it has a negative slope.

To find the slope of a line, use the following formula:

$$\text{Slope} = \frac{\text{rise}}{\text{run}} = \frac{\text{change in } y}{\text{change in } x}$$

Rise means the difference between the *y*-coordinate values of the two points on the line, and *run* means the difference between the *x*-coordinate values.

Example: What is the slope of the line that contains the points (1, 2) and (4, −5)?

$$\text{Slope} = \frac{-5-2}{4-1} = \frac{-7}{3} = -\frac{7}{3}$$

To determine the slope of a line from an equation, put the equation into the slope-intercept form: $y = mx + b$, where the slope is m.

Example: What is the slope of the equation $3x + 2y = 4$?

$$3x + 2y = 4$$
$$2y = -3x + 4$$
$$y = -\frac{3}{2}x + 2, \text{ so } m \text{ is } -\frac{3}{2}$$

LINES AND ANGLES EXERCISE

In #1–6, find the indicated value. (Answers are on the following page.)

1.

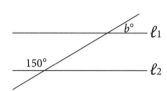

$\ell_1 \parallel \ell_2$
$b = ?$

2.

$\ell_1 \parallel \ell_2$
$s = ?$

3.

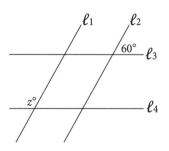

$\ell_1 \parallel \ell_2$
$\ell_3 \parallel \ell_4$
$z = ?$

4.

$z = ?$

5.

$3y° \quad 2y°$

$y = ?$

6.

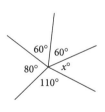

$x = ?$

**ANSWER KEY
BEGINS ON NEXT PAGE**

ANSWER KEY—LINES AND ANGLES EXERCISE

1. 30
2. 50
3. 120
4. 45
5. 36
6. 50

LINES AND ANGLES TEST

Solve the following problems and choose the best answers. (Answers and explanations are at the end of this chapter.)

Basic

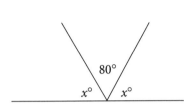

1. In the figure above, what is the value of x?

   ◯ 40

   ◯ 50

   ◯ 60

   ◯ 80

   ◯ 100

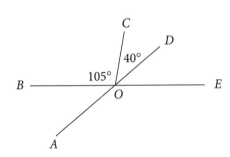

2. In the figure above, what is the measure of $\angle AOE$?

   ◯ 35°

   ◯ 45°

   ◯ 75°

   ◯ 105°

   ◯ 145°

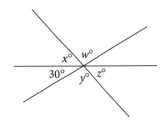

3. In the figure above, $w + x + y + z =$

   ◯ 330

   ◯ 300

   ◯ 270

   ◯ 240

   ◯ 210

4. In the figure above, what is the value of $x + y$?

   ◯ 30

   ◯ 60

   ◯ 90

   ◯ 110

   ◯ It cannot be determined from the information given.

5. In the figure above, if $y = 5x$, then $x =$

    ◯ 15
    ◯ 30
    ◯ 45
    ◯ 135
    ◯ 150

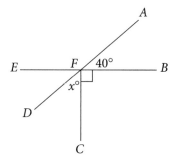

6. In the figure above, EB is perpendicular to FC, and AD and EB intersect at point F. What is the value of x?

    ◯ 30
    ◯ 40
    ◯ 50
    ◯ 60
    ◯ 130

Intermediate

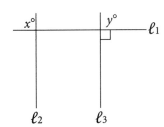

7. In the figure above, if $x = y$, which of the following MUST be true?

    I. $\ell_2 \| \ell_3$
    II. $\ell_1 \perp \ell_2$
    III. Any line that intersects ℓ_1 also intersects ℓ_2.

    ⭘ I only
    ⭘ II only
    ⭘ III only
    ⭘ I and II only
    ⭘ I, II, and III

8. In the figure above, $v = 2w$, $w = 2x$, and $x = \dfrac{y}{3}$. What is the value of y?

    ⭘ 18
    ⭘ 36
    ⭘ 45
    ⭘ 54
    ⭘ 60

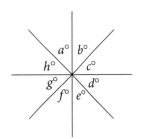

9. In the figure above, which of the following MUST equal 180?

    I. $a + b + e + h$
    II. $b + e + g + h$
    III. $a + b + d + g$

    ⭘ I only
    ⭘ II only
    ⭘ I and III only
    ⭘ II and III only
    ⭘ I, II, and III

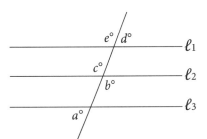

10. In the figure above, ℓ_1 is parallel to ℓ_2 and ℓ_2 is parallel to ℓ_3. What is the value of $a + b + c + d + e$?

    ⭘ 180
    ⭘ 270
    ⭘ 360
    ⭘ 450
    ⭘ It cannot be determined from the information given.

Advanced

11. Which of the following must be true of the angles marked in the figure above?

   I. $a + b = d + e$
   II. $b + e = c + f$
   III. $a + c + e = b + d + f$

   ⬭ I only
   ⬭ I and II only
   ⬭ I and III only
   ⬭ II and III only
   ⬭ I, II, and III

12. In the diagram above, $AD = BE = 6$ and $CD = 3(BC)$. If $AE = 8$, then $BC =$

   ⬭ 6
   ⬭ 4
   ⬭ 3
   ⬭ 2
   ⬭ 1

13. According to the diagram above, which of the following MUST be true?

   I. $p = x$ and $q = y$
   II. $x + y = 90$
   III. $x = y = 45$

   ⬭ I only
   ⬭ II only
   ⬭ III only
   ⬭ I and III only
   ⬭ I, II, and III

14. In the figure above, $x =$

   ⬭ 40
   ⬭ 60
   ⬭ 80
   ⬭ 100
   ⬭ 120

TRIANGLES

General Triangles

A **triangle** is a closed figure with three angles and three straight sides.

**The sum of the interior angles
of any triangle is 180 degrees.**

Each **interior angle** is supplementary to an adjacent **exterior angle**. The degree measure of an exterior angle is equal to the sum of the measures of the two non-adjacent (remote) interior angles, or 180° minus the measure of the adjacent interior angle.

In the figure below, a, b, and c are interior angles. Therefore $a + b + c = 180$. In addition, d is supplementary to c; therefore $d + c = 180$. So $d + c = a + b + c$, and $d = a + b$. Thus, the exterior angle d is equal to the sum of the two remote interior angles: a and b.

The **altitude** (or height) of a triangle is the perpendicular distance from a vertex to the side opposite the vertex. The altitude can fall inside the triangle, outside the triangle, or on one of the sides.

Altitude = AD

Altitude = EH

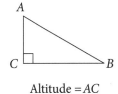

Altitude = AC

Sides and angles: The length of any side of a triangle is less than the sum of the lengths of the other two sides, and greater than the positive difference of the lengths of the other two sides.

$$b + c > a > b - c$$
$$a + b > c > a - b$$
$$a + c > b > a - c$$

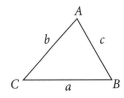

If the lengths of two sides of a triangle are unequal, the **greater angle** lies **opposite the longer side** and vice versa. In the figure above, if $\angle A > \angle B > \angle C$, then $a > b > c$.

Area of a triangle:

Example: In the diagram below, the base has length 4 and the altitude length 3, so we write:

> The area of a triangle is
> $\frac{1}{2}$ base × height

$$A = \frac{1}{2}bh$$
$$= \frac{1}{2} \cdot 4 \cdot 3 = 6$$

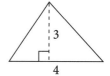

Remember that the height (or altitude) is perpendicular to the base. Therefore, when two sides of a triangle are perpendicular to each other, the area is easy to find. In a right triangle, we call the two sides that form the 90° angle the **legs**. Then the area is one half the product of the legs, or

$$A = \frac{1}{2}bh$$
$$= \frac{1}{2}\ell_1 \times \ell_2$$

Example: In the triangle below, we could treat the hypotenuse as the base, since that is the way the figure is drawn. If we did this, we would need to know the distance from the hypotenuse to the opposite vertex in order to determine the area of the triangle. A more straightforward method is to notice that this is a right triangle with legs of lengths 6 and 8, which allows us to use the alternative formula for area:

$$A = \frac{1}{2}\ell_1 \times \ell_2$$
$$= \frac{1}{2} \cdot 6 \cdot 8 = 24$$

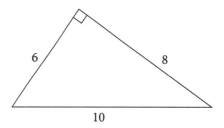

Perimeter of a triangle: The **perimeter** of a triangle is the distance around the triangle. In other words, the perimeter is equal to the sum of the lengths of the sides.

Example: In the triangle below, the sides are of length 5, 6, and 8. Therefore, the perimeter is 5 + 6 + 8 or 19.

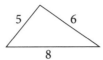

Isosceles triangles: An **isosceles triangle** is a triangle that has two sides of equal length. The two equal sides are called **legs** and the third side is called the **base**.

Since the two legs have the same length, the two angles opposite the legs must have the same measure. In the figure below, $PQ = PR$, and $\angle R = \angle Q$.

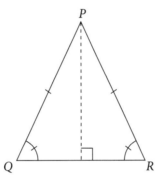

Equilateral triangles: An **equilateral triangle** has three sides of equal length and three 60° angles.

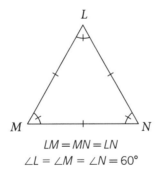

$LM = MN = LN$
$\angle L = \angle M = \angle N = 60°$

Similar triangles: Triangles are **similar** if they have the same shape—if corresponding angles have the same measure. For instance, any two triangles whose angles measure 30°, 60°, and 90° are similar. In similar triangles, corresponding sides are in the same ratio. Triangles are **congruent** if corresponding angles have the same measure and corresponding sides have the same length.

Example: What is the perimeter of $\triangle DEF$ below?

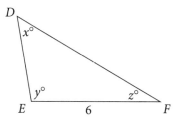

Each triangle has an $x°$ angle, a $y°$ angle, and a $z°$ angle; therefore, they are similar, and corresponding sides are in the same ratio. BC and EF are corresponding sides; each is opposite the $x°$ angle. Since EF is twice the length of BC, **each** side of $\triangle DEF$ will be twice the length of the corresponding side of $\triangle ABC$. Therefore $DE = 2(AB)$ or 4, and $DF = 2(AC)$ or 8. The perimeter of $\triangle DEF$ is $4 + 6 + 8 = 18$.

The ratio of the **areas** of two similar triangles is the **square** of the ratio of corresponding lengths. For instance, in the example above, since each side of $\triangle DEF$ is 2 times the length of the corresponding side of $\triangle ABC$, $\triangle DEF$ must have 2^2 or 4 times the area of $\triangle ABC$.

$$\frac{\text{Area } \triangle DEF}{\text{Area } \triangle ABC} = \left(\frac{DE}{AB}\right)^2 = \left(\frac{2}{1}\right)^2 = 4$$

Right Triangles

A right triangle has one interior angle of 90°. The longest side (which lies opposite the right angle, the largest angle of a right triangle) is called the **hypotenuse**. The other two sides are called the **legs**.

Pythagorean Theorem

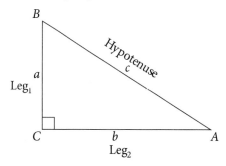

$$(\text{Leg}_1)^2 + (\text{Leg}_2)^2 = (\text{Hypotenuse})^2$$
or
$$a^2 + b^2 = c^2$$

The Pythagorean theorem holds for all right triangles, and states that the square of the hypotenuse is equal to the sum of the squares of the legs.

Some sets of integers happen to satisfy the Pythagorean theorem. These sets of integers are commonly referred to as "Pythagorean triples." One very common set that you might remember is 3, 4, and 5. Since $3^2 + 4^2 = 5^2$, you can have a right triangle with legs of lengths 3 and 4, and hypotenuse of length 5. This is probably the most common kind of right triangle on the GMAT. You should be familiar with the numbers, so that whenever you see a right triangle with legs of 3 and 4, you will immediately know the hypotenuse must have length 5. In addition, any multiple of these lengths makes another Pythagorean triple; for instance, $6^2 + 8^2 = 10^2$, so 6, 8, and 10 also make a right triangle. One other triple that appears occasionally is 5, 12, and 13.

The Pythagorean theorem is very useful whenever you're given the lengths of two sides of a right triangle; you can find the length of the third side with the Pythagorean theorem.

Example: What is the length of the hypotenuse of a right triangle with legs of length 9 and 10?

Use the theorem: the square of the length of the hypotenuse equals the sum of the squares of the lengths of the legs. Here the legs are 9 and 10, so we have:

$$\text{Hypotenuse}^2 = 9^2 + 10^2$$
$$= 81 + 100$$
$$= 181$$
$$\text{Hypotenuse} = \sqrt{181}$$

Example: What is the length of the hypotenuse of an isosceles right triangle with legs of length 4?

Since we're told the triangle is isosceles, we know two of the sides have the same length. We know the hypotenuse can't be the same length as one of the legs (the hypotenuse must be the longest side), so it must be the two legs that are equal. Therefore, in this example, the two legs have length 4, and we can use the Pythagorean theorem to find the hypotenuse.

$$\text{Hypotenuse}^2 = 4^2 + 4^2$$
$$= 16 + 16$$
$$= 32$$
$$\text{Hypotenuse} = \sqrt{32} = 4\sqrt{2}$$

You can always use the Pythagorean theorem to find the lengths of the sides in a right triangle. There are two special kinds of right triangles, though, that always have the same ratios. They are:

$1:1:\sqrt{2}$

(for isosceles right triangles)

$1:\sqrt{3}:2$

(for 30-60-90 triangles)

These triangles do not appear very frequently on the GMAT, and if one does, you can still use the Pythagorean theorem to calculate the length of a side, as we did in the last example.

TRIANGLES EXERCISE

Solve the following questions as directed. (Answers follow the exercise.)

> The sum of the measures of the angles
> in a triangle is 180°.

In #1–4, find the missing angle:

1.

$$x = ?$$

2.

$$t = ?$$

3.

$$v = ?$$

4.

$$AB = BC$$

$$x = ?$$

> In a right triangle, $\text{leg}^2 + \text{leg}^2 = \text{hyp}^2$.

In #5–12, find the missing side:

5.

$$b = ?$$

6.

$x = ?$

7.

$y = ?$

8.

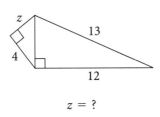

$z = ?$

The ratio of the sides in an isosceles right triangle is $1 : 1 : \sqrt{2}$.

9.

$x = ?$

10.

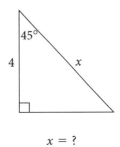

$x = ?$

> The ratio of the sides in a 30-60-90 triangle is $1 : \sqrt{3} : 2$.

11.

$b = ?$

12.

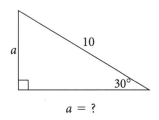

$a = ?$

> The area of a triangle is $\frac{1}{2}$(base × height).

In #13–16, find the area of the triangle:

13.

Area = ?

14.

Area = ?

15.

Area = ?

16.

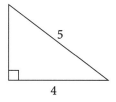

Area = ?

ANSWER KEY
BEGINS ON NEXT PAGE

ANSWER KEY—TRIANGLES EXERCISE

1. 60
2. 20
3. 70
4. 70
5. 40
6. $\sqrt{5}$
7. $\sqrt{8}$ or $2\sqrt{2}$
8. 3
9. $\sqrt{18}$ or $3\sqrt{2}$
10. $4\sqrt{2}$
11. 2
12. 5
13. 14
14. 14
15. 24
16. 6

TRIANGLES TEST

Solve the problems below and choose the best answer. (Answers and explanations are at the end of this chapter.)

Basic

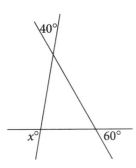

1. In the figure above, $x =$
    - ◯ 60
    - ◯ 80
    - ◯ 85
    - ◯ 90
    - ◯ 100

2. In the figure above, what is the value of x?
    - ◯ 120
    - ◯ 110
    - ◯ 90
    - ◯ 70
    - ◯ 60

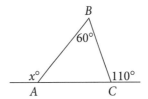

3. In the figure above, $x =$
    - ◯ 70
    - ◯ 110
    - ◯ 130
    - ◯ 150
    - ◯ 170

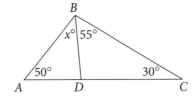

4. In ΔABC above, $x =$
    - ◯ 45
    - ◯ 55
    - ◯ 60
    - ◯ 75
    - ◯ 80

KAPLAN

Note: figure not drawn to scale.

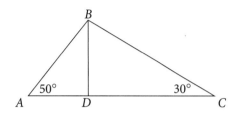

5. In the figure above, if BD bisects $\angle ABC$, then the measure of $\angle BDC$ is

    ○ 50°

    ○ 90°

    ○ 100°

    ○ 110°

    ○ 120°

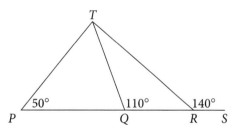

6. In the figure above, what is the measure of $\angle PTR$?

    ○ 30°

    ○ 50°

    ○ 65°

    ○ 70°

    ○ 90°

7. In the figure above, $x = 2z$ and $y = 3z$. What is the value of z?

    ○ 24

    ○ 30

    ○ 36

    ○ 54

    ○ 60

8. In the figure above, what is x in terms of y?

    ○ $150 - y$

    ○ $150 + y$

    ○ $80 + y$

    ○ $30 + y$

    ○ $30 - y$

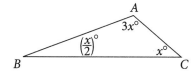

9. In $\triangle ABC$ above, $x =$

    ◯ 20
    ◯ 30
    ◯ 40
    ◯ 50
    ◯ 60

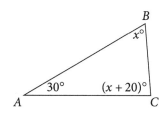

10. In $\triangle ABC$ above, $x =$

    ◯ 30
    ◯ 45
    ◯ 60
    ◯ 65
    ◯ 75

11. The angles of a triangle are in the ratio of $2:3:4$. What is the degree measure of the largest angle?

    ◯ 40
    ◯ 80
    ◯ 90
    ◯ 120
    ◯ 150

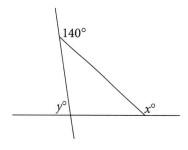

12. In the figure above, $x + y =$

    ◯ 40
    ◯ 120
    ◯ 140
    ◯ 180
    ◯ 220

Intermediate

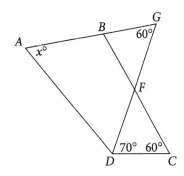

13. In the figure above, if $AD \parallel BC$, then $x =$

    ◯ 20
    ◯ 30
    ◯ 50
    ◯ 60
    ◯ 70

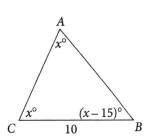

14. In $\triangle ABC$ above, which of the following must be true?

    I. $x > 50$
    II. $AC < 10$
    III. $AB > 10$

    ◯ I only
    ◯ III only
    ◯ I and II only
    ◯ I and III only
    ◯ I, II, and III

15. In the figure above, the area of $\triangle ABC$ is 6. If BC is $\dfrac{1}{3}$ the length of AB, then $AC =$

    ◯ $\sqrt{2}$
    ◯ 2
    ◯ 4
    ◯ 6
    ◯ $2\sqrt{10}$

16. What is the length of the hypotenuse of an isosceles right triangle of area 32?

    ◯ 4
    ◯ $4\sqrt{2}$
    ◯ 8
    ◯ $8\sqrt{2}$
    ◯ $8\sqrt{3}$

Advanced

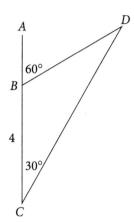

17. In the figure above, if ∠*DBA* has measure 60°, ∠*DCB* has measure 30°, and *BC* = 4, what is the length of *BD*?

- ○ $\sqrt{2}$
- ○ 4
- ○ $4\sqrt{2}$
- ○ $4\sqrt{3}$
- ○ 8

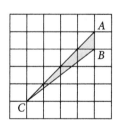

18. The figure consists of 36 squares each with a side of 1. What is the area of Δ*ABC*?

- ○ 8
- ○ 6
- ○ 4
- ○ 2
- ○ $\frac{1}{2}$

19. The lengths of two sides of a right triangle are $\frac{d}{3}$ and $\frac{d}{4}$, where $d > 0$. If one of these sides is the hypotenuse, what is the length of the third side of the triangle?

- ○ $\frac{5d}{12}$
- ○ $\frac{d}{\sqrt{7}}$
- ○ $\frac{d}{5}$
- ○ $\frac{d}{12}$
- ○ $\frac{d\sqrt{7}}{12}$

20. What is the length in feet of a ladder 24 feet from the foot of a building that reaches up 18 feet along the wall of the building?

- ○ 26
- ○ 28
- ○ 29
- ○ 30
- ○ 32

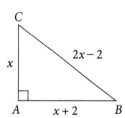

21. In right triangle *ABC* above, *x* =

- ○ 6
- ○ 8
- ○ $6\sqrt{2}$
- ○ 10
- ○ 13

POLYGONS

A **polygon** is a closed figure whose sides are straight line segments.
The **perimeter** of a polygon is the sum of the lengths of the sides.
A **vertex** of a polygon is the point where two adjacent sides meet.
A **diagonal** of a polygon is a line segment connecting two nonadjacent vertices.
A **regular polygon** has sides of equal length and interior angles of equal measure.

The number of sides determines the specific name of the polygon. A **triangle** has three sides, a **quadrilateral** has four sides, a **pentagon** has five sides, and a **hexagon** has six sides. Triangles and quadrilaterals are by far the most important polygons on the GMAT.

Interior and exterior angles: A polygon can be divided into triangles by drawing diagonals from a given vertex to all other nonadjacent vertices. For instance, the pentagon below can be divided into 3 triangles. Since the sum of the interior angles of each triangle is 180°, the sum of the interior angles of a pentagon is 3 × 180° = 540°.

The sum of the interior angles can also be found by using the formula 180° × (n − 2) where n represents the number of sides. For a pentagon that would be 180° × (5 − 2) = 180° × 3 = 540°.

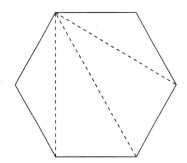

Example: What is the measure of one interior angle of the above regular hexagon?
Find the sum of the interior angles and divide by the number of interior angles, or 6. (Since all angles are equal, each of them is equal to one-sixth of the sum.)
Since we can draw 4 triangles in a 6-sided figure, the sum of the interior angles will be 4 × 180° or 720°. Therefore, each of the six interior angles has measure $\frac{720°}{6}$ or 120°.

Alternately, the sum can be calculated using the formula: 180° × (n − 2) = 180° × (6 − 2) = 180° × 4 = 720°

QUADRILATERALS

The most important quadrilaterals to know for the GMAT are the rectangle and square. Anything could show up on the test, but concentrate on the most important figures and principles. The lesser-known properties can readily be deduced from the way the figure looks, and from your knowledge of geometry.

Quadrilateral: A four-sided polygon. The sum of its four interior angles is 360°.

Rectangle: A quadrilateral with four equal angles, each a right angle.

$$AB = CD \qquad AD = CB$$

The opposite sides of a rectangle are equal in length. Also, the diagonals of a rectangle have equal length.

Square: A rectangle with four equal sides.

$$AB = BC = CD = DA$$

Areas of quadrilaterals: All formulas are based on common sense, observation, and deductions. Memorizing the formulas will save you time, but *understanding* how the formulas are derived will help you to remember them.

For the case of a rectangle, we multiply the lengths of any two adjacent sides, called the length and width, or:

Area of rectangle = ℓw

For the case of a square, since length and width are equal, we say:

Area of a square = (side)^2 = s^2

The areas of other figures can usually be found using the methods we'll discuss later in the Multiple Figures section.

QUADRILATERALS EXERCISE

Solve the problems below as directed. (Answers follow the exercise.)

> The sum of the measures of the interior angles of a quadrilateral is 360°.

In #1–6, find the indicated value.

1.

$z = ?$

2.

$y = ?$

3.

$x = ?$

4.

$a = ?$

5.

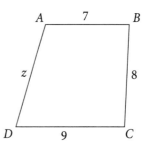

The perimeter of *ABCD* is 34.

$z = ?$

6.

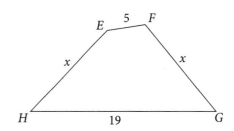

The perimeter of *EFGH* is 48.

$x = ?$

In #7–9, find the perimeter.

7.

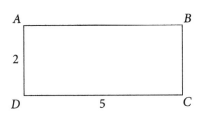

Rectangle *ABCD*

Perimeter = ?

8.

Rectangle *EFGH*

Perimeter = ?

9.

Square *QRST*

Perimeter = ?

Area of rectangle = length × width
Area of square = (side)²

In #10–12, find the area of the quadrilateral.

10.

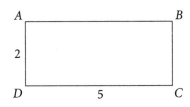

Rectangle *ABCD*

Area = ?

11.

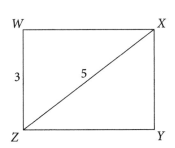

Rectangle *WXYZ*

Area = ?

12.

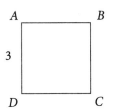

Square *ABCD*

Area = ?

In #13–15, find the indicated diagonal or side.

15.

13.

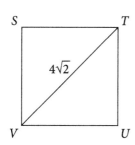

Square *STUV*

$ST = ?$

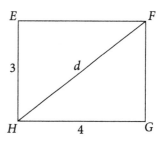

Rectangle *EFGH*

$d = ?$

14.

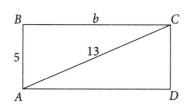

Rectangle *ABCD*

$b = ?$

ANSWER KEY—QUADRILATERALS EXERCISE

1. 90
2. 40
3. 65
4. 130
5. 10
6. 12
7. 14
8. 14
9. 20
10. 10
11. 12
12. 9
13. 4
14. 12
15. 5

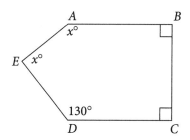

QUADRILATERALS AND OTHER POLYGONS TEST

Read the following problems and select the best answer choice. (Answers are at the end of the chapter.)

Basic

1. If each of the small squares in the figure above has area 1, what is the area of the shaded region?

   ◯ 50

   ◯ 55

   ◯ 59

   ◯ 60

   ◯ 61

2. In the figure above, $x =$

   ◯ 85

   ◯ 90

   ◯ 95

   ◯ 120

   ◯ 140

3. In pentagon $ABCDE$ above, $x =$

   ◯ 65

   ◯ 75

   ◯ 80

   ◯ 105

   ◯ 115

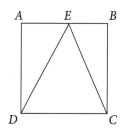

4. What is the ratio of the area of ΔDEC to the area of square $ABCD$ in the figure above?

   ◯ $\frac{1}{4}$

   ◯ $\frac{1}{3}$

   ◯ $\frac{1}{2}$

   ◯ $\frac{2}{1}$

   ◯ It cannot be determined from the information given.

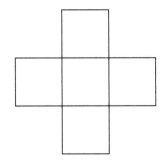

5. The figure above gives the floor dimensions, in meters, of a T-shaped room. If all the sides meet at right angles and 1 meter by 1 meter square tiles cost $2.00 each, how much would it cost to cover the entire room with these tiles?

   ◯ $48.00

   ◯ $72.00

   ◯ $96.00

   ◯ $192.00

   ◯ $198.00

6. The figure above is made up of 5 squares of equal area, with a total area of 20. What is the perimeter of the figure?

   ◯ 20

   ◯ 24

   ◯ 36

   ◯ 48

   ◯ 100

Intermediate

7. If the length of rectangle *A* is one-half the length of rectangle *B*, and the width of rectangle *A* is one-half the width of rectangle *B*, what is the ratio of the area of rectangle *A* to the area of rectangle *B*?

   ○ $\dfrac{1}{4}$

   ○ $\dfrac{1}{2}$

   ○ $\dfrac{1}{1}$

   ○ $\dfrac{2}{1}$

   ○ $\dfrac{4}{1}$

8. In the figure above, $AD \parallel BC$. What is the perimeter of quadrilateral *ABCD*?

   ○ 590

   ○ 600

   ○ 620

   ○ 640

   ○ 680

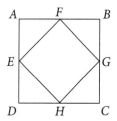

9. The midpoints of the sides of square *ABCD* above are connected to form square *EFGH*. What is the ratio of the area of square *EFGH* to the area of square *ABCD*?

   ○ $\dfrac{1}{4}$

   ○ $\dfrac{1}{3}$

   ○ $\dfrac{1}{2}$

   ○ $\dfrac{1}{\sqrt{2}}$

   ○ $\dfrac{2}{1}$

10. In the figure above, *A*, *B*, and *C* are squares. If the area of *A* is 9 and the area of *B* is 16, what is the area of *C*?

    ○ 25

    ○ 32

    ○ 36

    ○ 49

    ○ 50

11. A 1-inch-wide frame is placed around a 9-inch by 5-inch rectangular photograph. What is the area of the frame, in square inches?

    ○ 15

    ○ 32

    ○ 45

    ○ 60

    ○ 77

12. In quadrilateral $ABCD$, $\angle A + \angle B + \angle C = 2\angle D$. What is the degree measure of $\angle D$?

    ○ 90

    ○ 120

    ○ 135

    ○ 270

    ○ It cannot be determined from the information given.

13. If the area of a rectangle is 12, what is its perimeter?

    ○ 7

    ○ 8

    ○ 14

    ○ 16

    ○ It cannot be determined from the information given.

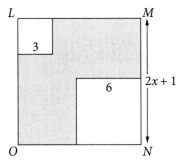

14. In the figure above, square $LMNO$ has a side of length $2x + 1$ and the two smaller squares have sides of lengths 3 and 6. If the area of the shaded region is 76, what is the value of x?

    ○ 5

    ○ 6

    ○ 7

    ○ 11

    ○ 14

Advanced

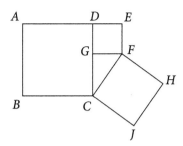

15. In the figure above, square *ABCD* has area 49 and square *DEFG* has area 9. What is the area of square *FCJH*?

    ◯ 25

    ◯ 32

    ◯ 40

    ◯ 48

    ◯ 69

16. A parallelogram is inscribed in a rectangle such that its vertices are the midpoints of the sides of the rectangle. If the area of the parallelogram is 60, and one of the dimensions of the rectangle is 12, what is the other dimension of the rectangle?

    ◯ 8

    ◯ 10

    ◯ 12

    ◯ 14

    ◯ 16

17. The perimeter of a rectangle is $6w$. If one side has length $\frac{w}{2}$, what is the area of the rectangle?

    ◯ $\frac{w^2}{4}$

    ◯ $\frac{5w^2}{4}$

    ◯ $\frac{5w^2}{2}$

    ◯ $\frac{11w^2}{4}$

    ◯ $\frac{11w^2}{2}$

18. The length of each side of square *A* is increased by 100 percent to make square *B*. If the length of the side of square *B* is increased by 50 percent to make square *C*, by what percent is the area of square *C* greater than the sum of the areas of squares *A* and *B*?

    ◯ 75%

    ◯ 80%

    ◯ 100%

    ◯ 150%

    ◯ 180%

19. A rectangle with integer side lengths has perimeter 10. What is the greatest number of these rectangles that can be cut from a piece of paper with width 24 and length 60?

    ◯ 144

    ◯ 180

    ◯ 240

    ◯ 360

    ◯ 480

CIRCLES

Circle: The set of all points in a plane at the same distance from a certain point. This point is called the **center** of the circle.

A circle is labeled by its center point: circle *O* means the circle with center point *O*. Two circles of different size with the same center are called **concentric**.

Diameter: A line segment that connects two points on the circle and passes through the center of the circle. In circle *O*, *AB* is a diameter.

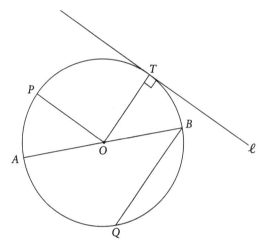

Radius: A line segment from the center of the circle to any point on the circle. The radius of a circle is one-half the length of the diameter. In circle *O*, *OA*, *OB*, *OP*, and *OT* are radii.

Chord: A line segment joining two points on the circle. In circle *O*, *QB* and *AB* are chords. The diameter of the circle is the longest chord of the circle.

Central Angle: An angle formed by two radii. In circle *O*, ∠*AOP*, ∠*POB*, ∠*BOA*, along with others, are central angles.

Tangent: A line that touches only one point on the circumference of the circle. A line drawn tangent to a circle is perpendicular to the radius at the point of tangency. Line ℓ is tangent to circle *O* at point *T*.

Circumference and arc length: The distance around a circle is called the **circumference**. The number π ("pi") is the ratio of a circle's circumference to its diameter. The value of π is 3.1415926…, usually approximated 3.14. For the GMAT, it is usually sufficient to remember that π is a little more than 3.

Since π equals the ratio of the circumference to the diameter, a formula for the circumference is:

$$C = \pi d$$

or

$$C = 2\pi r$$

An **arc** is a portion of the circumference of a circle. In the figure below, *AB* is an arc of the circle, with the same degree measure as central angle *AOB*. The shorter distance between *A* and *B* along the circle is called the **minor arc**; the longer distance *AXB* is the **major arc**. An arc which is exactly half the circumference of the circle is called a **semicircle** (in other words, half a circle).

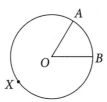

The length of an arc is the same fraction of a circle's circumference as its central angle is of the total measure of the circle (360°). For an arc with a central angle measuring *n* degrees,

$$\text{Arc length} = \left(\frac{n}{360}\right)(\text{circumference})$$

$$= \frac{n}{360} \times 2\pi r$$

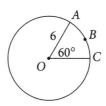

Example: What is the length of arc *ABC* of the circle with center *O* above?

Since $C = 2\pi r$, if the radius is 6, the circumference is $2 \times \pi \times 6 = 12\pi$.

Since $\angle AOC$ measures 60°, the arc is $\frac{60}{360}$, or one-sixth, of the circumference.

Therefore, the length of the arc is one-sixth of 12π, which is $\frac{12\pi}{6}$ or 2π.

Area of a circle: The area of a circle is given by the formula

$$\boxed{\text{Area} = \pi r^2}$$

A **sector** is a portion of the circle, bounded by two radii and an arc. In the circle below with center O, OAB is a sector. To determine the area of a sector of a circle, use the same method we used to find the length of an arc. Determine what fraction of 360° is the degree measure of the central angle of the sector, and multiply that fraction by the area of the circle. In a sector whose central angle measures n degrees,

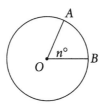

$$\text{Area of sector} = \left(\frac{n}{360}\right) \times (\text{Area of circle})$$

$$= \frac{n}{360} \times \pi r^2$$

Example: What is the area of sector AOC in the circle with center O above?

Since $\angle AOC$ measures 60°, a 60° "slice" is $\dfrac{60}{360}$, or one-sixth, of the circle. So the sector

has area $\dfrac{1}{6} \times \pi r^2 = \dfrac{1}{6} \times 36\pi = 6\pi$.

CIRCLES EXERCISE

Solve the following problems as indicated. (Answers follow the exercise.)

$$\boxed{\text{Circumference } = 2\pi r = \pi d}$$

1. What is the circumference of a circle with the radius 3?

2. What is the circumference of a circle with the diameter 8?

3. What is the circumference of a circle with diameter $\dfrac{3}{4\pi}$?

4. What is the radius of a circle with circumference $\dfrac{7}{2}\pi$?

5. What is the diameter of a circle with circumference $\dfrac{\pi}{2}$?

$$\boxed{\text{Area } = \pi r^2}$$

6. What is the area of a circle with radius 8?

7. What is the area of a circle with diameter 12?

8. What is the area of a circle with radius $\sqrt{2}$?

9. What is the area of a circle with circumference 8π?

10. What is the diameter of a circle with area 49π?

11. What is the circumference of a circle with area 18π?

$$\boxed{\text{Arc length } = \left(\frac{n}{360}\right)2\pi r}$$

In #12–15, find the length of minor arc AB.

12.

Arc $AB = ?$

13.

Arc $AB = ?$

14.

Arc $AB = ?$

15.

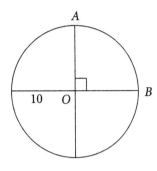

Arc AB = ?

$$\text{Area of sector} = \left(\frac{n}{360}\right)\pi r^2$$

In #16–19, find the area of sector AOB.

16.

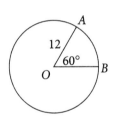

Area of sector = ?

17.

Area of sector = ?

18.

Area of sector = ?

19.

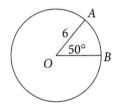

Area of sector = ?

**ANSWER KEY
BEGINS ON NEXT PAGE**

ANSWER KEY—CIRCLES EXERCISE

1. 6π

2. 8π

3. $\dfrac{3}{4}$

4. $\dfrac{7}{4}$

5. $\dfrac{1}{2}$

6. 64π

7. 36π

8. 2π

9. 16π

10. 14

11. $6\pi\sqrt{2}$

12. 2π

13. 4π

14. π

15. 5π

16. 24π

17. $\dfrac{\pi}{2}$

18. $\dfrac{15\pi}{4}$

19. 5π

CIRCLES TEST

Solve the following problems and choose the best answer. (Answers and explanations are at the end of this chapter.)

Basic

1. If the area of a circle is 64π, then the circumference of the circle is

   ○ 8π

   ○ 16π

   ○ 32π

   ○ 64π

   ○ 128π

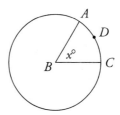

3. In the figure above, the ratio of the circumference of circle B to the length of arc ADC is $8:1$. What is the value of x?

   ○ 30

   ○ 45

   ○ 60

   ○ 75

   ○ 90

2. If points A, B, and C are the centers of the above circles and the circles have radii of 2, 3, and 4 respectively, what is the perimeter of triangle ABC?

   ○ 9

   ○ 3π

   ○ 12

   ○ 18

   ○ 9π

4. The figure above displays two semicircles, one with diameter AB and one with diameter AC. If AB has a length of 4 and AC has a length of 6, what fraction of the larger semicircle does the shaded region represent?

   ○ $\dfrac{1}{3}$

   ○ $\dfrac{4}{9}$

   ○ $\dfrac{1}{2}$

   ○ $\dfrac{5}{9}$

   ○ $\dfrac{2}{3}$

Intermediate

5. A line segment joining two points on the circumference of a circle is one inch from the center of the circle at its closest point. If the circle has a two-inch radius, what is the length of the line?

    ○ 1

    ○ $\sqrt{2}$

    ○ 2

    ○ $2\sqrt{2}$

    ○ $2\sqrt{3}$

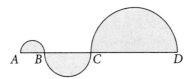

6. Each of the three shaded regions above is a semicircle. If $AB = 4$, $CD = 2BC$, and $BC = 2AB$, then the area of the entire shaded figure is

    ○ 28π

    ○ 42π

    ○ 84π

    ○ 96π

    ○ 168π

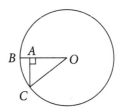

7. In the figure above, if the area of the circle with center O is 100π and CA has a length of 6, what is the length of AB?

    ○ 2

    ○ 3

    ○ 4

    ○ 5

    ○ 6

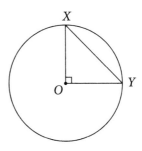

8. In the figure above, O is the center of the circle. If the area of triangle XOY is 25, what is the area of the circle?

    ○ 25π

    ○ $25\pi\sqrt{2}$

    ○ 50π

    ○ $50\pi\sqrt{3}$

    ○ 625π

Advanced

9. If the diameter of a circle increases by 50 percent, by what percent will the area of the circle increase?

   ○ 25%

   ○ 50%

   ○ 100%

   ○ 125%

   ○ 225%

10. A lighthouse emits a light which can be seen for 60 miles in all directions. If the intensity of the light is strengthened so that its visibility is increased by 40 miles in all directions, by approximately how many square miles is its region of visibility increased?

    ○ 6,300

    ○ 10,000

    ○ 10,300

    ○ 20,000

    ○ 31,400

11. If an arc with a length of 12π is $\dfrac{3}{4}$ of the circumference of a circle, what is the shortest distance between the endpoints of the arc?

    ○ 4

    ○ $4\sqrt{2}$

    ○ 8

    ○ $8\sqrt{2}$

    ○ 16

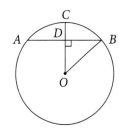

12. In the figure above, O is the center of the circle. If AB has a length of 16 and OB has a length of 10, what is the length of CD?

    ○ 2

    ○ 4

    ○ $2\sqrt{3}$

    ○ $8 - \sqrt{35}$

    ○ $8 - \sqrt{39}$

13. The total area of the four equal circles in the figure above is 36π, and the circles are all tangent to one another. What is the diameter of the small circle?

    ○ $6\sqrt{2}$

    ○ $6 + \sqrt{2}$

    ○ $3\sqrt{2} - 3$

    ○ $6\sqrt{2} - 6$

    ○ $6\sqrt{2} + 6$

KAPLAN)

MULTIPLE FIGURES

You can expect to see some problems on the exam that involve several different types of figures. They test your **understanding** of various geometrical concepts and relationships, not just your ability to memorize a few formulas. The hypotenuse of a right triangle may be the side of a neighboring rectangle, or the diameter of a circumscribed circle. Keep looking for the relationships between the different figures until you find one that leads you to the answer.

One common kind of multiple figures question involves irregularly shaped regions formed by two or more overlapping figures, often with one region shaded. When you are asked to find the area of such a region, any or all of the following methods may work:

(1) Break up that shaded area into smaller pieces; find the area of each piece using the proper formula; add those areas together.

(2) Find the area of the whole figure and the area of the **unshaded** region, and subtract the latter from the former.

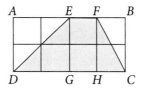

Example: Rectangle *ABCD* above has an area of 72 and is composed of 8 equal squares. Find the area of the shaded region.

For this problem you can use either of the two approaches. First, divide 8 into 72 to get the area of each square, which is 9. Since the area of a square equals its side squared, each side of the small squares must have length 3. Now you have a choice of methods.

(1)   You can break up the trapezoid into right triangle *DEG*, rectangle *EFHG*, and right triangle *FHC*.
The area of triangle *DEG* is $\frac{1}{2} \times 6 \times 6$, or 18. The area of rectangle *EFHG* is 3×6, or 18. The area of triangle *FHC* is $\frac{1}{2} \times 6 \times 3$, or 9. The total area is 18 + 18 + 9, or 45.

(2)   The area of the whole rectangle *ABCD* is 72. The area of unshaded triangle *AED* is $\frac{1}{2} \times 6 \times 6$, or 18. The area of unshaded triangle *FBC* is $\frac{1}{2} \times 6 \times 3$, or 9.
Therefore, the total unshaded area is 18 + 9 = 27. The area of the shaded region is the area of the rectangle minus the unshaded area, or 72 − 27 = 45.

Inscribed and Circumscribed Figures: A polygon is **inscribed** in a circle if all the vertices of the polygon lie on the circle. A polygon is **circumscribed** about a circle if all the sides of the polygon are tangent to the circle.

Square *ABCD* is inscribed in circle *O*.

(We can also say that circle *O* is circumscribed about square *ABCD*.)

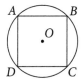

Square *PQRS* is circumscribed about circle *O*.

(We can also say that circle *O* is inscribed in square *PQRS*.)

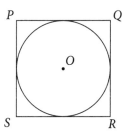

A triangle inscribed in a semicircle such that one side of the triangle coincides with the diameter of the semicircle is a right triangle.

MULTIPLE FIGURES EXERCISE

Solve the following problems as directed. (Answers follow the exercise.)

1.

Area of circle = 25π

Perimeter of square = ?

3.

Circumference of circle = 6π

Area of square = ?

2.

Area of square = 16

Area of circle = ?

4.

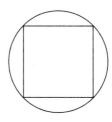

Area of square = 4

Area of circle = ?

**ANSWER KEY
BEGINS ON NEXT PAGE**

ANSWER KEY—MULTIPLE FIGURES EXERCISE

1. 40

2. 4π

3. 36

4. 2π

MULTIPLE FIGURES TEST

Solve the following problems and choose the best answer. (Answers and explanations are at the end of this chapter.)

Basic

1. If a rectangle with a diagonal of 5 inches is inscribed in circle O, what is the circumference of circle O, in inches?

   ○ 5
   ○ $\frac{5\pi}{2}$
   ○ 5π
   ○ 6π
   ○ 10π

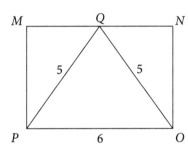

2. In the figure above, triangle PQO is an isosceles triangle with sides of lengths 5, 5, and 6. What is the area of rectangle $MNOP$?

   ○ 12
   ○ 18
   ○ 24
   ○ 30
   ○ 36

3. In the circle above, three right angles have vertices at the center of the circle. If the radius of the circle is 8, what is the combined area of the shaded regions?

   ○ 8π
   ○ 9π
   ○ 12π
   ○ 13π
   ○ 16π

4. If a square of side x and a circle of radius r have equal areas, what is the ratio $\frac{x}{r}$?

   ○ $\frac{2}{\pi}$
   ○ $\sqrt{\pi}$
   ○ $\frac{\sqrt{\pi}}{2}$
   ○ π
   ○ π^2

KAPLAN

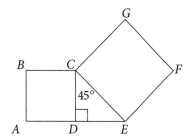

5. In the figure above, *ABCD* and *CEFG* are squares. If the area of *CEFG* is 36, what is the area of *ABCD*?

- ⬭ 6
- ⬭ $6\sqrt{2}$
- ⬭ 9
- ⬭ 18
- ⬭ 24

6. A triangle and a circle have equal areas. If the base of the triangle and the diameter of the circle each have length 5, what is the height of the triangle?

- ⬭ $\dfrac{5}{2}$
- ⬭ $\dfrac{5}{2}\pi$
- ⬭ 5π
- ⬭ 10π
- ⬭ It cannot be determined from the information given.

Intermediate

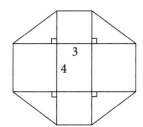

7. The figure above is composed of nine regions: four squares, four triangles, and one rectangle. If the rectangle has length 4 and width 3, what is the perimeter of the entire figure?

- ⬭ 24
- ⬭ 28
- ⬭ 34
- ⬭ 40
- ⬭ 44

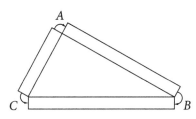

8. Rectangles lie on sides *AB*, *BC*, and *AC* of △*ABC* above. What is the sum of the measures of the angles marked?

- ⬭ 90°
- ⬭ 180°
- ⬭ 270°
- ⬭ 360°
- ⬭ It cannot be determined from the information given.

9. The two semicircles above both have radii of 7. If *AB* is tangent to the semicircles as shown, what is the shaded area, to the nearest integer?

- ⬭ 21
- ⬭ 42
- ⬭ 49
- ⬭ 54
- ⬭ 77

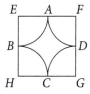

10. In the figure above, if *EFGH* is a square and the arcs are all quarter-circles of length π, what is the perimeter of *EFGH*?

- ⬭ 1
- ⬭ 2
- ⬭ 4
- ⬭ 8
- ⬭ 16

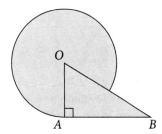

11. In the figure above, if radius *OA* is 8 and the area of right triangle *OAB* is 32, what is the area of the shaded region?

⬭ $64\pi + 32$

⬭ $60\pi + 32$

⬭ $56\pi + 32$

⬭ $32\pi + 32$

⬭ $16\pi + 32$

Advanced

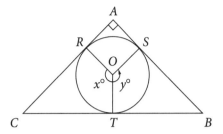

12. Point *O* is the center of the circle in which triangle *ABC* is inscribed. What is the area of triangle *ABC*?

   ◯ $75\sqrt{2}$

   ◯ $100\sqrt{2}$

   ◯ 150

   ◯ 300

   ◯ It cannot be determined from the information given.

13. In the figure above, right triangle *ABC* is circumscribed about circle *O*. If *R*, *S*, and *T* are the three points at which the triangle is tangent to the circle, then what is the value of $x + y$?

   ◯ 180

   ◯ 210

   ◯ 240

   ◯ 270

   ◯ It cannot be determined from the information given.

14. In the figure above, *AB* is an arc of a circle with center *O*. If the length of arc *AB* is 5π and the length of *CB* is 4, what is the sum of the areas of the shaded regions?

   ◯ $25\pi - 60$

   ◯ $25\pi - 48$

   ◯ $25\pi - 36$

   ◯ $100\pi - 48$

   ◯ $100\pi - 36$

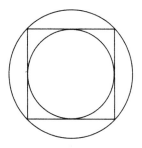

15. In the figure above, the smaller circle is inscribed in the square and the square is inscribed in the larger circle. If the length of each side of the square is *s*, what is the ratio of the area of the larger circle to the area of the smaller circle?

○ $2\sqrt{2}:1$

○ $2:1$

○ $\sqrt{2}:1$

○ $2s:1$

○ $s\sqrt{2}:1$

SOLIDS

A **solid** is a three-dimensional figure (a figure having length, width, and height), and is therefore rather difficult to represent accurately on a two-dimensional page. Figures are drawn "in perspective," giving them the appearance of depth. If a diagram represents a three-dimensional figure, it will be specified in the accompanying text.

Fortunately, there are only a few types of solids that appear with any frequency on the GMAT: rectangular solids, including cubes; and cylinders.

Other types, such as spheres, may appear, but typically will only involve understanding the solid's properties and not any special formula. Here are the terms used to describe the common solids:

Vertex: The vertices of a solid are the points at its corners. For example, a cube has eight vertices.

Edge: The edges of a solid are the line segments which connect the vertices and form the sides of each face of the solid. A cube has twelve edges.

Face: The faces of a solid are the polygons that are the boundaries of the solid. A cube has six faces, all squares.

Volume: The volume of a solid is the amount of space enclosed by that solid. The volume of any uniform solid is equal to the area of its base times its height.

Surface Area: In general, the surface area of a solid is equal to the sum of the areas of the solid's faces.

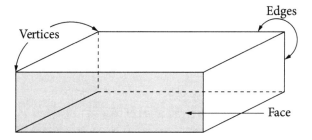

Rectangular Solid: A solid with six rectangular faces (all edges meet at right angles). Examples are cereal boxes, bricks, etc.

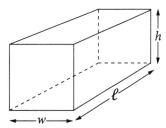

Volume = area of base × height = length × width × height = $\ell \times w \times h$.

Surface area = sum of areas of faces = $2\ell w + 2\ell h + 2wh$.

Cube: A special rectangular solid with all edges equal ($\ell = w = h$), such as a die or a sugar cube. All faces of a cube are squares.

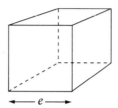

Volume = area of base × height = $\ell \times w \times h = e^3$.
Surface area = sum of areas of faces = $6e^2$.

Cylinder: A uniform solid whose horizontal cross section is a circle; for example, a soup can. We need two pieces of information for a cylinder: the radius of the base, and the height.

Volume = area of base × height = $\pi r^2 \times h$
Lateral surface area = circumference of base × height = $2\pi r \times h$
Total surface area = areas of bases + LSA = $2\pi r^2 + 2\pi rh$.

You can think of the surface area of a cylinder as having two parts: one part is the top and bottom (the circles), and the other part is the lateral surface. In a can, for example, the area of both the top and the bottom is just the area of the circle, or lid, which represents the top; hence, πr^2 for the top and πr^2 for the bottom, yielding a total of $2\pi r^2$. For the lateral surface, the area around the can, think of removing the can's label. When unrolled, it's actually in the shape of a rectangle. One side is the height of the can, and the other side is the distance around the circle, or circumference. Hence, its area is $h \times (2\pi r)$, or $2\pi rh$. And so, the total surface area is $2\pi r^2 + 2\pi rh$.

Sphere: A sphere is made up of all the points in space a certain distance from a center point; it's like a three-dimensional circle. The distance from the center to a point on the sphere is the radius of the sphere. A basketball is a good example of a sphere. A sphere is not a uniform solid; the cross sections are all circles, but are of different sizes. (In other words, a slice of a basketball from the middle is bigger than a slice from the top.)

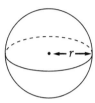

It is not important to know how to find the volume or surface area of a sphere, but occasionally a question might require you to understand what a sphere is.

SOLIDS EXERCISE

Find the volume and surface area of each of the solids in #1–5. (Answers follow the exercise.)

1. A rectangular solid with dimensions 4, 6, and 8.

2. A rectangular solid with dimensions 3, 4, and 12.

3. A cube with edge 6.

4. A cube with edge $\sqrt{2}$.

5. A cylinder with height 12 and radius 6. (Find the total surface area.)

6. What is the area of a face of a cube with volume 64?

ANSWER KEY
BEGINS ON NEXT PAGE

ANSWER KEY—SOLIDS EXERCISE

1. 192, 208
2. 144, 192
3. 216, 216
4. $2\sqrt{2}$, 12
5. 432π, 216π
6. 16

SOLIDS TEST

1. What is the ratio of the volume of a cylinder with radius r and height h to the volume of a cylinder with radius h and height r?

    ○ $\dfrac{r}{h}$

    ○ $\dfrac{h}{r}$

    ○ $\dfrac{1}{1}$

    ○ $\dfrac{\pi r}{h}$

    ○ $\dfrac{h}{\pi r}$

2. A cube and a rectangular solid are equal in volume. If the lengths of the edges of the rectangular solid are 4, 8, and 16, what is the length of an edge of the cube?

    ○ 4

    ○ 8

    ○ 12

    ○ 16

    ○ 64

3. When 16 cubic meters of water are poured into an empty cubic container, it fills the container to 25 percent of its capacity. What is the length of one edge of the container, in meters?

    ○ $2\sqrt{2}$

    ○ 4

    ○ $4\sqrt{2}$

    ○ 8

    ○ 16

4. The outside surface of a white cube with a volume of 64 is painted purple. The cube is then cut evenly into smaller $2 \times 2 \times 2$ cubes, such that sides that originally faced outside are painted purple while the sides that faced inside the original cube remain white. What is the ratio of the total purple surface area of the smaller cubes to the total white surface area of the smaller cubes?

    ○ 3:1

    ○ 2:1

    ○ 1:1

    ○ 1:2

    ○ 1:3

5. A motor scooter has an empty rectangular gas tank with dimensions of $4 \times 8 \times 10$ inches. The tank is filled completely with gasoline from a cylindrical container with a diameter of 8 inches. If the gasoline fills the cylindrical container to a height of 20 inches before the gas tank is filled, how high, in inches, is the gasoline in the cylindrical container after the tank is filled?

    ○ $\dfrac{20}{\pi}$

    ○ $80(4\pi - 3)$

    ○ 10

    ○ $\dfrac{5(\pi - 1)}{4}$

    ○ $\dfrac{20(\pi - 1)}{\pi}$

KAPLAN)

6. What is the radius of the largest sphere that can be placed inside a cube of volume 64?

   ◯ $6\sqrt{2}$

   ◯ 8

   ◯ 4

   ◯ $2\sqrt{2}$

   ◯ 2

7. Each dimension of a certain rectangular solid is an integer less than 10. If the volume of the rectangular solid is 24 and one edge has length 4, which of the following could be the total surface area of the solid?

   ◯ 48

   ◯ 52

   ◯ 56

   ◯ 60

   ◯ 96

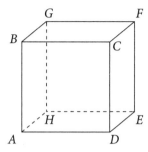

8. Which of the following statements about the cube above must be true?

   I. *FD* is parallel to *GA*.

   II. △*GCF* and △*AHD* have the same area.

   III. *AF = GD*

   ◯ I only

   ◯ I and II only

   ◯ I and III only

   ◯ II and III only

   ◯ I, II, and III

LINES AND ANGLES TEST
ANSWERS AND EXPLANATIONS

1. 50

Since the three marked angles form a straight angle, the sum of their measures is 180°. So we can set up an equation to solve for x:

$$x + x + 80 = 180$$
$$2x + 80 = 180$$
$$2x = 100$$
$$x = 50$$

2. 145°

Notice that $\angle AOE$ and $\angle BOD$ are vertical angles, and therefore must have equal measures. $\angle BOD$ is made up of one angle with a measure of 105°, and a second angle with a measure of 40°; it must have a measure of 105° + 40°, or 145°. Therefore, $\angle AOE$ must also have a measure of 145°.

3. 300

In the diagram, the unmarked angle and the 30° angle are vertical angles; therefore, the unmarked angle must also have a measure of 30°. The sum of the measures of the angles around a point is 360°, so we can set up the following equation:

$$30 + x + w + 30 + z + y = 360$$

Rearranging the terms on the left side of the equation gives:

$$w + x + y + z + 60 = 360$$
$$w + x + y + z = 360 - 60 = 300$$

4. 90

There's no way to find either x or y alone, but their sum is a different story. Since AD is a straight line, the angle marked $x°$, the angle marked $y°$, and the right angle together make up a straight angle, which measures 180°.

$$x + y + 90 = 180$$
$$x + y = 180 - 90 = 90$$

5. 30

Together, the angle marked $x°$ and the angle marked $y°$ form a straight angle, so $x + y$ equals 180. We're also told that $y = 5x$.

Substitute 5x for y:

$$x + y = 180$$
$$x + 5x = 180$$
$$6x = 180$$
$$x = 30$$

6. 50

$\angle AFD$ is a straight angle. The angle marked 40°, the right angle, and the angle marked $x°$ together form $\angle AFD$; therefore, they must sum to 180°.

$$x + 90 + 40 = 180$$
$$x + 130 = 180$$
$$x = 50$$

7. I and II only

From the diagram, we see that the angle marked $y°$ is supplementary to a right angle, which measures 90°. This means that y must be $180 - 90$, or 90. We are told that x equals y, so x must also be 90. This means that ℓ_2 and ℓ_3 are each perpendicular to ℓ_1; therefore, they must be parallel to each other. Thus, statements I and II are true. But statement III is not necessarily true. For instance, ℓ_3 intersects ℓ_1, but never meets ℓ_2.

8. 54

The sum $v + w + x + y$ must equal 180 since the angles with these measures together form a straight line. Since the question asks for the value of y, define all variables in terms of y. If $w = 2x$ and $x = \dfrac{y}{3}$, then $w = \dfrac{2y}{3}$. Similarly, $v = 2w$, so $v = 2\left(\dfrac{2y}{3}\right)$, or $\dfrac{4y}{3}$. Substitute the angles in terms of y into the equation:

$$v + w + x + y = 180$$
$$\frac{4y}{3} + \frac{2y}{3} + \frac{y}{3} + y = 180$$
$$\frac{7y}{3} + y = 180$$
$$\frac{10y}{3} = 180$$
$$y = \frac{3}{10} \times 180 = 3 \times 18 = 54$$

9. **II and III only**

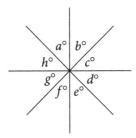

Check each expression to see which sets of angles sum to 180°.

I: $a + b + e + h$. Since angles $h, a, b,$ and c together make up a straight angle, $h + a + b + c = 180$. Since we don't know whether $e = c$, we can't be sure that $a + b + e + h = 180$. So statement I is out. Eliminate choices **(A)**, **(C)**, and **(E)**.

This leaves **(B)**, II only, and **(D)**, II and III only. Therefore, statement II must be included in the correct answer. So we immediately skip to checking statement III.

III: $a + b + d + g$. Angles $a, b, c,$ and d sum to 180, and $g = c$ (vertical angles), so it's also true that $a + b + d + g = 180$. Therefore, statement III must be true, and choice **(D)** is correct.

As a check, we can test the expression in statement II (although it's not necessary to do so during the actual exam):

II: $b + e + g + h$. Angles $e, f, g,$ and h sum to 180°. Is b equal to f? Yes, since they are a pair of vertical angles. So, sure enough, statement II must be true as well.

10. **It cannot be determined from the information given.**

We're given that $\ell_1, \ell_2,$ and ℓ_3 are all parallel to one another. Remember, when parallel lines are cut by a transversal, all acute angles formed by the transversal are equal, all obtuse angles are equal, and any acute angle is supplementary to any obtuse angle. We can get 2 pairs of supplementary angles from the 5 marked angles:

$$\underset{180}{\underline{a + b}} + \underset{180}{\underline{c + d}} + e$$

We're left with $360 + e$. Since we don't know the value of e, we cannot find the sum.

11. I and III only

We have three pairs of vertical angles around the point of intersection: a and d, b and e, and c and f. Therefore, $a = d$, $b = e$, and $c = f$. Let's look at the three statements one at a time.

I: $a + b = d + e$. Since $a = d$ and $b = e$, this is true. Eliminate choice (**D**).

II: $b + e = c + f$. We know that $b = e$ and $c = f$, but not how the pairs relate to each other. Statement II does not have to be true. Eliminate choices (**B**) and (**E**).

III: $a + c + e = b + d + f$. This is true, since $a = d$, $c = f$, and $b = e$. That is, we can match each angle on one side of the equation with a different angle on the other side. Statement III must be true.

Statements I and III must be true.

12. 1

Since AE is a line segment, all the lengths are additive, so $AE = AD + DE$. We're told that $AD = 6$ and $AE = 8$. So $DE = AE - AD = 8 - 6 = 2$. We're also told that $BE = 6$. So $BD = BE - DE = 6 - 2 = 4$. We have the length of BD, but still need the length of BC. Since $CD = 3(BC)$, the situation looks like this:

Here x stands for the length of BC. Since $BD = 4$, we can write:

$$x + 3x = 4$$
$$4x = 4$$
$$x = 1$$

13. II only

Before we look at the choices, let's see what information we can get from the diagram. We can see that angles p and x together are supplementary to the right angle, so p and x together must form a right angle. The same is true for the angles q and y. We also have these two pairs of vertical angles: $p = y$ and $x = q$. Now let's look at the three statements.

I: $p = x$ and $q = y$. This will be true only if $p = 45$. Since we have no way of knowing the exact measure of p, this can be true, but doesn't have to be. Eliminate choices **(A)**, **(D)**, and **(E)**.

II: $x + y = 90$. This is true since $q + y = 90$ and $x = q$. Eliminate choice **(C)**.

Since we've eliminated four answer choices, we can safely pick choice **(B)** without checking statement III. For practice, though, let's have a look anyway:

III: $x = y = 45$. There is no indication from the diagram that the angles x and y must have the same degree measure. Statement III does not have to be true.

Statement II only must be true.

14. 40

The angle marked $(2x - 20)°$ and the angle marked $3x°$ together form a straight angle. This means that the sum of their degree measures must be 180.

$$(2x - 20) + (3x) = 180$$
$$2x - 20 + 3x = 180$$
$$5x = 200$$
$$x = \frac{200}{5} = 40$$

TRIANGLES TEST
ANSWERS AND EXPLANATIONS

1. **80**

Notice that each marked angle makes a pair of vertical angles with one of the interior angles of the triangle.

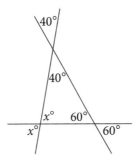

Since these marked angles have the same degree measure as the corresponding interior angles, the sum of their measures must equal 180.

$$x + 40 + 60 = 180$$
$$x = 180 - 100$$
$$= 80$$

2. **60**

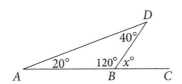

Notice that the angle marked $x°$ is supplementary to $\angle ABD$, and $\angle ABD$ is an interior angle of $\triangle ABD$. The sum of the measures of the two marked angles in $\triangle ABD$ is $20° + 40°$, or $60°$. Therefore, the third angle, $\angle ABD$, must have a measure of $180° - 60°$, or $120°$. So $x = 180 - 120$, or 60.

A quicker way to get this problem is to remember that the measure of an exterior angle is equal to the sum of the measures of the two remote interior angles. Angle x is an exterior angle, so $x = 20 + 40$, or 60.

3. 130

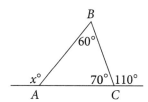

The angle with measure $x°$ is an exterior angle of the triangle; therefore it must equal the sum of the two remote interior angles: ∠ABC and ∠BCA. ∠ABC has a measure of 60°. ∠BCA is supplementary to the angle marked 110°; its measure must be 180° − 110°, or 70°. Therefore, $x = 60 + 70$, or 130.

4. 45

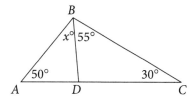

What are the three interior angles of △ABC? They are ∠BAD, with measure 50°, ∠ACB, with measure 30°, and ∠ABC, which is made up of the angle marked $x°$ and the angle with measure 55°. All these angles combined sum to 180°. Therefore,

$$50 + 30 + x + 55 = 180$$
$$135 + x = 180$$
$$x = 180 − 135$$
$$= 45$$

5. 100°

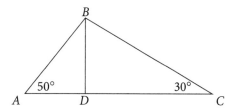

Notice that we're given the measure of two interior angles in △ABC: ∠BAC measures 50° and ∠BCA measures 30°. Therefore, ∠ABC, the third interior angle in △ABC, measures 180 − (50 + 30), or 180 − 80, or 100°. Since BD bisects ∠ABC, BD splits up ∠ABC into two smaller angles equal in measure, ∠ABD and ∠DBC. Therefore, the measure of ∠DBC is half the measure of ∠ABC, so ∠DBC measures $\frac{1}{2}$(100), or 50°. Now we can use this information along with the fact that ∠*BCA* measures 30° to find ∠*BDC*. Since these three angles are interior angles of △*BDC*, their measures sum to 180°. So ∠*BDC* measures 180 − (50 + 30), or 100°.

6. **90°**

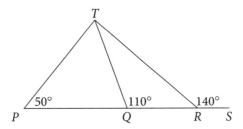

Identify the two interior angles of △*PRT* remote to the exterior angle marked 140°. ∠*TPR* with measure 50° is one of them and ∠*PTR*, whose measure we're trying to find, is the other. Since 50° plus the measure of ∠*PTR* must sum to 140°, the measure of ∠*PTR* = 140° − 50°, or 90°.

7. **36**

Since the angle marked $x°$ and the angle marked $y°$ together form a straight angle, their measures must sum to 180°.

Substitute in $2z$ for x and $3z$ for y, and solve for z.

$$x + y = 180$$
$$2z + 3z = 180$$
$$5z = 180$$
$$z = \frac{1}{5} \cdot 180 = 36$$

8. $150 - y$

Once again, we are dealing with the sum of the interior angles in a triangle. We can write:

$$x + y + 30 = 180$$
$$x + y = 180 - 30$$
$$x + y = 150$$

Subtracting y from each side, we find that $x = 150 - y$.

9. 40

In $\triangle ABC$, the measures of the three interior angles must sum to 180:

$$\frac{x}{2} + 3x + x = 180$$
$$\frac{9}{2}x = 180$$
$$x = 180 \cdot \frac{2}{9} = 40$$

10. 65

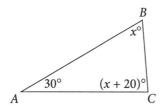

In $\triangle ABC$, the sum of the degree measures of the interior angles is 180:

$$x + (x + 20) + 30 = 180$$
$$2x + 50 = 180$$
$$2x = 180 - 50$$
$$2x = 130$$
$$x = \frac{130}{2} = 65$$

11. 80

The measures of the three interior angles are in the ratio of $2:3:4$, and they must add up to $180°$. So the three angles must have degree measures that are $2x$, $3x$, and $4x$, where x is a number to be found.

$$2x + 3x + 4x = 180$$
$$9x = 180$$
$$x = 20$$

The largest angle has measure $4x$, or $4(20)$, which is 80.

12. 220

Since the $140°$ angle is an exterior angle, it is equal to the sum of the two remote interior angles. One of these is supplementary to angle x, and the other is supplementary to angle y. So these two interior angles have measures $180 - x$ and $180 - y$:

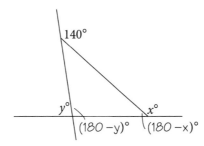

So

$$140 = (180 - x) + (180 - y)$$
$$140 = 360 - x - y$$
$$140 = 360 - (x + y)$$
$$x + y + 140 = 360$$
$$x + y = 220$$

13. 70

Since *BC* is parallel to *AD*, ∠*GBF* must have the same degree measure as *x* (two parallel lines cut by transversal *AG*). Finding *x*, then, is the same as finding the measure of ∠*GBF*.

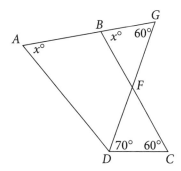

Let's look at triangles Δ*BFG* and Δ*DCF*. The two interior angles of these two triangles at point *F* must have the same degree measure, since they are a pair of vertical angles. In addition, each triangle has a 60° angle. Since we have two triangles with two pairs of equal angles, the third pair of angles must be equal, too, because the sum of all three angles in any triangle is 180°. The third angle in Δ*DCF* has measure 70°; therefore, ∠*GBF* = *x*° = 70°.

14. I and II only

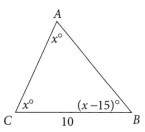

Statement I:

We could solve for the value of *x* here, but it's easier to ask "could *x* be 50?" If *x* were 50, then the triangle would have two 50° angles and a third angle with measure less than 50°. But this would make the total less than 180°. Therefore, *x* must be greater than 50, and Statement I is true. Eliminate choice **(B)**.

Statement II:

The shortest side of a triangle will always be opposite the angle of smallest measure. Two of the angles have measure *x*; the third, ∠*CBA*, has a measure less than that: *x* − 15. Since ∠*CBA* is the smallest angle, the side opposite it, side *AC*, must be the shortest side. Since *CB* has length 10, *AC* must be less than 10. Statement II is true. Eliminate choices **(A)** and **(D)**.

Statement III:

∠*ACB* and ∠*BAC* both have a measure of *x*°, so Δ*ABC* is isosceles. Therefore, *AB* has the same length as *CB* (they're opposite the equal angles). Since *BC* has a length of 10, *AB* must also have a length of 10. Statement III is not true.

Statements I and II only must be true.

15. $2\sqrt{10}$

First, solve for the length of BC, the shortest side. We can then find the length of AB and the length of AC using the Pythagorean theorem.

The area of any right triangle equals one-half the product of the legs. If BC has a length of x, then AB has a length of $3x$. (If BC is one-third the length of AB, then AB is three times the length of BC.) The area of the triangle is one-half their product, or $\frac{1}{2}(x)(3x)$. This equals 6.

$$\frac{1}{2}(x)(3x) = 6$$
$$3x^2 = 12$$
$$x^2 = 4$$
$$x = 2$$

BC has a length of 2. So AB, which is $3x$, is 6. Now use the Pythagorean theorem to find AC.

$$AC^2 = AB^2 + BC^2$$
$$AC^2 = 6^2 + 2^2$$
$$AC^2 = 36 + 4$$
$$AC = \sqrt{40} = \sqrt{4 \cdot 10} = \sqrt{4}\sqrt{10} = 2\sqrt{10}$$

16. $8\sqrt{2}$

Draw yourself a diagram so that the picture is clearer:

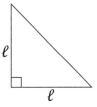

In an isosceles right triangle, both legs have the same length. So,

$$\text{area} = \frac{1}{2}\ell \times \ell = \frac{\ell^2}{2}$$

We're given that the area is 32, so we can set up an equation to solve for ℓ:

$$\frac{\ell^2}{2} = 32$$
$$\ell^2 = 64$$
$$\ell = 8$$

Remember, the ratio of the length of the legs to the length of the hypotenuse in any isosceles right triangle is $1 : \sqrt{2}$.

Since the legs have a length of 8, the hypotenuse is $\sqrt{2}$ times 8, or $8\sqrt{2}$.

An alternative is to use the Pythagorean theorem to find the hypotenuse:

$$\text{hypotenuse}^2 = 8^2 + 8^2$$
$$\text{hypotenuse}^2 = 64 + 64$$
$$\text{hypotenuse}^2 = 128$$
$$\text{hypotenuse} = \sqrt{128} = \sqrt{64 \cdot 2} = 8\sqrt{2}$$

17. 4

If $\angle DBA$ has a measure of 60°, $\angle CBD$, which is supplementary to it, must have a measure of $180 - 60$, or 120°. $\angle DCB$ has a measure of 30°; that leaves $180 - (120 + 30)$, or 30 degrees for the remaining interior angle: *BDC*.

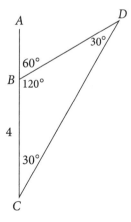

Since $\angle BCD$ has the same measure as $\angle BDC$, $\triangle BCD$ is an isosceles triangle, and the sides opposite the equal angles will have equal lengths. Therefore, *BD* must have the same length as *BC*, 4.

18. 2

Note that we've added point *D* for clarity.

The area of a triangle is $\frac{1}{2} \times$ base $\times$ height. If we treat *AB* as the base of $\triangle ABC$, then the triangle's height is *CD*. Each square has side 1, so we can just count the squares. $AB = 1$, $CD = 4$, so the area is $\frac{1}{2} \times 1 \times 4 = 2$.

19. $\dfrac{d\sqrt{7}}{12}$

We know one of the sides we're given is the hypotenuse; since the hypotenuse is the longest side, it follows that it must be the larger value we're given. The side of length $\frac{d}{3}$ must be the hypotenuse, since *d* is positive (all lengths are positive), and $\frac{1}{3}$ of a positive value is always greater than $\frac{1}{4}$ of a positive value. Now we can use the Pythagorean theorem to solve for the unknown side, which we'll call *x*.

$$(\text{hypotenuse})^2 = (\text{leg})^2 + (\text{leg})^2$$

$$\left(\frac{d}{3}\right)^2 = \left(\frac{d}{4}\right)^2 + x^2$$

$$\frac{d^2}{9} = \frac{d^2}{16} + x^2$$

$$\frac{d^2}{9} - \frac{d^2}{16} = x^2$$

$$\frac{16d^2 - 9d^2}{144} = x^2$$

$$\frac{7d^2}{144} = x^2$$

$$x = \frac{d\sqrt{7}}{12}$$

Another way we can solve this, that avoids the tricky, complicated algebra is by picking a number for *d*. Let's pick a number divisible by both 3 and 4 to get rid of the fractions: 12 seems like a logical choice. Then the two sides have lengths, $\frac{12}{3}$, or 4, and $\frac{12}{4}$, or 3. If one of these is the hypotenuse, that must be 4, and 3 must be a leg. Now use the Pythagorean theorem to find the other leg:

$$(\text{leg})^2 + (\text{leg})^2 = (\text{hypotenuse})^2$$
$$(\text{leg})^2 + (3)^2 = (4)^2$$
$$(\text{leg})^2 + 9 = 16$$
$$(\text{leg})^2 = 7$$

Now plug in 12 for *d* into each answer choice; the one which equals $\sqrt{7}$ is correct.

$$\frac{5 \times 12}{12} = 5 \qquad \text{Discard.}$$
$$\frac{12}{\sqrt{7}} \neq \sqrt{7} \qquad \text{Discard.}$$
$$\frac{12}{5} \neq \sqrt{7} \qquad \text{Discard.}$$
$$\frac{12}{12} = 1 \qquad \text{Discard.}$$
$$\frac{12\sqrt{7}}{12} = \sqrt{7} \qquad \text{Correct.}$$

20. 30

Drawing a diagram makes visualizing the situation much easier. Picture a ladder leaning against a building:

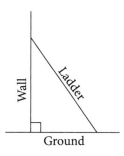

This forms a right triangle, since the side of the building is perpendicular to the ground. The length of the ladder, then, is the hypotenuse of the triangle; the distance from the foot of the building to the base of the ladder is one leg; the distance from the foot of the building to where the top of the ladder touches the wall is the other leg. We can write these dimensions into our diagram:

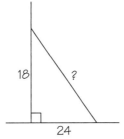

The one dimension we're missing (what we're asked to find) is the length of the ladder, or the hypotenuse. Well, we could use the Pythagorean theorem to find that, but these numbers are fairly large, and calculating will be troublesome. When you see numbers this large in a right triangle, you should be a little suspicious; perhaps the sides are a multiple of a more familiar Pythagorean triple. One leg is 18 and another leg is 24; 18 is just 6×3, and 24 is just 6×4. So we have a multiple of the familiar 3-4-5 right triangle. That means that our hypotenuse, the length of the ladder, is 6×5 or 30.

21. 6

This problem involves as much algebra as geometry. The Pythagorean theorem states that the sum of the squares of the legs is equal to the square of the hypotenuse, or, in this case:

$$x^2 + (x + 2)^2 = (2x - 2)^2$$

and from here on in it's a matter of algebra:

$$x^2 + x^2 + 4x + 4 = 4x^2 - 8x + 4$$
$$12x = 2x^2$$
$$2x^2 - 12x = 0$$
$$2x (x - 6) = 0$$

When the product of two factors is 0, one of them must equal 0. So we find that

EITHER	OR
$2x = 0$	$x - 6 = 0$
$x = 0$	$x = 6$

According to the **equation,** the value of x could be either 0 or 6, but according to the **diagram,** x is the length of one side of a triangle, which must be a positive number. This means that x must equal 6 (which makes this a $6:8:10$ triangle).

Another way to do this problem is to try plugging each answer choice into the expression for x, and see which one gives side lengths which work in the Pythagorean theorem. Choice **(A)** gives us 6, 8, and 10 (a Pythagorean triple) for the three sides of the triangle, so it must be the answer.

QUADRILATERALS AND OTHER POLYGONS TEST
ANSWERS AND EXPLANATIONS

1. 55

The fastest way to get the total area is to count the number of shaded small squares in each row (there's a pattern here: each row has one more shaded square than the row above it), and add. This gives a total of $1 + 2 + 3 + 4 + 5 + 6 + 7 + 8 + 9 + 10$, or 55 shaded squares.

2. 85

Keep in mind that the measures of the interior angles of a quadrilateral sum to 360°. Is this useful to us in this problem? Well, the angles marked 75° and 60° are both supplementary to the two unmarked interior angles in the diagram. There are four interior angles in the quadrilateral: the two unmarked angles, and the angle marked 50° and the one marked $x°$. The angle supplementary to the 75° angle must have a measure of $180 - 75$, or 105°. The angle supplementary to the 60° angle must have a measure of $180 - 60$, or 120°.

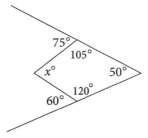

Now that we know the measures of three of the interior angles, we can set up an equation to solve for x:

$$x + 105 + 50 + 120 = 360$$
$$x + 275 = 360$$
$$x = 360 - 275 = 85$$

3. 115

What is the sum of the interior angles of a pentagon? Drawing two diagonals from a single vertex, we can divide a pentagon into three triangles.

The sum of the interior angles must be three times the sum of each triangle: $3 \times 180 = 540°$. Therefore, the two angles with measure x, the two right angles, and the $130°$ angle must sum to $540°$. So we can set up an equation to solve for x:

$$x + x + 90 + 90 + 130 = 540$$
$$2x + 310 = 540$$
$$2x = 230$$
$$x = 115$$

4. $\dfrac{1}{2}$

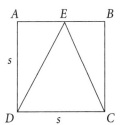

The height of ΔDEC is the perpendicular distance from point E to base DC, and that's the same as the length of side AD or side BC of the square. The base of ΔDEC is also a side of the square, so the area of ΔDEC must equal one half the length of a side of the square times the length of a side of the square. Or, calling the length of a side s, the area of ΔDEC is $\dfrac{1}{2}s^2$, while the area of the square is just s^2. Since the triangle has half the area of the square, the ratio is $1:2$, or $\dfrac{1}{2}$.

5. **$192.00**

We can break the figure up into two rectangles, as shown in the diagram.

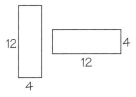

The area of a rectangle equals length $\times$ width, so each of these rectangles has an area of 4×12, or 48 square meters. Adding these areas together gives us $48 + 48$, or 96 square meters. Each square meter of tile costs $2.00, so the total cost for 96 square meters is 2×96, or $192.

6. 24

Each of these squares must have an area equal to one-fifth of the area of the whole figure: $\frac{1}{5} \times 20 = 4$. For squares, area = side², or $\sqrt{\text{area}}$ = side. Since $\sqrt{4} = 2$, the length of each side of the squares must be 2. How many of these sides make up the perimeter? The perimeter consists of three sides from each of four squares, for a total of 3 × 4, or 12 sides. Each side has a length of 2, for a total perimeter of 12 × 2, or 24.

7. $\frac{1}{4}$

Watch out for the trap: the ratio of areas is *not* the same as the ratio of lengths. We can pick numbers for the length and width of rectangle A. Let's pick 4 for the length and 2 for the width. The area of rectangle A is then 4 × 2, or 8. The length of rectangle B is twice the length of rectangle A : 2 × 4 = 8; the width of rectangle B is twice the width of rectangle A : 2 × 2 = 4. So the area of rectangle B is 8 × 4, or 32. Therefore, the ratio of the area of rectangle A to the area of rectangle B is $\frac{8}{32}$, or $\frac{1}{4}$.

As a general rule for similar polygons, the ratio of areas is equal to the square of the ratio of lengths.

8. 620

We're given the lengths of three of the four sides of ABCD; all we need to find is the length of side AD. If we drop a perpendicular line from point C to side AD and call the point where this perpendicular line meets side AD point E, we divide the figure into rectangle ABCE and right triangle CDE.

Since ABCE is a rectangle, AE has the same length as BC: 250. Similarly, EC has the same length as AB: 40. We can now find the length of ED: it is a leg of a right triangle with hypotenuse 50 and other leg 40. This is just 10 times as big as a 3:4:5 right triangle; therefore, ED must have a length of 10 × 3, or 30. So AD, which is AE + ED, is 250 + 30, or 280. Now we can find the perimeter:

$$\text{perimeter} = AB + BC + CD + AD$$
$$= 40 + 250 + 50 + 280 = 620$$

9. $\frac{1}{2}$

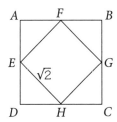

The key here is that *E*, *F*, *G*, and *H* are all midpoints of the sides of square *ABCD*. Therefore, the four triangles inside square *ABCD* are isosceles right triangles. We can pick a value for the length of each leg of the isosceles right triangles (all the legs have the same length). Let's pick 1 for the length of each leg. Then the length of each side of square *ABCD*, which is twice as long as each leg, is 2. So the area of square *ABCD* is 2 × 2, or 4. At the same time, the length of each hyptenuse is $1 \times \sqrt{2}$, or $\sqrt{2}$. This is the same as the length of each side of square *EFGH*, so the area of square *EFGH* is $\sqrt{2} \times \sqrt{2}$, or 2. Therefore, the ratio of the area of *EFGH* to the area of *ABCD* is $\frac{2}{4}$, or $\frac{1}{2}$.

We can also attack this problem by using a more common sense approach. If we connect *EG* and *FH*, we'll have eight isosceles right triangles which are all the same size:

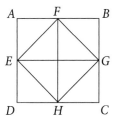

Square *EFGH* is composed of four of these triangles, and square *ABCD* is composed of eight of these triangles. Since all of these triangles are the same size, square *EFGH* is half the size of square *ABCD*, and the ratio we're looking for is $\frac{1}{2}$.

10. 49

From the diagram we see the top side of square *C* is made up of a side of *A* and a side of *B*. So we can find the length of the sides of squares *A* and *B* to get the length of each side of square *C*. Since the area of square *A* is 9, each of its sides must have a length of $\sqrt{9}$, or 3. Similarly, since the area of square B is 16, each of its sides must have a length of $\sqrt{16}$, or 4. So, the length of each side of square C must be 4 + 3, or 7. The area of a square is the length of a side squared; therefore, square C has area 7^2, or 49.

11. 32

The photograph is $9 \times 5 = 45$ square inches. A frame adds 1 inch to *each* side of the photograph, so the total dimensions of the photograph and the frame are 11 by 7.

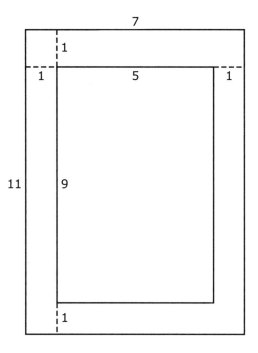

This gives a total area of $11 \times 7 = 77$ square inches. Now we need to subtract the area of the photo from this total to get an area of $77 - 45 = 32$ square inches for the frame itself.

12. 120

Since the sum of the interior angles of a quadrilateral is 360°, $A + B + C + D = 360°$. At the same time, $A + B + C = 2D$. So we can make a substitution for $A + B + C$ in our first equation to get:

$$2D + D = 360°$$
$$3D = 360°$$
$$D = 120°$$

13. It cannot be determined from the information given.

The area ($L \times W$) of a rectangle by itself tells us very little about its perimeter ($2L + 2W$). We can pick different values for the length and width to see what we get for the perimeter. For example, the length could be 4 and the width 3 ($4 \times 3 = 12$). In this case, the perimeter is $(2)(4) + (2)(3)$, or 14. On the other hand, the length could be 6 and the width 2 ($6 \times 2 = 12$). In this case the perimeter is $(2)(6) + (2)(2)$, or 16. Since more than one perimeter is possible based on the given information, the answer must be choice **(E)**.

14. 5

The shaded area and the two small squares all combine to form the large square, *LMNO*. Therefore the area of square *LMNO* equals the sum of the shaded area and the area of the two small squares. We know the shaded area; we can find the areas of the two small squares since we're given side lengths for each square. The smallest square has a side of length 3; its area is 3^2, or 9. The other small square has a side of length 6; its area is 6^2, or 36. The area of square *LMNO*, then, is $9 + 36 + 76 = 121$. If square *LMNO* has an area of 121, then each side has a length of $\sqrt{121}$, or 11. Since we have an expression for the length of a side of the large square in terms of *x*, we can set up an equation and solve for *x*:

$$2x + 1 = 11$$
$$2x = 10$$
$$x = 5$$

15. 25

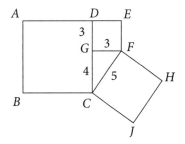

In order to determine the area of square *FCJH*, we can find the length of side *FC*, which is the hypotenuse of $\triangle FGC$. We can find the length of *FC* by finding the lengths of *FG* and *GC*.

Since *ABCD* has area 49, each side must have length $\sqrt{49}$, or 7. Therefore, *DC* has length 7. Since *DEFG* has area 9, side *FG* must have length $\sqrt{9}$, or 3. *DG* is also a side of the same square, so its length is also 3. The length of *CG* is the difference between the length of *DC* and the length of *DG*: $7 - 3 = 4$. Now we have the lengths of the legs of $\triangle FGC$: 3 and 4, so this must be a 3-4-5 right triangle. Thus *CF* has length 5. The area of square *FCJH* is the square of the length of *CF*: $5^2 = 25$.

16. 10

When a geometry problem does not provide us with a diagram, it can often be helpful to draw our own:

If we now add two lines like this...

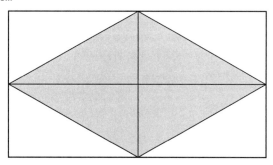

...we split the original rectangle into four smaller rectangles, each of which is half in and half out of the parallelogram. So the area of the parallelogram must be half the area of the rectangle.

Once we've made this deduction, the rest is straightforward. The area of the rectangle is twice the area of the parallelogram: $2 \times 60 = 120$. Since one dimension of the rectangle is 12, the other is $\frac{120}{12} = 10$.

17. $\dfrac{5w^2}{4}$

The sum of all four sides is $6w$. The two short sides add up to $\frac{w}{2} + \frac{w}{2}$, or w. This leaves $6w - w$, or $5w$, for the **sum** of the other two sides. So **each** long side is $\frac{1}{2}(5w)$, or $\frac{5}{2}w$.

So,

$$\text{Area} = \left(\frac{w}{2}\right)\left(\frac{5w}{2}\right) = \frac{5w^2}{4}$$

18. **80%**

The best way to solve this problem is to pick a value for the length of a side of square *A*. We want our numbers to be easy to work with, so let's pick 10 for the length of each side of square *A*. The length of each side of square *B* is 100 percent greater, or twice as great as a side of square *A*. So the length of a side of square *B* is 2 × 10, or 20. The length of each side of square *C* is 50 percent greater, or $1\frac{1}{2}$ times as great as a side of square *B*.

So the length of a side of square *C* is $1\frac{1}{2}$ × 20, or 30. The area of square *A* is 10^2, or 100. The area of square *B* is 20^2, or 400. The sum of the areas of squares *A* and *B* is 100 + 400, or 500. The area of square *C* is 30^2, or 900. The area of square *C* is greater than the sum of the areas of squares *A* and *B* by 900 − 500, or 400. The percent that the area of square *C* is greater than the sum of the areas of squares *A* and *B* is $\frac{400}{500}$ × 100%, or 80%.

19. **360**

First of all, if a rectangle has perimeter 10, what could its dimensions be? Perimeter = 2*L* + 2*W* = 2(*L* + *W*). The perimeter is 10, so 2(*L* + *W*) = 10, or *L* + *W* = 5. Since *L* and *W* must be integers, there are two possibilities: *L* = 4 and *W* = 1 (4 + 1 = 5), or *L* = 3 and *W* = 2 (3 + 2 = 5). Let's consider each case separately. If *L* = 4, then how many of these rectangles would fit along the length of the larger rectangle? The length of the larger rectangle is 60: 60 ÷ 4 = 15, so 15 smaller rectangles would fit, if they were lined up with their longer sides against the longer side of the large rectangle. The width of the smaller rectangles is 1, and the width of the large rectangle is 24; 24 ÷ 1 = 24, so 24 small rectangles can fit against the width of the large rectangle. The total number of small rectangles that fit inside the large rectangle is the number along the length times the number along the width: 15 × 24 = 360. In the second case, *L* = 3 and *W* = 2. 60 ÷ 3 = 20, so 20 small rectangles fit along the length; 24 ÷ 2 = 12, so 12 small rectangles fit along the width. So the total number of small rectangles is 20 × 12, or 240. We're asked for the greatest number, which we got from the first case: 360.

CIRCLES TEST
ANSWERS AND EXPLANATIONS

1. 16π

We need to find the radius in order to get the circumference. We're given that the area is 64π, so we can use the area formula to get the radius:

$$\text{Area} = \pi r^2 = 64\pi$$
$$r^2 = 64$$
$$r = 8$$

The circumference, which is $2\pi r$, is $2\pi(8)$, or 16π.

2. 18

Each side of $\triangle ABC$ connects the centers of two tangent circles, and each side passes through the point where the circumference of the circles touch. Therefore, each side is composed of the radii of two of the circles: AB is made up of a radius of B, BC is made up of a radius of B and a radius of C, and AC is made up of a radius of A and a radius of C:

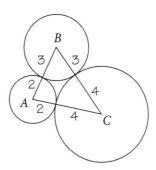

The sum of the lengths of these sides is the perimeter. Since we have two radii of each circle, the perimeter is twice the sum of the radii: $2(2 + 3 + 4) = 18$.

3. 45

We need to use the following ratio:

$$\frac{\text{length of arc}}{\text{circumference}} = \frac{\text{measure of arc's central angle}}{360°}$$

The measure of the arc's central angle is marked x degrees, and we're given that the length of the arc is $\frac{1}{8}$ of the circumference. So,

$$\frac{1}{8} = \frac{x}{360}$$
$$x = 45$$

4. $\frac{5}{9}$

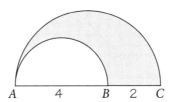

Method I:

The area of the shaded region equals the difference in areas of the two semicircles; to find the fraction of the larger semicircle occupied by the shaded region, we first find the area of the shaded region, then divide this by the area of the larger semicircle. The area of a semicircle is $\frac{1}{2}$ the area of the whole circle, or $\frac{1}{2}\pi r^2$. Here, the larger semicircle has a diameter of 6. Its radius is $\frac{1}{2}$ the diameter, or 3, and its area equals $\frac{1}{2}\pi r^2 = \frac{1}{2}\pi(3)^2 = \frac{9}{2}\pi$. The smaller circle has a diameter of 4 and a radius of 2, for an area of $\frac{1}{2}\pi(2)^2 = 2\pi$. The area of the shaded region equals:

$$\frac{9\pi}{2} - 2\pi = \frac{9\pi}{2} - \frac{4\pi}{2} = \frac{5\pi}{2}$$

The fraction of the larger semicircle the shaded region occupies is:

$$\frac{\frac{5\pi}{2}}{\frac{9\pi}{2}} = \frac{5\pi}{2} \times \frac{2}{9\pi} = \frac{5}{9}$$

Method II:

Avoid most of this work by exploring the ratios involved here. Any two semicircles are similar. The ratio of *AB* to *AC* is 4 to 6 or 2 to 3. The ratio of all linear measures of the two circles (circumference, radius) will also have this ratio. The area ratio will be the **square** of this, or 4 to 9. The small semicircle has $\frac{4}{9}$ the area of the large semicircle, leaving $\frac{5}{9}$ of the area of the large semicircle for the shaded region.

5. $2\sqrt{3}$

Sketch a diagram:

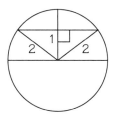

Since the radius of the circle is 2, the end-points of the line are both 2 inches from the center. The line can be seen as the legs of two right triangles, each of which has a hypotenuse of 2 and a leg of 1. Each of the legs that make up the line must have a length equal to $\sqrt{2^2 - 1^2}$, or $\sqrt{3}$. The total length of the line is twice this, or $2\sqrt{3}$.

6. 42π

Since we're given the diameter of the semicircle around *AB*, we should begin with this semicircle. The radius of semicircle *AB* is $\frac{1}{2}(4)$, or 2. The area of a semicircle is half the area of the circle, or $\frac{1}{2}\pi r^2$. So the area of semicircle *AB* is $\frac{1}{2}\pi(2)^2$, or 2π.

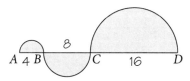

BC = 2*AB*, so *BC* = 2(4) = 8. The radius of semicircle *BC* is 4, so the area of semicircle *BC* is $\frac{1}{2}\pi(4)^2$, or 8π.
CD = 2*BC*, so *CD* = 2(8) = 16.

The radius of semicircle *CD* is 8, so the area of semicircle *CD* is $\frac{1}{2}\pi(8)^2$, or 32π. Adding the three areas together gives us $2\pi + 8\pi + 32\pi$, or 42π.

7. **2**

Since we know the area of circle *O*, we can find the radius of the circle. And if we find the length of *OA*, then *AB* is just the difference of *OB* and *OA*.

Since the area of the circle is 100π, the radius must be $\sqrt{100}$ or 10. Radius *OC*, line segment *CA*, and line segment *OA* together form a right triangle, so we can use the Pythagorean theorem to find the length of *OA*. But notice that 10 is twice 5 and 6 is twice 3, so right triangle *ACO* has sides whose lengths are in a 3 : 4 : 5 ratio.

OA must have a length of twice 4, or 8. *AB* is the segment of radius *OB* that's not a part of *OA*; its length equals the length of *OB* minus the length of *OA*, or $10 - 8 = 2$.

8. **50π**

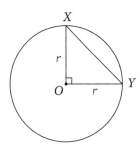

Each leg of right triangle *XOY* is also a radius of circle *O*. If we call the radius *r*, then the area of $\triangle XOY$ is $\frac{1}{2}(r)(r) = \frac{r^2}{2}$.

At the same time, the area of circle *O* is πr^2. So, we can use the area of $\triangle XOY$ to find r^2, and then multiply r^2 by π to get the area of the circle.

$$\text{Area of } \triangle XOY = \frac{r^2}{2} = 25$$
$$r^2 = 50$$
$$\text{Area of circle } O = \pi r^2 = \pi(50) = 50\pi$$

Note that it's unnecessary (and extra work) to find the actual value of *r*, since the value of r^2 is sufficient to find the area.

9. **125%**

The fastest method is to pick a value for the diameter of the circle. Let's suppose that the diameter is 4. Then the radius is $\frac{4}{2}$, or 2, which means that the area is $\pi(2)^2$, or 4π. Increasing the diameter by 50% means adding on half of its original length: $4 + (50\% \text{ of } 4) = 4 + 2 = 6$. So the new radius is $\frac{6}{2}$, or 3, which means that the area of the circle is now $\pi(3)^2$, or 9π. The percent increase is $\frac{9\pi - 4\pi}{4\pi} \times 100\% = \frac{5\pi}{4\pi} \times 100\% = 125\%$.

10. **20,000**

Since the lighthouse can be seen in all directions, its region of visibility is a circle with the lighthouse at the center. Before the change, the light could be seen for 60 miles, so the area of visibility was a circle with radius 60 miles. Now it can be seen for 40 miles further, or for a total of $60 + 40$, or 100 miles. The area is now a circle with radius 100 miles:

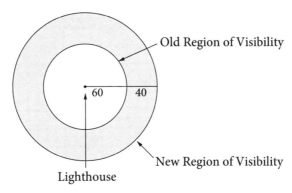

The increase is just the difference in these areas; that is, the shaded region on the above diagram.

$$\text{Increase} = \text{New area} - \text{old area}$$
$$= \pi(100)^2 - \pi(60)^2$$
$$= 10{,}000\pi - 3{,}600\pi$$
$$= 6{,}400\pi$$

The value of π is a bit more than 3, so $6{,}400\pi$ is a bit more than $3 \times 6{,}400$, or just over 19,200. The only choice close to this is 20,000.

11. **$8\sqrt{2}$**

Let's call the end-points of the arc A and B and the center of the circle C. Major arc AB represents $\frac{3}{4}$ of 360°, or 270°. Therefore, minor arc AB is $360° - 270°$, or 90°. Since AC and CB are both radii of the circle, $\triangle ABC$ must be an isosceles right triangle:

We can find the distance between A and B if we know the radius of the circle. Major arc AB, which takes up $\frac{3}{4}$ of the circumference, has a length of 12π, so the entire circumference is 16π. The circumference of any circle is 2π times the radius, so a circle with circumference 16π must have radius 8. The ratio of a leg to the hypotenuse in an isosceles right triangle is $1:\sqrt{2}$. The length of AB is $\sqrt{2}$ times the length of a leg, or $8\sqrt{2}$.

12. 4

We're looking for the length of CD. Note that OC is a radius of the circle, and if we knew the length of OC and OD, we could find CD, since $CD = OC - OD$. Well, we're given that OB has a length of 10, which means the circle has a radius of 10, and therefore OC is 10. All that remains is to find OD and subtract. The only other piece of information we have to work with is that AB has length 16. How can we use this to find OD? If we connect O and A, then we create two right triangles, $\triangle ADO$ and $\triangle BDO$:

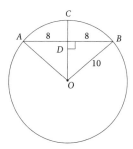

Since both of these right triangles have a radius as the hypotenuse, and both have a leg in common (OD), then they must be equal in size. Therefore, the other legs, AD and DB, must also be equal. That means that D is the midpoint of AB, so DB is $\frac{1}{2}(16)$, or 8. Considering right triangle BDO, we have a hypotenuse of 10 and a leg of 8; thus the other leg has length 6. (It's a 6-8-10 Pythagorean triple.) So OD has length 6, and $CD = 10 - 6 = 4$.

13. $6\sqrt{2} - 6$

Connect the centers of the circles O, P, and Q as shown. Each leg in this right triangle consists of two radii. The hypotenuse consists of two radii plus the diameter of the small circle.

We can find the radii of the large circles from the given information. Since the total area of the four large circles is 36π, each large circle has area 9π. Since the area of a circle is πr^2, we know that the radii of the large circles all have length 3.

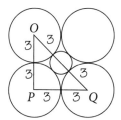

Therefore, each leg in the isosceles right triangle OPQ is 6. The hypotenuse then has length $6\sqrt{2}$. (The hypotenuse of an isosceles right triangle is always $\sqrt{2}$ times a leg.) The hypotenuse is equal to two radii plus the diameter of the small circle, so $6\sqrt{2} = 2(3) +$ diameter, or diameter $= 6\sqrt{2} - 6$.

MULTIPLE FIGURES TEST
ANSWERS AND EXPLANATIONS

1. **5π**

It may be helpful to draw your own diagram.

If a rectangle is inscribed in a circle, all four of its vertices are on the circumference of the circle and its diagonals pass through the center of the circle. This means that the diagonals of the rectangle are diameters of the circle. Here we are told that the diagonals have length 5, which means that the diameter of the circle is 5. The circumference of a circle is $2\pi r$, or πd, which in this case is 5π.

2. **24**

Area $= b \times h$. We are given the base of this rectangle ($PO = 6$), but we need to find the height. Let's draw a perpendicular line from point Q to OP and label the point R as shown below:

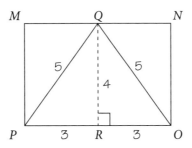

Now look at right triangle PQR. In isosceles triangle PQO, the altitude bisects the base, so QR bisects OP. Therefore, $PR = \frac{1}{2}(6) = 3$.

Hypotenuse QP is 5. This is an example of the famous 3-4-5 right triangle. Therefore, segment QR must have length 4. This is equal to the height of rectangle $MNOP$, so the area of the rectangle is $b \times h = 6 \times 4 = 24$.

3. 16π

The three right angles define three sectors of the circle, each with a central angle of 90°. Together, the three sectors account for $\frac{270°}{360°}$, or $\frac{3}{4}$ of the area of the circle, leaving $\frac{1}{4}$ of the circle for the shaded regions. So the total area of the shaded regions is $\frac{1}{4} \times \pi(8)^2$, or 16π.

4. $\sqrt{\pi}$

The area of a square with side x is x^2. The area of a circle with radius r is πr^2. Since the two areas are equal, we can write:

$$x^2 = \pi r^2$$

We need to solve for $\frac{x}{r}$:

$$\frac{x^2}{r^2} = \pi$$

$$\frac{x}{r} = \sqrt{\pi}$$

5. 18

Notice that both squares share a side with right triangle CDE. Since square $CEFG$ has an area of 36, CE has a length of $\sqrt{36}$, or 6. Since right triangle CDE has a 45° angle, CDE must be an isosceles right triangle. Therefore, CD and DE are the same length. Let's call that length x:

Remember, we're looking for the area of square *ABCD*, which will be x^2. Using the Pythagorean theorem on ΔCDE, we get:

$$(\text{leg})^2 + (\text{leg})^2 = (\text{hypotenuse})^2$$
$$x^2 + x^2 = 6^2$$
$$2x^2 = 36$$
$$x^2 = 18$$

So the area is 18. (There's no need to find x.)

6. $\dfrac{5}{2}\pi$

We can easily find the area of the circle given its diameter. The diameter is 5, so the radius is $\dfrac{5}{2}$ and the area is $\pi\left(\dfrac{5}{2}\right)^2$ or $\dfrac{25}{4}\pi$. This is equal to the area of the triangle. We know the base of the triangle is 5, so we can solve for the height:

$$\frac{1}{2}(5)(h) = \frac{25}{4}\pi$$
$$5h = \frac{25}{2}\pi$$
$$h = \frac{5}{2}\pi$$

7. **34**

The central rectangle shares a side with each of the four squares, and the four squares form the legs of the four right triangles. So we need to use the information that we're given about the rectangle. Two of its sides have a length of 4, so the two squares that share these sides must also have sides of length 4. The other two sides of the rectangle have a length of 3, so the other two squares, which share these sides, must also have sides of length 3. Each triangle shares a side with a small square and a side with a large square, so the legs of each triangle have lengths of 3 and 4, respectively.

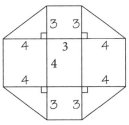

Since the legs are of length 3 and 4, the hypotenuse of each triangle must have a length of 5. To get the perimeter, we use the lengths of the hypotenuse and a side from each square:

$$\text{Perimeter} = 4(5) + 2(4) + 2(3)$$
$$= 20 + 8 + 6$$
$$= 34$$

8. **360°**

There are four angles at each of the three vertex points of the triangle, making a total of 12 angles. The sum of the angles around each vertex is equal to the measure of a full circle, 360°. The total measure of the 12 angles around all three points is 3(360°) = 1,080°. At each point there are two right angles and one angle of the triangle. For all three points there are six right angles for a total of 540°, and the three interior angles of the triangle for another 180°. Therefore,

$$540 + 180 + \angle A + \angle B + \angle C = 1,080$$
$$\angle A + \angle B + \angle C = 360$$

9. **21**

Drop radii *AO* and *BP* to form rectangle *ABPO*. (We've added points *O* and *P* into the diagram for clarity.)

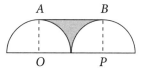

The shaded area is equal to the area of the rectangle minus the area of the two quarter-circles. The base of the rectangle is two radii, or 14, and the height is one radius, or 7. Therefore, the area of the rectangle = $bh = 14 \times 7 = 98$.

The area of two quarter circles is the same as the area of one semi-circle, or $\frac{1}{2}\pi r^2$. Since the radius is 7,

the area is $\frac{1}{2}\pi(7)^2 = \frac{49}{2}\pi$. We only need to estimate the answer, and the answer choices are far enough apart for

us to approximate. Since $\frac{49}{2}$ is almost 25 and π is close to 3, the area of the semicircle is about 75. Therefore, the

shaded area is approximately $98 - 75$, or 23. Choice **(A)**, 21, is closest to this.

10. 16

Each side of square *EFGH* consists of 2 radii of the quarter-circles. So we need to find the radius of each quarter-circle to get the length of the square's sides. If we put these four quarter-circles together we'd get a whole circle with a circumference of $4 \times \pi$, or 4π. We can use the circumference formula to solve for the radius of each quarter-circle:

$$\text{Circumference} = 2\pi r = 4\pi$$
$$r = 2$$

So each side of square *EFGH* has length 2×2, or 4. Therefore, the perimeter of the square is 4(4), or 16.

11. $56\pi + 32$

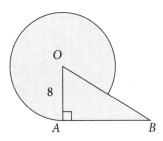

The total area of the shaded region equals the area of the circle plus the area of the right triangle minus the area of overlap. The area of circle *O* is $\pi(8)^2$, or 64π. We're told that the area of right triangle *OAB* is 32. So we just need to find the area of overlap, the area of right triangle *OAB* inside circle *O*, which forms a sector of the circle. Let's see what we can find out about $\angle AOB$, the central angle of the sector.

The area of right triangle *OAB* is 32, and the height is the radius. So $\frac{1}{2}(8)(AB) = 32$, or $AB = 8$.

Since $AB = OA$, $\triangle OAB$ is an isosceles right triangle. Therefore, $\angle AOB$ has a measure of 45°. So the area of the sector is $\frac{45}{360}(64\pi)$, or 8π. Now we can get the total area of the shaded region:

$$64\pi + 32 - 8\pi = 56\pi + 32$$

12. $100\sqrt{2}$

The key to solving a problem with multiple figures is to transfer information from one figure to another. Redraw the figure before examining the circle.

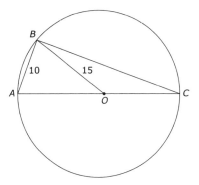

We are given that $OB = 15$. Since OA, OB, and OC are all radii of the circle, $OA = OB = OC = 15$. Let's add this information to the figure and then have a look at the triangle.

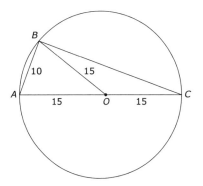

Whenever a triangle is inscribed in a circle such that one side of the triangle is the diameter of the circle, the triangle is a right triangle with the diameter of the circle as the triangle's hypotenuse. Because AC is the diameter of circle O, angle ABC must be 90 degrees, and the area of triangle ABC is equal to $\frac{1}{2}(AB \times BC)$.

We can now use the Pythagorean theorem:

$AB^2 + BC^2 = AC^2$

$10^2 + BC^2 = 30^2$

$100 + BC^2 = 900$

$BC^2 = 800$

$BC = \sqrt{800} = 20\sqrt{2}$

The area of the triangle is $\frac{1}{2}(AB \times BC) = \frac{10 \times 20\sqrt{2}}{2} = 100\sqrt{2}$.

13. 270

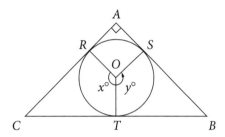

A line tangent to a circle is perpendicular to the radius of the circle at the point of tangency. Since AC is tangent to circle O at R and AB is tangent to circle O at S, $\angle ARO$ and $\angle ASO$ are 90° angles. Since three of the angles in quadrilateral $RASO$ are right angles, the fourth, $\angle ROS$, must also be a right angle. $\angle ROS$, x, and y sum to 360°, so we can set up an equation to solve for $x + y$.

$$x + y + 90 = 360$$
$$x + y = 360 - 90$$
$$x + y = 270$$

14. $25\pi - 48$

The total area of the shaded regions equals the area of the quarter-circle minus the area of the rectangle. Since the length of arc AB (a quarter of the circumference of circle O) is 5π, the whole circumference equals $4 \times 5\pi$, or 20π. Thus, the radius OE has length 10. (We've added point E in the diagram for clarity.) Since OB also equals 10, $OC = 10 - 4$, or 6. This tells us that ΔOEC is a 6-8-10 right triangle and $EC = 8$.

Now we know the dimensions of the rectangle, so we can find its area: area $= \ell \times w = 8 \times 6 = 48$. Finally, we can get the total area of the shaded regions:

$$\text{Area of shaded regions} = \frac{1}{4} \times \pi \times (10)^2 - 48$$
$$= 25\pi - 48$$

15. $2 : 1$

The length of each side of the square is given as s. A side of the square has the same length as the diameter of the smaller circle. (You can see this more clearly if you draw the vertical diameter in the smaller circle. The diameter you draw will connect the upper and lower tangent points where the smaller circle and square intersect.)

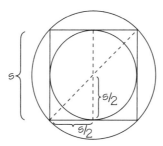

This means that the radius of the smaller circle is $\frac{s}{2}$, so its area is $\left(\frac{s}{2}\right)^2 \pi$, or $\frac{s^2}{4}\pi$. Now draw a diagonal of the square, and you'll see that it's the diameter of the larger circle. The diagonal breaks the square up into two isosceles right triangles, where each leg has length s as in the diagram above. So the diagonal must have length $s\sqrt{2}$. Therefore, the radius of the larger circle is $\frac{s\sqrt{2}}{2}$, so its area is $\left(\frac{s\sqrt{2}}{2}\right)^2 \pi$, or $\frac{2s^2}{4}\pi$, or $\frac{s^2}{2}\pi$. This is twice the area of the smaller circle.

SOLIDS TEST ANSWERS AND EXPLANATIONS

1. $\dfrac{r}{h}$

Let's express the volume of a cylinder with radius r and height h first. (Call it cylinder A.)

$$\text{Volume} = \text{area of base} \times \text{height} = \pi r^2 h$$

For the cylinder with radius h and height r (cylinder B),

$$\text{Volume} = \pi h^2 r$$

Then the ratio of the volume of A to the volume of B is $\dfrac{\pi r^2 h}{\pi h^2 r}$. We can cancel the factor πrh from both numerator and denominator, leaving us with $\dfrac{r}{h}$.

2. 8

We can immediately determine the volume of the rectangular solid since we're given all its dimensions: 4, 8, and 16. The volume of a rectangular solid is equal to the product $\ell \times w \times h$. So the volume of this solid is $16 \times 8 \times 4$, and this must equal the volume of the cube as well. The volume of a cube is the length of an edge cubed, so we can set up an equation to solve for e:

$$e^3 = 16 \times 8 \times 4$$

To avoid the multiplication, let's break the 16 down into 2×8:

$$e^3 = 2 \times 8 \times 8 \times 4$$

We can now combine 2×4 to get another 8:

$$e^3 = 8 \times 8 \times 8$$
$$e = 8$$

The length of an edge of the cube is 8.

3. 4

Once we find the cube's volume, we can get the length of one edge. Since 16 cubic meters represents 25 percent, or $\dfrac{1}{4}$, of the volume of the whole cube, the cube has a volume of 4×16, or 64 cubic meters. The volume of a cube is the length of an edge cubed, so $e^3 = 64$. Therefore e, the length of an edge, is 4.

4. **1:1**

This problem may seem complicated, but solving is actually straightforward. If a cube has a volume of 64, its edges are $\sqrt[3]{64} = 4$. Therefore, when cubes 2 on a side are formed, each edge will be split in half, and all of the resulting cubes are identical. We can visualize each smaller cube as a corner of the original cube with three outward-facing purple sides and three inward-facing white sides. The ratio is therefore 1:1, and there is no need to spend time doing any math.

5. $\dfrac{20(\pi - 1)}{\pi}$

This problem may seem difficult, but it is quite manageable if we approach it step-by-step. We are pouring gasoline from a cylindrical container into a rectangular tank, so we'll need to find the volume of each solid before we address the question itself. The volume of a solid is the area of its base multiplied by its height. In the case of the gas tank, that's $4 \times 8 \times 10 = 320$ cubic inches.

Now we find the volume of gasoline in the cylinder in a similar way: The base of the cylinder has a diameter of 8, so its radius is 4. The area of the base is therefore 16π. We are told that the gasoline reached a height of 20 inches before the tank was filled, so the cylinder began with $16\pi \times 20 = 320\pi$ cubic inches of gasoline.

After filling the tank, the cylindrical container has $(320\pi - 320)$ cubic inches of gasoline remaining. The base of the cylinder is 16π, so the new height is

$$\frac{320\pi - 320}{16\pi} = \frac{320(\pi - 1)}{16\pi} = \frac{20(\pi - 1)}{\pi}$$

6. **2**

It may be helpful to draw a quick diagram, like this one:

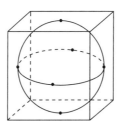

The sphere will touch the cube at six points. Each point will be an endpoint of a diameter and will be at the center of one of the cubic faces. (If this isn't clear, imagine putting a beach ball inside a cube-shaped box.) So, the diameter extends directly from one face of the cube to the other, and is perpendicular to both faces that it touches. This means that the diameter must have the same length as an edge of the cube. The cube's volume is 64, so each edge has length $\sqrt[3]{64}$, or 4. Thus, the diameter of the sphere is 4, which means that the radius is 2.

7. **52**

The given conditions narrow down the possibilities for the solid's dimensions. The volume of a rectangular solid is length $\times$ width $\times$ height. Since one of these dimensions is 4, and the volume is 24, the other two dimension must have a product of $\dfrac{24}{4}$, or 6. Since the dimensions are integers, there are two possibilities: 2 and 3 ($2 \times 3 = 6$), or 1 and 6 ($1 \times 6 = 6$). We can work with either possibility to determine the total surface area. If our result matches an answer choice, we can stop. If not, we can try the other possibility. Let's try 4, 2, and 3:

$$\text{Surface area} = 2\ell w + 2\ell h + 2wh$$
$$= 2(4)(2) + 2(4)(3) + 2(2)(3)$$
$$= 16 + 24 + 12 = 52$$

Since choice **(B)** is 52, we've found our answer.

8. I, II, and III

We need to go through the statements one at a time.

Statement I:

Intuitively or visually, you might be able to see that *FD* and *GA* are parallel. It's a little trickier to prove mathematically. Remember, two line segments are parallel if they're in the same plane and if they do not intersect each other. Imagine slicing the cube in half, diagonally from *FG* to *AD*.

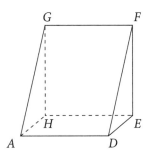

The diagonal face will be a flat surface, with sides *AD*, *FD*, *FG*, and *GA*. So *FD* and *GA* are in the same plane. They both have the same length, since each is a diagonal of a face of the cube. *FG* and *DA* also have the same length, since they're both edges of the cube. Since both pairs of opposite sides have the same length, *ADFG* must be a parallelogram. (In fact, it's a rectangle.) So *FD* and *GA*, which are opposite sides, are parallel. Eliminate choice **(D)**.

Statement II:

$\triangle GCF$ is half of square *BCFG*, and $\triangle AHD$ is half of square *ADEH*. Both squares have the same area, so both triangles must also have the same area. Eliminate choices **(A)** and **(C)**.

Statement III:

Draw in diagonals *AE* and *AF* to get right triangle *AEF*. Also draw in diagonals *HD* and *GD* to get right triangle *DGH*.

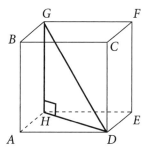

AE and *HD* are both diagonals of the same square, so *AE* = *HD*. *FE* and *GH* are both edges of the cube, so *FE* = *GH*. Since right triangle *AEF* and right triangle *DGH* have corresponding legs of the same length, they must also have hypotenuses of the same length. *AF* and *GD* are the respective hypotenuses, so *AF* = *GD*.

Therefore, statements I, II, and III are true.

Question Type Review

Chapter 5:
Problem Solving

Problem Solving questions account for the majority of the math problems on the GMAT, about two-thirds of the math section. Each question contains a question stem and five answer choices, similar to what you have seen throughout this book. These questions can test your understanding of any of the math concepts on the GMAT.

PROBLEM SOLVING—DIRECTIONS

Directions: Solve the problems and choose the best answer.

Note: Unless otherwise indicated, the figures accompanying the questions have been drawn as accurately as possible and may be used as sources of information for answering the questions.

All figures lie in a plane except where noted.

All numbers used are real numbers.

THE KAPLAN FOUR-STEP METHOD FOR PROBLEM SOLVING

1. Analyze the question.
Read through the whole problem first, without pausing for details, to get a sense of the overall problem. Be sure to glance at the answer choices: they might trigger an important insight.

2. State the task.
Make sure you know what you're solving for. The right answer to the wrong question is a wrong answer. Identify the variables and name them in a way that makes it easy to remember what they stand for. For example, call the unknown quantity Bill's age B, and the unknown quantity Al's age A. And note that you might be able to solve for what you need without calculating the value of every single variable involved in the problem.

3. Approach strategically.
Analyze the problem to find the most straightforward approach that allows you to make sense of the problem. There is rarely a "right approach." Choose the easiest for you given the current problem.

4. Confirm your answer.

You can't go back to check your work after completing the section, so build that step into your work on each problem by rereading the question. If you notice a wrinkle to the problem that you missed earlier, redo the problem (if you have time) or change your answer.

While working through Problem Solving questions, there are two important strategies you can rely on. The first is Picking Numbers and the second is Backsolving. Knowing these two methods on Test Day will allow you to get to the correct answers much more quickly and efficiently.

Picking Numbers

Picking numbers is often an easier way to tackle ratio or percent word problems, and provides a useful backup strategy if you cannot solve the problem using more traditional techniques. Picking numbers is especially helpful in ratio and percent problems. But be careful—try to pick a number that is easy to work with. In a ratio problem pick a number that is divisible by all the numerators and denominators. In percent problems it is almost always best to pick 100, since calculating percents of 100 is easy.

Example:　At the Frosty Ice Cream store, the number of cones sold fell by 20 percent in November. If sales fell by a further 25 percent in December, what was the percent decrease in the number of cones sold in the whole two-month period?

- ⬭ 10%
- ⬭ 20%
- ⬭ 35%
- ⬭ 40%
- ⬭ 45%

Let the original number of cones sold be 100. The number of cones sold in November is 20% less than this. 20% of 100 is 20, so the number of cones sold in November is $100 - 20 = 80$.

The number of cones sold in December is 25% less than this amount. 25% of $80 = \frac{1}{4}$ of $80 = 20$. So the number of cones sold in December is $80 - 20 = 60$. The difference between the original number of cones sold and the number of cones sold in December is $100 - 60 = 40$ cones. If sales fell by 40 cones, the percent decrease in sales was $\frac{40}{100} \times 100\%$, or 40%.

Backsolving

Backsolving can be used on many problems, especially if running answer choices through the question stem seems like it would be quicker than setting up equations and solving.

Example: An insurance company provides coverage according to the following rules: the policy pays 80 percent of the first $1,200 of cost and 50 percent of the cost above $1,200. If a patient had to pay $490 of the cost of a certain procedure himself, how much did the procedure cost?

⬭ $1,200

⬭ $1,300

⬭ $1,500

⬭ $1,700

⬭ $1,800

Since each answer choice represents a possible amount of the procedure's cost, we can pick a choice, assume that this was the cost of the procedure, and apply the insurance company's rules on that choice. The answer choice that results in the patient paying $490 is correct.

Let's start with **choice (B)**. If it is correct, then the procedure costs **$1,300**. We know that the policy pays 80% of the first $1,200, so the patient pays 20% of the first $1,200 of the cost. We also know that the policy pays 50% of any cost above $1,200, so that means the patient must pay 50% of the cost above $1,200. Looking at **choice (B)**, **$1,300**: the patient pays 20% of the first $1,200, or 0.2 × $1,200 = $240. The part of the cost above $1,200 is **$1,300** − $1,200, or **$100**. Because the patient pays 50% of that, the patient's share is one-half of $100, or $50. That's a total expense for the patient of **$240 + $50 = $290**.

So, if the procedure cost **$1,300**, then the patient would have paid **$290**. But we know from the question stem that the patient paid $490. So we know that the choice is too small. In order for the patient to have spent $490, the procedure must have cost more than **$1,300**. So that means that **choices (A) and (B) are both wrong** and we can eliminate them. **Next, try choice (D). If it is too large, choice (C) must be the correct answer. If it is too small, choice (E) must be the correct answer.**

Looking at **choice (D)**, $1,700, again the patient pays $240 of the first $1,200. Now the excess amount is $1,700 − $1,200 = $500. Since the patient pays 50% of the excess, this part of the charge is 0.5 × $500, or $250. That's a total of $250 + $240 = $490. This is the same as the amount the patient pays in the + question stem, so this choice is correct.

Backsolving often allows you to find the correct answer by checking at most two possibilities. It's primarily useful on problems with numerical answer choices, and problems where you're able to determine whether the choice you tried was too high or too low.

WORD PROBLEMS LEVEL ONE

Basic Arithmetic and Algebraic Operations in Word Problems

There are word problems in which only numbers are involved—some of these can be quite complicated. These complications become even more challenging when variables are used instead of numbers. If you don't see immediately what operations to use, imagine that the variables are numbers and see whether that gives you a clue.

In this section, we give examples of when to use each of the four basic operations: addition, subtraction, multiplication, and division.

Addition—You add when:

You are given the amounts of individual quantities and you want to find the total.

Example: If the sales tax on a $12.00 lunch check is $1.20, the total amount of the check is 12.00 + 1.20, or $13.20.

You are given an original amount and the amount of increase.

Example: If the bus fare increased from 55 cents by 35 cents, the new fare is 55 + 35 = 90 cents.

Subtraction—You subtract when:

You are given the total and one part of the total. You want to find the other part (the rest).

Example: If there are 50 children and 32 of them are girls, then the number of boys is 50 − 32 = 18 boys.

You are given two numbers and you want to know how much **more** or how much **less** one number is than the other. The amount is called the **difference**.

Example: How much larger than 30 is 38?

$$38 \quad - \quad 30 \quad = \quad 8$$
$$\uparrow \qquad\qquad \uparrow$$
$$\text{larger} \qquad \text{smaller}$$
$$\downarrow \qquad\qquad \downarrow$$

Example: How much less is a than b?

$$b \quad - \quad a \quad = \quad b - a$$

Note: In word problems, difference typically means **absolute** difference; that is larger − smaller.

Multiplication—You multiply when:

You are given the value for one item; you want to find the total value for **many** of these items.

Example: If 1 book costs $6.50, then 12 copies of the same book cost 12 × $6.50 = $78.

Division—You divide when:

> You are given the amount for **many** items, and you want the amount for **one**. (Division is the inverse of multiplication.)

> **Example:** If the price of 5 pounds of apples is $6.75, then the price of one pound of apples is $6.75 ÷ 5 or $1.35.

> You are given the amount of one group and the total amount for all groups, and you want to know how many of the small groups fit into the larger one.

> **Example:** If 240 students are divided into groups of 30 students, then there are 240 ÷ 30 = 8 groups of 30 students.

Word problems, or problem solving questions, account for the majority of the math problems on the GMAT. Word problems test the same concepts covered in algebra, arithmetic, and geometry, but do so in a different way. The question is presented in ordinary language; indeed it often involves some ordinary situation such as the price of goods. To be able to solve the problem mathematically, however, we must be able to translate the problem into mathematical terms.

Suppose the core of a problem involves working with the equation

$$3J = S - 4$$

In a word problem, this might be presented as follows:

> If the number of macaroons John had tripled, he would have four macaroons less than Susan.

Your job will be to translate the problem from English to math. A phrase like "three times as many" translates as "$3J$"; the phrase "four less than Susan" becomes "$S - 4$."

The key to solving word problems is isolating the words and phrases that relate to a particular mathematical process. In this chapter you will also find a Translation Table, showing the most common key words and phrases and their mathematical translation.

Many people dislike word problems and not unreasonably, since turning a word problem into a straightforward question means you first must go to the trouble of translating the problem before you can start working on it. But in some ways this actually makes the problem easier. Once you have translated the problem, you will generally find that the concepts and processes involved are rather simple. The test makers figure that they have made the problem difficult enough by adding the extra step of translating from English to math. So, once you have passed this step you stand an excellent chance of being able to solve the problem.

Translating English into Algebra

In some word problems, especially those involving variables, the best approach is to translate directly, from an English sentence into an algebraic "sentence," i.e., into an equation. You can then deal with the equation by using the techniques we have discussed in the previous chapters.

The Translation Table below lists some common English words and phrases, and the corresponding algebraic symbols.

TRANSLATION TABLE

Equals, is, was, will, be, has, costs, adds up to, is the same as	$=$
Times, of, multiplied by, product of, twice, double, triple	$\cdot$ or $\times$
Divided by, per, out of, each, ratio of __ to __	$\div$
Plus, added to, sum, combined, and, more than, total	$+$
Minus, subtracted from, less than, decreased by, difference between	$-$
What, how much, how many, a number	x, n, etc.

Example: Beatrice   gets   3 dollars more than   twice Alan's wage

↓   ↓

B   =   2A   +3

Some word problems can be fairly complicated; nonetheless, the solution merely involves understanding the scenario presented, translating the given information, and taking things one step at a time.

Example: Steve is now five times as old as Craig was 5 years ago. If the sum of Craig's and Steve's ages is 35, in how many years will Steve be twice as old as Craig?

○ 2

○ 5

○ 10

○ 15

○ 25

Let c = Craig's current age
Let s = Steve's current age

Translate the first sentence to get the first equation:

s	$=$	$5(c - 5)$
Steve's current age	is	Five times Craig's age 5 years ago

Translate the first part of the second sentence to get the second equation:

$c + s$	$=$	35
The sum of Craig's and Steve's ages	is	35

Now we are ready to solve for the two unknowns. Solve for c in terms of s in the second equation:

$$c + s = 35$$
$$c = 35 - s$$

Now plug this value for c into the first equation and solve for s:

$$s = 5(c - 5)$$
$$s = 5(35 - s - 5)$$
$$s = 5(30 - s)$$
$$s = 150 - 5s$$
$$6s = 150$$
$$s = 25$$

Plug this value for s into either equation to solve for c:

$$c = 35 - s$$
$$c = 35 - 25$$
$$c = 10$$

So Steve is currently 25 and Craig is currently 10. We still haven't answered the question asked, though; we need to set up an equation to find the number of years after which Steve will be twice as old as Craig.

Let x be the number of years from now in which Steve will be twice as old as Craig.

$$25 + x = 2(10 + x)$$

Solve this equation for x.

$$25 + x = 20 + 2x$$
$$x = 5$$

So Steve will be twice as old as Craig in 5 years. Answer choice **(B)** is correct.

WORD PROBLEMS LEVEL ONE EXERCISE

Translate the following directly into algebraic form. Do not reduce the expressions. (Answers are on the following page.)

1. z is x less than y.

2. The sum of 5, 6, and a.

3. If n is greater than m, the positive difference between twice n and m.

4. The ratio of $4q$ to $7p$ is 5 to 2.

5. The product of a decreased by b and twice the sum of a and b.

6. A quarter of the sum of a and b is 4 less than a.

7. Double the ratio of z to a plus the sum of z and a equals z minus a.

8. If \$500 were taken from F's salary, then the combined salaries of F and G will be double what F's salary would be if it were increased by a half of itself.

9. The sum of a, b and c is twice the sum of a minus b and a minus c.

10. The sum of y and 9 decreased by the sum of x and 7 is the same as dividing x decreased by z by 7 decreased by x.

**ANSWER KEY
BEGINS ON NEXT PAGE**

ANSWER KEY—WORD PROBLEMS LEVEL ONE EXERCISE

1. $z = y - x$

2. $5 + 6 + a$

3. $2n - m$

4. $\dfrac{4q}{7p} = \dfrac{5}{2}$

5. $(a - b) \cdot 2(a + b)$

6. $\dfrac{a + b}{4} = a - 4$

7. $\dfrac{2z}{a} + z + a = z - a$

8. $F - 500 + G = 2\left(F + \dfrac{F}{2}\right)$

9. $a + b + c = 2[(a - b) + (a - c)]$

10. $(y + 9) - (x + 7) = \dfrac{x - z}{7 - x}$

WORD PROBLEMS LEVEL ONE TEST

Solve the following problems and choose the best answer. (Answers and explanations are at the end of the chapter.)

Basic

1. Before the market opens on Monday, a stock is priced at $25. If its price decreases $4 on Monday, increases $6 on Tuesday, and then decreases $2 on Wednesday, what is the final price of the stock on Wednesday?

   ○ $12

   ○ $21

   ○ $25

   ○ $29

   ○ $37

2. Between 1950 and 1960 the population of Country A increased by 3.5 million people. If the increase between 1960 and 1970 was 1.75 million more than the increase between 1950 and 1960, what was the total amount of increase in population in Country A between 1950 and 1970?

   ○ 1.75 million

   ○ 3.5 million

   ○ 5.25 million

   ○ 7 million

   ○ 8.75 million

3. Greg's weekly salary is $70 less than Joan's, whose weekly salary is $50 more than Sue's. If Sue earns $280 per week, how much does Greg earn per week?

   ○ $160

   ○ $260

   ○ $280

   ○ $300

   ○ $400

4. During the 19th century a certain tribe collected 10 pieces of copper for every camel passing through Timbuktu in a caravan. If in 1880 an average of 8 caravans passed through Timbuktu every month, and there was an average of 100 camels in each caravan that year, how many pieces of copper did the tribe collect from the caravans over the year?

   ○ 800

   ○ 8,000

   ○ 9,600

   ○ 80,000

   ○ 96,000

5. A painter charges $12 an hour while his son charges $6 an hour. If father and son work the same amount of time together on a job, how many hours does each of them work if their combined charge for labor is $108?

   ○ 6

   ○ 8

   ○ 9

   ○ 12

   ○ 18

6. A certain book costs $12 more in hardcover than in softcover. If the softcover price is $\frac{2}{3}$ of the hardcover price, how much does the book cost in hardcover?

    ◯ $8

    ◯ $15

    ◯ $18

    ◯ $20

    ◯ $36

7. During a certain week, a post office sold $280 worth of 14-cent stamps. How many of these stamps did they sell?

    ◯ 20

    ◯ 2,000

    ◯ 3,900

    ◯ 20,000

    ◯ 39,200

8. Liza was 2*n* years old *n* years ago. What will be her age, in years, *n* years from now?

    ◯ 4*n*

    ◯ 3*n*

    ◯ 2*n* + 2

    ◯ 2*n*

    ◯ 2*n* − 2

9. During a drought the amount of water in a pond was reduced by a third. If the amount of water in the pond was 48,000 gallons immediately after the drought, how many thousands of gallons of water were lost during the drought?

    ◯ 16

    ◯ 24

    ◯ 36

    ◯ 64

    ◯ 72

10. A man has an estate worth $15 million that he will either divide equally among his 10 children or among his 10 children and 5 stepchildren. How much more will each of his children inherit if his 5 stepchildren are excluded?

    ◯ $500,000

    ◯ $1,000,000

    ◯ $1,500,000

    ◯ $2,500,000

    ◯ $5,000,000

Intermediate

11. An office has 27 employees. If there are 7 more women than men in the office, how many employees are women?

   - ⬭ 8
   - ⬭ 10
   - ⬭ 14
   - ⬭ 17
   - ⬭ 20

12. If the product of 3 and x is equal to 2 less than y, which of the following must be true?

   - ⬭ $6x - y - 2 = 0$
   - ⬭ $6x - 6 = 0$
   - ⬭ $3x - y - 2 = 0$
   - ⬭ $3x + y - 2 = 0$
   - ⬭ $3x - y + 2 = 0$

13. Four partners invested $1,600 each to purchase 1,000 shares of a certain stock. If the total cost of the stock is $8,000 plus a 2 percent commission, each partner should additionally invest what equal amount to cover the purchase of the stock?

   - ⬭ $100
   - ⬭ $110
   - ⬭ $220
   - ⬭ $440
   - ⬭ $880

14. At garage A, it costs $8.75 to park a car for the first hour and $1.25 for each additional hour. At garage B, it costs $5.50 for the first hour and $2.50 for each additional hour. What is the difference between the cost of parking a car for 5 hours at garage A and garage B?

   - ⬭ $1.50
   - ⬭ $1.75
   - ⬭ $2.25
   - ⬭ $2.75
   - ⬭ $3.25

15. At a certain high school, $\frac{2}{3}$ of the students play on sports teams. Of the students who play sports, $\frac{1}{4}$ play on the football team. If there are a total of 240 students in the high school, how many students play on the football team?

   - ⬭ 180
   - ⬭ 160
   - ⬭ 80
   - ⬭ 60
   - ⬭ 40

16. Ed has 100 dollars more than Robert. After Ed spends twenty dollars on groceries, Ed has 5 times as much money as Robert. How much money does Robert have?

   - ⬭ $20
   - ⬭ $30
   - ⬭ $40
   - ⬭ $50
   - ⬭ $120

KAPLAN

17. Diane finds that $2\frac{1}{2}$ cans of paint are just enough to paint $\frac{1}{3}$ of her room. How many more cans of paint will she need to finish her room and paint a second room of the same size?

   ○ 5

   ○ $7\frac{1}{2}$

   ○ 10

   ○ $12\frac{1}{2}$

   ○ 15

18. In a typical month, $\frac{1}{2}$ of the UFO sightings in the state are attributable to airplanes and $\frac{1}{3}$ of the remaining sightings are attributable to weather balloons. If there were 108 UFO sightings during one typical month, how many would be attributable to weather balloons?

   ○ 18

   ○ 24

   ○ 36

   ○ 54

   ○ 72

19. At a certain photography store, it costs Pete $1.65 for the first print and $0.85 for each additional print. How many prints of a particular photograph can Pete get for $20.00?

   ○ 19

   ○ 20

   ○ 21

   ○ 22

   ○ 23

20. There are enough peanuts in a bag to give 12 peanuts to each of 20 children, with no peanuts left over. If 5 children do not want any peanuts, how many peanuts can be given to each of the others?

   ○ 12

   ○ 15

   ○ 16

   ○ 18

   ○ 20

Advanced

21. The total fare for 2 adults and 3 children on an excursion boat is $14.00. If each child's fare is one half of each adult's fare, what is the adult fare?

    ◯ $2.00

    ◯ $3.00

    ◯ $3.50

    ◯ $4.00

    ◯ $4.50

22. Doris spent $\frac{2}{3}$ of her savings on a used car, and she spent $\frac{1}{4}$ of her remaining savings on a new carpet. If the carpet cost her $250, how much were Doris' original savings?

    ◯ $1,000

    ◯ $1,200

    ◯ $1,500

    ◯ $2,000

    ◯ $3,000

23. Gheri is n years old. Carl is 6 years younger than Gheri and 2 years older than Jean. What is the sum of the ages of all three?

    ◯ $3n + 16$

    ◯ $3n + 4$

    ◯ $3n - 4$

    ◯ $3n - 8$

    ◯ $3n - 14$

24. A class of 40 students is to be divided into smaller groups. If each group is to contain 3, 4, or 5 people, what is the largest number of groups possible?

    ◯ 8

    ◯ 10

    ◯ 12

    ◯ 13

    ◯ 14

25. Philip has twice as many salamanders as Matt. If Philip gives Matt 10 of his salamanders, he will have half as many as Matt. How many salamanders do Philip and Matt have together?

    ◯ 10

    ◯ 20

    ◯ 30

    ◯ 40

    ◯ 60

26. In a group of 60 workers, the average salary is $80 a day per worker. If some of the workers earn $75 a day and the rest earn $100 a day, how many workers earn $75 a day?

    ◯ 12

    ◯ 24

    ◯ 36

    ◯ 48

    ◯ 54

PERCENT, RATIO, AND RATES WORD PROBLEMS

Percent Problems

Many word problems are percent problems; in fact, the majority of percent problems are presented in this form. We have already looked at percents in the Arithmetic chapter; let's just look at a few examples using terms that you will often find in percent word problems.

Profit: The profit made on an item is the selling price minus the cost to the seller.
(If the cost is more than the selling price, it is a loss.)

Example: A store is selling a video monitor for $600. If the store makes a profit of 20 percent of its cost, what was the cost of the monitor to the store?

If we let C represent the cost, then we set up an equation to find the cost:

$$\text{Cost} + \text{Profit} = \text{Selling Price}$$

$$C + (20\%)C = \$600$$

$$C + \frac{1}{5}C = \$600$$

$$\frac{6}{5}C = \$600$$

$$C = \$600 \times \frac{5}{6} = \$500$$

The cost of the monitor to the store was $500.

Gross and net: Gross is the total amount before any deductions are made, while **net** is the amount after deductions are made. For instance, gross pay is the total amount of money earned, while net pay is gross pay minus any deductions, such as tax.

Discount: The discount on an item is usually a percent of a previous price for the item.

Example: If a dress usually selling for $120 is sold at a 40% discount, what is the sale price of the dress?

The discount is 40% of $120, or $40\% \times \$120 = \frac{2}{5} \times \$120$
$$= \$48$$

So the sale price is $\$120 - \$48 = \$72$.

Notice that if the dress is sold at a 40% discount, the sale price is $(100\% - 40\%)$ or 60% of the original price:

$$60\% \times \$120 = \frac{3}{5} \times \$120$$
$$= \$72$$

Ratios and Rates

Other common word problems are those involving ratios and rates. This is not really surprising, as many of the math topics that we commonly encounter in the real world (percent profits, rates of work, etc.) are often presented as word problems.

We have already looked at ratios in the Arithmetic chapter. Let's just have a look at how we can deal with them as word problems.

Example: There are 36 marbles in a bag containing only blue and red marbles. If there are three red marbles for every blue marble, how many blue marbles are there in the bag?

Translate from English into math: "three red marbles for every blue marble" means the ratio of red:blue = 3:1.

Set up a proportion with a part to whole ratio to find the number of blue marbles. The ratio of the number of blue marbles to the total number of marbles is 1 : [1 + 3] or 1:4.

Using b for the number of blue marbles, we have the proportion:

$$\frac{1}{4} = \frac{b}{36}$$

$$4b = 36$$

$$b = 9$$

So there are 9 blue marbles in the bag.

Rates are even more common than ratios in word problems. Rates were touched upon in the Arithmetic chapter, but let's examine them in more detail now. A rate is simply a ratio that relates two different quantities that are measured in different units. Examples include speed, which can be measured in miles per hour, or cost, which is dollars per item, or work, which can be measured in pay per hour.

The two most common types of rate problems involve motion and work.

Motion: The basic formula for motion problems is

Distance = Rate × Time

which can also be arranged as $\text{Rate} = \dfrac{\text{Distance}}{\text{Time}}$ or $\text{Time} = \dfrac{\text{Distance}}{\text{Rate}}$.

This is a very important formula and you should remember it. It is perhaps easiest to remember if you consider the everyday situation of driving a car. The distance travelled (in miles) = the speed of the car (in miles per hour) × time driving at that speed (in hours). For instance, if you are driving at 50 miles per hour for two hours, how far do you travel? The distance travelled is 50 miles per hour × 2 hours = 100 miles. (Notice how the unit 'hours' cancels out when you multiply.)

Example: Bob travels 60 miles in $1\frac{1}{2}$ hours. If he travels at the same rate for another 3 hours, how many more miles will he travel?

First find the speed at which he is traveling.

$$\text{Distance} = \text{Rate} \times \text{Time}$$

$$60 \text{ miles} = \text{Rate} \times 1\frac{1}{2} \text{ Hours}$$

$$\frac{60 \text{ miles}}{1\frac{1}{2} \text{ hours}} = \text{Rate}$$

$$40 \text{ miles per hour} = \text{Rate}$$

If he travels for 3 hours at 40 miles per hour he will travel:

$$\text{Distance} = 3 \text{ hours} \times 40\frac{\text{miles}}{\text{hour}} = 120 \text{ miles}$$

Notice how units divide and multiply just like numbers. When we say 40 miles per hour we mean:

$$\frac{40 \text{ miles}}{1 \text{ hour}}$$

So then when we multiply 40 miles per hour by 3 hours we get:

$$\frac{40 \text{ miles}}{1 \text{ hour}} \times 3 \text{ hours} = 120 \text{ miles}$$

It is often useful to have the units we want to end up with in mind when we do the problem, as in the following example:

Example: If David paints houses at the rate of h houses per day, how many houses does he paint in d days, in terms of h and d?

- $\frac{h}{d}$

- hd

- $\frac{h+d}{2}$

- $h-d$

- $\frac{d}{h}$

First note that the answer should tell us a number of houses. Now look at the units of the given information. We have $h\,\dfrac{\text{houses}}{\text{days}}$ and d days.

Find a combination of the units $\dfrac{\text{"houses"}}{\text{days}}$ and "days" that will leave us with "houses." Notice that if we multiply the terms

$$h\,\frac{\text{houses}}{\text{days}} \times d\ \text{days} = hd\ \text{houses}$$

the "days" cancel out and we are left with "houses," the desired result. Thus, the answer is hd.

Units are important in many types of word problems. Units can measure time, length, weight, etc. We can multiply and divide units, and even raise them to higher powers. We must be especially careful when changing from one unit to another, such as minutes to hours, or feet to inches.

To change to smaller units: you need a greater number of smaller units, so multiply.

To change to larger units: you need a smaller number of larger units, so divide.

Don't worry about memorizing any obscure conversion factors, like feet to miles, or fluid ounces to gallons—if you need to convert units, the conversion factors will be given to you. An exception to this is time. You are expected to know the divisions of time—days in a week, seconds in a minute, months in the year, etc.

Example: Change 10 hours to minutes.

There will be **more** minutes than hours, so we multiply by 60, the number of minutes in one hour.

$$10\ \text{hours} = 10\ \text{hours} \times \frac{60\ \text{minutes}}{1\ \text{hour}} = 600\ \text{minutes}$$

The Units Cancellation Method (UCM) is a useful way of keeping track of units. When multiplying or dividing by a conversion factor, the units cancel in the same way as numbers or variables; for instance, inches in a numerator cancels with inches in a denominator. If you are unsure whether to multiply or divide by a conversion factor, check to see which will leave you with only the desired units.

Example: Change 120 minutes to hours.

We want to cancel out the minutes, so we have to multiply 120 minutes by a fraction (equal to 1) with hours in the numerator and minutes in the denominator:

$$120\ \text{minutes} = 120\ \text{minutes} \times \frac{1\ \text{hour}}{60\ \text{minutes}} = 2\ \text{hours}$$

Example: Convert 10 inches per second to feet per minute. (1 foot = 12 inches)

Use the UCM successively to eliminate the unwanted units.

$$\frac{10 \text{ inches}}{\text{second}} = \frac{10 \text{ inches}}{\text{second}} \times \frac{1 \text{ foot}}{12 \text{ inches}} \times \frac{60 \text{ seconds}}{\text{minute}}$$

$$= \frac{10 \times 60}{12} \times \frac{\text{feet}}{\text{minute}}$$

$$= 50 \text{ feet per minute}$$

One other thing worth bearing in mind is that metric units are commonly used on the GMAT. While it is not essential to know the conversions between these units, it helps to be somewhat familiar with what they measure.

Volume is measured in liters. A milliliter is $\frac{1}{1,000}$ of a liter.

Length is measured in meters. A centimeter is $\frac{1}{100}$ of a meter.

Weight is measured in grams. A kilogram is 1,000 grams.

Work: Work problems tend to be harder than other rate problems. Happily, they appear irregularly on the test, and are usually among the hardest questions on the exam. It is useful to keep in mind that the greater the rate (the faster you work), the sooner you get the job done. If you can imagine how varying the parameters affects the time it takes to do the job, you can usually solve the problem by using logic.

Example: It takes 6 people 6 days to do a job. How many days would it take 2 people working at the same rate to do the job?

- ⬭ 3
- ⬭ 6
- ⬭ 12
- ⬭ 16
- ⬭ 18

We have **fewer** people so it would take **more** time. (Discard the first two answer choices.) First find out how long it takes 1 person to do the job. If 6 people take 6 days, then 1 person will take 6 times as long, i.e., 6 × 6 days = 36 days. If 1 person takes 36 days, 2 people will take half as long, i.e., 36 days ÷ 2 = 18 days.

Work problems often involve people working together.

Example: John can weed a garden in 3 hours. If Mary can weed the garden in 2 hours, how long will it take them to weed the garden at this rate, working together but independently?

Determine how much work John can do in a certain unit of time (one hour is convenient), and how much work Mary can do in the same hour, then add the results to find how much they can do together in an hour. From that, we can find how long it will take them to finish the job.

If John needs 3 hours to do the whole job, then in each hour, $\frac{1}{3}$ of the time, he will do $\frac{1}{3}$ of the job. Similarly, if Mary can do everything in 2 hours, each hour she will do $\frac{1}{2}$ of the job. Then in 1 hour, John and Mary together will do

$$\frac{1}{3} + \frac{1}{2} = \frac{2}{6} + \frac{3}{6} = \frac{5}{6} \text{ of the job.}$$

Now if they do $\frac{5}{6}$ of the job in 1 hour, how long will it take them to do the whole job? It will take the inverse of $\frac{5}{6}$, or $\frac{6}{5}$ hours. (Try it with easier numbers: if you do $\frac{1}{2}$ of the job in 1 hour, you will do the whole job in the inverse of $\frac{1}{2}$, or 2, hours.)

There is a general formula that can be used to find out how long it takes a number of people working together to complete a task: the Work Formula. Let's say we had three people; the first takes t_1 units of time to complete the job, the second t_2 units of time to complete the job, and the third t_3 units of time. If the time it takes all three working together to complete the job is T then

$$\frac{1}{t_1} + \frac{1}{t_2} + \frac{1}{t_3} = \frac{1}{T}$$

For instance, in the example above, we can call the amount of time it takes John to weed the garden t_1 and the amount of time it takes Mary t_2. That is, $t_1 = 3$ hours and $t_2 = 2$ hours. So, if T represents how much time it takes them working together (but independently), we get $\frac{1}{3} + \frac{1}{2} = \frac{1}{T}$. So, $\frac{5}{6} = \frac{1}{T}$ and $T = \frac{6}{5}$ hours.

Alternatively, you can use the following combined work formula. This shortcut formula should be used when you are working with two rates. The combined rate problem with John and Mary is just such a problem.

If A represents the number of hours it takes John to weed the garden, and B represents the number of hours it takes Mary to weed the garden, then the time it takes for them to weed the garden working together is:

$$\frac{AB}{A+B} = \frac{(3)(2)}{3+2} = \frac{6}{5} \text{ hours}$$

In general, with work problems, you can assume that each person works at the same rate as he does even when working with another person—don't worry that John and Mary will spend so much time chatting they won't get any of that garden done. That's what the "working together but independently" meant in the question stem.

PERCENT, RATIO, AND RATES WORD PROBLEMS TEST

Solve the following problems and choose the best answer. (Answers and explanations are at the end of the chapter.)

Basic

1. What is the percent profit made on the sale of 1,000 shares of stock bought at $10 per share and sold at $12 per share?

   ○ 0.2%

   ○ 2%

   ○ $16\frac{2}{3}$%

   ○ 20%

   ○ 25%

2. A subway car passes an average of 3 stations every 10 minutes. At this rate, how many stations will it pass in one hour?

   ○ 2

   ○ 12

   ○ 15

   ○ 18

   ○ 30

3. What is the percent discount on a jacket marked down from $120 to $100?

   ○ $16\frac{2}{3}$%

   ○ 20%

   ○ 30%

   ○ $33\frac{1}{3}$%

   ○ 40%

4. If a car travels $\frac{1}{100}$ of a kilometer each second, how many kilometers does it travel per hour?

   ○ $\frac{3}{5}$

   ○ $3\frac{3}{5}$

   ○ 36

   ○ 72

   ○ 100

5. If John buys a stereo marked down 7 percent from its $650 original price while Sally buys the same stereo marked down only 5 percent, how much more does Sally pay for the stereo?

   ○ $2

   ○ $12

   ○ $13

   ○ $78

   ○ $618

6. If a train travels m miles in 5 hours, how many miles will it travel in 25 hours?

   ○ $\frac{m}{25}$

   ○ $\frac{m}{5}$

   ○ $5m$

   ○ $25m$

   ○ $\frac{5}{m}$

7. At a record store, a record is priced at 60 percent of the price of the compact disk of the same title. If a compact disk is priced at $15, how much less does the record cost?

⬭ $5

⬭ $6

⬭ $9

⬭ $10

⬭ $12

8. A certain mule travels at $\frac{2}{3}$ the speed of a certain horse. If it takes the horse 6 hours to travel 20 miles, how many hours will the trip take the mule?

⬭ 4

⬭ 8

⬭ 9

⬭ 10

⬭ 30

9. What is the percent profit an ice cream seller makes on vanilla ice cream if vanilla ice cream costs him 90 cents per scoop to make and he sells it at $1.20 per scoop?

⬭ 25%

⬭ 30%

⬭ $33\frac{1}{3}$%

⬭ 40%

⬭ 50%

10. Two cars travel away from each other in opposite directions at 24 miles per hour and 40 miles per hour respectively. If the first car travels for 20 minutes and the second car for 45 minutes, how many miles apart will they be at the end of their trips?

⬭ 22

⬭ 24

⬭ 30

⬭ 38

⬭ 42

11. An encyclopedia salesman makes a 10 percent commission on any sales. If he sells a set of encyclopedias at $700 instead of the original price of $800, how much less of a commission does he earn?

⬭ $7

⬭ $8

⬭ $10

⬭ $70

⬭ $80

12. A car travels 60 kilometers in one hour before a piston breaks, then travels at 30 kilometers per hour for the remaining 60 kilometers to its destination. What is its average speed in kilometers per hour for the entire trip?

⬭ 20

⬭ 40

⬭ 45

⬭ 50

⬭ 60

13. A survey finds that 80 percent of the apartments in City G have smoke alarms installed. Of these, 20 percent have smoke alarms that are not working. What percent of the apartments in City G were found to have working smoke alarms?

   ○ 60%

   ○ 64%

   ○ $66\frac{2}{3}\%$

   ○ 70%

   ○ 72%

14. If a tree grew 5 feet in n years, how many inches did the tree grow per year on average during those years? (1 foot = 12 inches.)

   ○ $60n$

   ○ $\dfrac{5}{n}$

   ○ $\dfrac{5}{12n}$

   ○ $\dfrac{12n}{5}$

   ○ $\dfrac{60}{n}$

15. A baseball team increased its home attendance 20 percent in each of two successive years. If home attendance was 1 million the year before the first increase, what was the attendance the year of the second increase?

   ○ 1,200,000

   ○ 1,400,000

   ○ 1,440,000

   ○ 1,500,000

   ○ 1,600,000

16. If Bill can mow $\dfrac{3}{4}$ of his lawn in one hour, how many minutes does it take Bill to mow his entire lawn?

   ○ 45

   ○ 75

   ○ 80

   ○ 90

   ○ 100

17. If a camera priced at $360 represents a potential profit of 20 percent to a store if sold, what was the original cost of the camera to the store?

   ○ $288

   ○ $300

   ○ $310

   ○ $320

   ○ $342

Intermediate

18. If an item costs $800 after a 20 percent discount, what was the amount of the discount?

    ◯ $200

    ◯ $160

    ◯ $120

    ◯ $80

    ◯ $20

19. John buys R pounds of cheese to feed N people at a party. If $N + P$ people come to the party, how many more pounds of cheese must John buy in order to feed everyone at the original rate?

    ◯ $\dfrac{NP}{R}$

    ◯ $\dfrac{N}{RP}$

    ◯ $\dfrac{N+P}{R}$

    ◯ $\dfrac{P}{NR}$

    ◯ $\dfrac{PR}{N}$

20. A store sells a watch for a profit of 25 percent of the cost. What percent of the selling price is the profit?

    ◯ 5%

    ◯ $16\dfrac{2}{3}\%$

    ◯ 20%

    ◯ $33\dfrac{1}{3}\%$

    ◯ 45%

21. If it takes ten minutes to fill $\dfrac{5}{12}$ of a hole, how many minutes will it take to fill the rest of the hole at this rate?

    ◯ 12

    ◯ 14

    ◯ 16

    ◯ 18

    ◯ 24

22. A builder purchases 25 windows at 25 percent off the total price of $1,200. If the builder receives an additional discount of $75 for the purchase, how much did each window cost her?

    ◯ $48

    ◯ $45

    ◯ $36

    ◯ $33

    ◯ $25

23. If Carol can finish a job in 5 hours and Steve can finish the same job in 10 hours, how many minutes will it take both of them together to finish the job?

    ◯ 160

    ◯ 180

    ◯ 200

    ◯ 210

    ◯ 220

24. One class in a school is 30 percent boys. If a second class that is half the size of the first is 40 percent boys, what percent of both classes are boys?

   ○ 20%
   ○ 25%
   ○ 28%
   ○ 30%
   ○ $33\frac{1}{3}\%$

25. If John can paint a room in 30 minutes and Tom can paint it in 1 hour, how many minutes will it take them to paint the room working together?

   ○ 10
   ○ 15
   ○ 18
   ○ 20
   ○ 24

26. If a driver travels m miles per hour for 4 hours and then travels $\frac{3}{4}m$ miles per hour every hour thereafter, how many miles will she drive in 10 hours?

   ○ $\frac{15}{2}m$
   ○ $8m$
   ○ $\frac{17}{2}m$
   ○ $10m$
   ○ $\frac{21}{2}m$

27. Joan spends 20 percent of her income on taxes and 20 percent of the remainder on rent. What percent of her income does she spend on rent?

   ○ 8%
   ○ 10%
   ○ 16%
   ○ 20%
   ○ 24%

28. Phil is making a 40-kilometer canoe trip. If he travels at 30 kilometers per hour for the first 10 kilometers, and then at 15 kilometers per hour for the rest of the trip, how many minutes longer will it take him than if he makes the entire trip at 20 kilometers per hour?

   ○ 15
   ○ 20
   ○ 35
   ○ 45
   ○ 50

29. In a certain school, 50 percent of all male students and 60 percent of all female students play a varsity sport. If 40 percent of the students at the school are male, what percent of the entire student body DO NOT play a varsity sport?

   ○ 44%
   ○ 50%
   ○ 55%
   ○ 56%
   ○ 60%

30. Tammy bikes the course of a race at 30 miles per hour, then returns home along the same route at 10 miles per hour. If the total time it takes her to travel the course and return home is 2 hours, and if the time spent turning around is negligible, what is the length, in miles, of the race course?

   ○ 15
   ○ 20
   ○ 25
   ○ 30
   ○ 35

31. The workforce of a company is 20 percent part-time workers, with the rest of the workers full-time. At the end of the year 30 percent of the full-time workers received bonuses. If 72 full-time workers received bonuses, how many workers does the company employ?

   ○ 132
   ○ 240
   ○ 280
   ○ 300
   ○ 360

Advanced

32. Pipe A can fill a tank in 3 hours. If pipe B can fill the same tank in 2 hours, how many minutes will it take both pipes to fill $\frac{2}{3}$ of the tank?

  ○ 30

  ○ 48

  ○ 54

  ○ 60

  ○ 72

33. A factory cut its labor force by 16 percent, but then increased it by 25 percent of the new amount. What was the net percent change in the size of the workforce?

  ○ a 5% decrease

  ○ no net change

  ○ a 5% increase

  ○ a 9% increase

  ○ a 10% increase

34. If snow falls at a rate of x centimeters per minute, how many hours would it take for y centimeters to fall?

  ○ $\dfrac{x}{60y}$

  ○ $\dfrac{y}{60x}$

  ○ $\dfrac{60x}{y}$

  ○ $\dfrac{60y}{x}$

  ○ $60xy$

35. If a dealer had sold a stereo for $600, he would have made a 20 percent profit. Instead, the dealer sold it for a 40 percent loss. At what price was the stereo sold?

  ○ $300

  ○ $315

  ○ $372

  ○ $400

  ○ $440

36. If four men working at the same rate can do $\frac{2}{3}$ of a job in 40 minutes, how many minutes would it take one man working at this rate to do $\frac{2}{5}$ of the job?

  ○ 80

  ○ 88

  ○ 92

  ○ 96

  ○ 112

37. Bob and Alice can finish a job together in 3 hours. If Bob can do the job by himself in 5 hours, what percent of the job does Alice do?

  ○ 20%

  ○ 30%

  ○ 40%

  ○ 50%

  ○ 60%

GENERAL PROBLEM SOLVING TEST

Solve the following problems and choose the best answer. (Answers and explanations are at the end of the chapter.)

2008	$250
2009	$300
2010	$360

1. Robert's rent increased each year by the same percent, as shown in the chart above. At that rate, what was his rent in 2011?

   ○ $420

   ○ $430

   ○ $432

   ○ $438

   ○ $440

2. In a certain baseball league, each team plays 160 games. After playing half of their games, team A has won 60 games and team B has won 49 games. If team A wins half of its remaining games, how many more games must team B win to have the same record as team A at the end of the season?

   ○ 48

   ○ 49

   ○ 50

   ○ 51

   ○ 52

3. If a man earns $200 for his first 40 hours of work in a week and is then paid $1\frac{1}{2}$ times his regular hourly rate for any additional hours, how many hours must he work to make $230 in a week?

   ○ 4

   ○ 5

   ○ 6

   ○ 44

   ○ 45

4. If 10 millimeters equal 1 centimeter, how many square centimeters does 1 square millimeter equal?

   ○ 0.01

   ○ 0.1

   ○ 1

   ○ 10

   ○ 100

5. Team X and team Y have a tug of war. From their starting positions team X pulls team Y forward 3 meters, and is then pulled forward 5 meters. Team Y then pulls team X forward 2 meters. If the first team to be pulled forward 10 meters loses, how many more meters must team Y pull team X forward to win?

   ○ 0

   ○ 4

   ○ 6

   ○ 8

   ○ 14

6. An hour-long test has 60 problems. If a student completes 30 problems in 20 minutes, how many seconds does he have on average for completing each of the remaining problems?

   ○ 60
   ○ 70
   ○ 80
   ○ 90
   ○ 100

7. The sum of the lengths of all the roads in county Z is 1,400 miles. If the sum of the lengths of unpaved roads is $\frac{3}{4}$ the sum of the lengths of paved roads, how many more miles of paved than unpaved roads are there in county Z?

   ○ 200
   ○ 400
   ○ 600
   ○ 800
   ○ 1,000

8. In a certain class, 3 out of 24 students are in student organizations. What is the ratio of students in organizations to students not in organizations?

   ○ $\frac{1}{8}$
   ○ $\frac{1}{7}$
   ○ $\frac{1}{6}$
   ○ $\frac{1}{5}$
   ○ $\frac{1}{4}$

9. On the face of a regular die, the dots are arranged in such a way that the total number of dots on any two opposite faces is 7. If the figure above shows a regular die, what is the total number of dots on the faces that are not shown?

   ○ 7
   ○ 9
   ○ 12
   ○ 13
   ○ 14

10. A student averages 72 on 5 tests. If the lowest score is dropped, the average rises to 84. What is the lowest score?

   ○ 18
   ○ 24
   ○ 32
   ○ 43
   ○ 48

11. Achmed finds that by wearing different combinations of the jackets, shirts and pairs of trousers that he owns, he can make up 90 different outfits. If he owns 5 jackets and 3 pairs of trousers, how many shirts does he own?

   ○ 3
   ○ 6
   ○ 12
   ○ 18
   ○ 30

12. Jean is driving from Mayville to a county fair in Yorkville. After driving for two hours at an average speed of 70 kilometers per hour, she still has 80 kilometers left to travel. What is the distance between the two towns, in kilometers?

   ○ 220

   ○ 250

   ○ 260

   ○ 270

   ○ 280

13. A store offers a variety of discounts that range between 10 percent and 25 percent inclusive. If a book is discounted to a price of $2.40, what was its greatest possible price originally?

   ○ $2.64

   ○ $3.00

   ○ $3.20

   ○ $10.80

   ○ $24.00

14. A man earns N dollars a month and spends S dollars a month on rent. If he then spends $\frac{3}{8}$ of the remainder on food, how much, in dollars, is left over for other expenses, in terms of N and S?

   ○ $\frac{3}{8}(N - S)$

   ○ $\frac{3}{8}(N + S)$

   ○ $\frac{5}{8}(N - S)$

   ○ $\frac{5}{8}(N + S)$

   ○ $\frac{8}{3}(N - S)$

15. If a sequence of consecutive integers of increasing value has a sum of 63 and a first term of 6, how many integers are in the sequence?

   ○ 11

   ○ 10

   ○ 9

   ○ 8

   ○ 7

16. The kinetic energy K, in joules, provided by the mass of a particle m, in kilograms, with a velocity of v meters per seconds, is given by the equation $K = \frac{1}{2}mv^2$. If a particle had a velocity of 4 meters per second and a kinetic energy of 144 joules, then the mass, in kilograms, of this particle must be

   ○ 16

   ○ 18

   ○ 24

   ○ 44

   ○ 64

17. Bill purchases an item and receives no change. Before the purchase, he had only a five-dollar bill, two ten-dollar bills, and a twenty-dollar bill. How many distinct possibilities are there for the total amount of his purchase?

$\bigcirc$ 3

$\bigcirc$ 4

$\bigcirc$ 6

$\bigcirc$ 9

$\bigcirc$ 10

Type of Pet	Number of Households	Average Number of Pets per Household
Dogs Only	16	1.5
Cats Only	24	1.25
Dogs & Cats	8	3.25

18. The table above gives the type and number of pets owned by a group of 48 households that own cats or dogs. If the ratio of the total number of cats to the total number of dogs is 5 : 3, how many dogs are there?

$\bigcirc$ 18

$\bigcirc$ 24

$\bigcirc$ 30

$\bigcirc$ 36

$\bigcirc$ 48

19. Jane knits 72 stitches to the line and uses $\frac{1}{4}$ inch of yarn in each of the stitches. How many lines can she knit with 10 yards of yarn? (1 yard = 3 feet; 1 foot = 12 inches)

$\bigcirc$ 10

$\bigcirc$ 20

$\bigcirc$ 30

$\bigcirc$ 40

$\bigcirc$ 50

20. Robert purchased $2,000 worth of U.S. savings bonds. If bonds are sold in $50 or $100 denominations only, which of the following CANNOT be the number of U.S. savings bonds that Robert purchased?

$\bigcirc$ 20

$\bigcirc$ 27

$\bigcirc$ 30

$\bigcirc$ 40

$\bigcirc$ 50

21. A supply of sugar lasts for 30 days. If its use is increased by 50 percent, how many days would the same amount of sugar last?

$\bigcirc$ 15

$\bigcirc$ 20

$\bigcirc$ 25

$\bigcirc$ 30

$\bigcirc$ 45

22. Bucky leaves Amity for Truro, which is 8 miles away, at the same time that Robin leaves Truro for Amity. If neither of them stops along the way, and they meet along the road 2 miles from Amity, what is the ratio of Bucky's average speed to Robin's average speed?

$\bigcirc$ $\frac{1}{4}$

$\bigcirc$ $\frac{1}{3}$

$\bigcirc$ $\frac{1}{1}$

$\bigcirc$ $\frac{3}{1}$

$\bigcirc$ $\frac{4}{1}$

23. On a scaled map, a distance of 10 centimeters represents 5 kilometers. If a street is 750 meters long, what is its length on the map, in centimeters? (1 kilometer = 1,000 meters)

○ 0.015

○ 0.15

○ 1.5

○ 15

○ 150

24. Oak trees line both sides of a street for a length of $\frac{3}{8}$ of a kilometer. If there is 16 meters of space between the trees, and each tree is 1 meter wide, how many trees are there along the street? (1 kilometer = 1,000 meters)

○ 36

○ 40

○ 42

○ 44

○ 46

25. A lighthouse blinks regularly 5 times a minute. A neighboring lighthouse blinks regularly 4 times a minute. If they blink simultaneously, after how many seconds will they blink together again?

○ 20

○ 24

○ 30

○ 60

○ 300

26. A vault holds only 8-ounce tablets of gold and 5-ounce tablets of silver. If there are 130 ounces of gold and silver total, what is the greatest amount of gold that can be in the vault, in ounces?

○ 40

○ 80

○ 120

○ 128

○ 130

27. At a parade, balloons are given out in the order blue, red, red, yellow, yellow, yellow, blue, red, red, yellow, yellow, yellow, etc. If this pattern continues, how many red balloons will have been given out when a total of 70 balloons have been distributed?

○ 18

○ 22

○ 24

○ 26

○ 35

28. If the cost of p plums priced at 25 cents each equals the cost of $p - 6$ nectarines priced at 28 cents each, then p equals

○ 26

○ 42

○ 52

○ 56

○ 66

29. In July the price of a stock increased by 10 percent. In August, it declined by 20 percent. If in September the price increased by 10 percent, by what percent of the original July price has the stock changed between the start of July and the end of September?

- ◯ 0%
- ◯ 3.2%
- ◯ 4.4%
- ◯ 20%
- ◯ 40%

30. If 1 tic equals 3 tacs and 2 tacs equal 5 tocs, what is the ratio of one tic to one toc?

- ◯ $\dfrac{15}{2}$
- ◯ $\dfrac{6}{5}$
- ◯ $\dfrac{5}{6}$
- ◯ $\dfrac{3}{10}$
- ◯ $\dfrac{1}{15}$

31. If John gives Allen 5 dollars and Allen gives Frank 2 dollars, the three boys will have the same amount of money. How much more money does John have than Allen?

- ◯ $3
- ◯ $5
- ◯ $6
- ◯ $7
- ◯ $8

32. If sheets of paper are 0.08 centimeters thick and 500 sheets cost $3.00, how much will a stack of paper 4 meters thick cost?
(1 meter = 100 centimeters)

- ◯ $30
- ◯ $45
- ◯ $60
- ◯ $72
- ◯ $96

33. Ms. Smith drove a total of 700 miles on a business trip. If her car averaged 35 miles per gallon of gasoline, and gasoline cost an average of $1.25 per gallon, how much did she spend on gasoline during the trip?

- ◯ $17.50
- ◯ $25.00
- ◯ $35.00
- ◯ $70.00
- ◯ $250.00

34. There are 7 people on committee A and 8 people on committee B. If three people serve on both committees, how many people serve on only one of the committees?

- ◯ 8
- ◯ 9
- ◯ 10
- ◯ 11
- ◯ 12

35. Anne owes Bob $4, Bob owes Carol $3, and Carol owes Anne $5. If Carol settles all the debts by giving money to both Anne and Bob, how much will she give Anne?

    ⬭ $1

    ⬭ $2

    ⬭ $3

    ⬭ $4

    ⬭ $5

36. John can shovel a driveway in 50 minutes. If Mary can shovel the driveway in 20 minutes, how long will it take them, to the nearest minute, to shovel the driveway if they work together?

    ⬭ 12

    ⬭ 13

    ⬭ 14

    ⬭ 16

    ⬭ 18

37. A butcher buys 240 kilograms of beef for $380. If 20 percent of the beef is unusable, at approximately what average price per kilogram must he sell the rest of the beef in order to make a profit of 25 percent?

    ⬭ $2.30

    ⬭ $2.40

    ⬭ $2.45

    ⬭ $2.47

    ⬭ $2.55

38. A vending machine dispenses gumballs in a regularly repeating cycle of 10 different colors. If a quarter buys 3 gumballs, what is the minimum amount of money that must be spent before 3 gumballs of the same color are dispensed?

    ⬭ $1.00

    ⬭ $1.75

    ⬭ $2.00

    ⬭ $2.25

    ⬭ $2.50

39. During a season in a certain baseball league every team plays every other team in the league 10 times. If there are ten teams in the league, how many games are played in the league in one season?

    ⬭ 45

    ⬭ 90

    ⬭ 450

    ⬭ 900

    ⬭ 1,000

40. Henry and Eleanor are waiting in line for a movie. If Henry is fourth in line, and there are n people ahead of Eleanor, where $n > 4$, how many people are between Henry and Eleanor?

    ⬭ $n - 5$

    ⬭ $n - 4$

    ⬭ $n - 3$

    ⬭ $n + 3$

    ⬭ $n + 4$

WORD PROBLEMS LEVEL ONE TEST ANSWERS AND EXPLANATIONS

1. $25

Translate directly into math. A price decrease makes the price smaller, so we subtract. A price increase makes the price greater, so we add. So for the final price we get:

$$\$25 - \$4 + \$6 - \$2 = \$25 + \$0 = \$25$$

So the final price is $25.

2. 8.75 million

In Country A, the population increase between 1960 and 1970 was 1.75 million **more** than the increase between 1950 and 1960, or 1.75 million **more** than 3.5 million. It must have been 1.75 + 3.5 million or 5.25 million. The total growth in population over the two decades equals 3.5 million, the amount of growth during the 50's, plus 5.25 million, the amount of growth during the 60's, for a total increase of 8.75 million.

3. $260

Sue makes $280. If Joan makes $50 **more** than this, then Joan must make $280 + $50, or $330. Greg makes $70 **less** than this amount, or $330 − $70 or $260.

4. 96,000

Find out how many camels passed through Timbuktu over the course of the year, then multiply that by the number of pieces of copper collected for each camel. Each month an average of 8 caravans with an average of 100 camels per caravan passed through the town; therefore, an average of 8 × 100 or 800 camels a month passed through Timbuktu. Over a year there must have been 12 times this amount, or 12 × 800 or 9,600 camels. They collected 10 pieces of copper for each of these. Over the year they collected 10 × 9,600, or 96,000 pieces of copper.

5. 6

When the painter and his son work together, they'll charge the sum of their hourly rates, $12 + $6 or $18 per hour. Their bill equals the product of this combined rate and the number of hours they work. Therefore $108 must equal $18 per hour times the number of hours they work. We need to divide $108 by $18 per hour to find the number of hours. $108 ÷ $18 = 6. They must have worked 6 hours.

6. $36

The price of the softcover edition plus the difference in price between the hardcover and softcover editions equals the price of the hardcover edition. We're told that this difference is $12. We're also told that the softcover price is simply two-thirds of the hardcover price. Calling the hardcover price H (since that's what we're ultimately looking for), we can set up an equation:

Softcover price + 12 = Hardcover price

$$\frac{2}{3}H + 12 = H$$

$$12 = H - \frac{2}{3}H$$

$$12 = \frac{1}{3}H$$

$$H = 36$$

The hardcover price is $36.

7. 2,000

To calculate the number of 14¢ stamps sold by the post office, divide the total amount of money spent on these stamps by the cost for each stamp. This means dividing $280 by 14¢. Since the units are not the same, we convert $280 to cents by multiplying by 100, to give 28,000¢, so that we are dividing cents by cents. We get:

$$\begin{array}{r} 2,000 \\ 14\overline{)28,000} \\ \underline{28} \\ 0 \end{array}$$

8. 4*n*

Lisa was 2*n* years old *n* years ago. Since it is now *n* years later, she must be 2*n* + *n* or 3*n* years old now. And in another *n* years? She will have aged *n* more years by then, so she will be 3*n* + *n* or 4*n* years old.

This type of problem is ideal for picking numbers. We can choose a value for *n*, determine the result we need, and then evaluate each answer choice using the same value to see which one gives the same result. Say *n* = 5. Then Lisa was 10 years old 5 years ago. So she is currently 15. In another 5 years, she'll be 20.

Which answer choice equals 20 when *n* is 5? Choice **(A)**, 4*n* = 20. This looks promising, but we still need to check the other choices. If you substitute 5 for *n*, you'll find none of the other choices equals 20.

9. 24

One third of the original volume of water in the pond was lost during the drought. The amount of water that remains must be two thirds of the original amount, that is, twice as much as was lost. So the one third that was lost is equal to half of what was left. That is, the amount of water lost = 48,000 ÷ 2 = 24,000 gallons of water.

Or, set up an equation where *W* represents how much water was originally in the pond:

$$W - \frac{1}{3}W = 48,000$$

$$\frac{2}{3}W = 48,000$$

$$W = 72,000$$

The amount lost was $\frac{1}{3}$ of the original amount, or $\frac{1}{3}$ of *W*, which is $\frac{1}{3}(72,000) = 24,000$.

10. $500,000

The amount each of the children stands to gain equals the difference between what he or she will make if the stepchildren are excluded and what he or she will make if they're included. If the stepchildren are excluded, the children will inherit $15 million divided by 10 (the number of children) or $1.5 million each. If the stepchildren are included, they'll inherit $15 million divided by 15 (the number of children and stepchildren combined), or $1 million each. The difference is $1.5 million − $1 million or $500,000.

11. 17

What two numbers seven apart add up to 27? With trial and error you should be able to find them soon; 10 and 17; there must be 17 women working at the office.

Alternatively, set up two equations each with two unknowns. There are 27 employees at the office total, all either men or women, so m (the number of men) $+ w$ (the number of women) $= 27$.
There are 7 more women than men, so:

$$m + 7 = w$$
$$m = w - 7$$

Substituting $w - 7$ for m into the first equation, we get:

$$(w - 7) + w = 27$$
$$2w - 7 = 27$$
$$2w = 34$$
$$w = 17$$

There are 17 women in the office. (In a problem like this, it's a good idea to check at the end to make sure you answered the right question. It would have been easy here to misread the question and solve for the number of men.)

12. $3x - y + 2 = 0$

Translate into math, remembering "2 less than y" means $y - 2$, not $2 - y$.

The product of 3 and x is equal to 2 less than y.

$$3x = y - 2$$

We must determine which of the answer choices corresponds to this. Since all the choices are equations where the right side is equal to zero, move all the terms to the left side. We get:

$$3x - y + 2 = 0$$

13. **$440**

The cost of stock = $8,000 + 2% of $8,000
= $8,000 + $160
= $8,160

The 4 partners have already invested $1,600 each, that is 4 × $1,600 = $6,400. They need to invest $8,160 − $6,400 = $1,760 more in total, and $1,760 ÷ 4 = $440 more per partner.

Or, since each invests an equal amount, each will ultimately invest $8,160 ÷ 4 = $2,040. If each partner already invested $1,600, the amount each one still needs to invest is $2,040 − $1,600 = $440. (Notice how it's a little less arithmetic to divide the whole amount into quarters first and then subtract.)

14. **$1.75**

We need to compute the cost of 5 hours at each garage. Since the two garages have a split-rate system of charging, the cost for the first hour is different from the cost of each remaining hour. The remaining hours after the first one (in this case, there are 4 of them) are charged at an hourly rate.

The first hour at garage *A* costs $8.75.
The next 4 hours cost 4 × $1.25 = $5.00.
The total cost for parking at garage
   A = $8.75 + 5.00 = $13.75

The first hour at garage *B* costs $5.50.
The next 4 hours cost 4 × $2.50 = $10.00.
The total cost for parking at garage
   B = $5.50 + 10.00 = $15.50
The difference in cost = $15.50 − $13.75 = $1.75.

15. **40**

Find the number of students who play on any sports team, then multiply by $\frac{1}{4}$ to find the number of students who play football. $\frac{2}{3}$ of the 240 students play some sport, or $\frac{2}{3} \times 240$ or 160 students. $\frac{1}{4}$ of these play football; that equals $\frac{1}{4} \times 160$ or 40 students. Therefore, 40 students play football.

16. **$20**

We can translate to get two equations. Let *E* be the amount Ed has and *R* the amount Robert has.

"Ed has $100 **more** than Robert" becomes *E* = *R* + 100.

"Ed **spends** $20" means he'll end up with $20 less, or $E - 20$. "5 **times as much as** Robert" becomes $5R$. So $E - 20 = 5R$.

Substitute $R + 100$ for E in the second equation and solve for R:

$$E - 20 = 5R$$
$$R + 100 - 20 = 5R$$
$$R + 80 = 5R$$
$$80 = 4R$$
$$20 = R$$

So Robert has $20.

17. **$12\frac{1}{2}$**

Diane has painted $\frac{1}{3}$ of a room with $2\frac{1}{2}$ cans of paint. We know that the whole room will need 3 times as much paint as $\frac{1}{3}$ of the room, so the amount of paint needed to paint the room equals $3 \times 2\frac{1}{2}$ cans, or $7\frac{1}{2}$ cans. To paint 2 rooms, she would need $2 \times 7\frac{1}{2}$ cans, or 15 cans. But the question asks how many **more** cans of paint Diane needs; she has already used $2\frac{1}{2}$ cans. We subtract: 15 cans minus $2\frac{1}{2}$ cans leaves $12\frac{1}{2}$ cans to finish the first room and paint the second.

18. **18**

We need to find a fraction of a fraction. The total number of UFO sightings is 108. Of these, $\frac{1}{2}$ turn out to be airplanes: $\frac{1}{2} \times 108 = 54$. If $\frac{1}{2}$ are airplanes, $\frac{1}{2}$ are not, so 54 sightings remain that are not airplanes. Of these 54, $\frac{1}{3}$ are weather balloons. We multiply $\frac{1}{3} \times 54$, which equals 18, to get the number of weather balloons.

19. **22**

One thing we must do here before we start is pick a unit to work with: either dollars or cents. It doesn't matter which we choose; it's a personal preference. We'll work with dollars. The first print uses up $1.65 of the $20.00 Pete has available. This leaves him $20.00 − $1.65, or $18.35 for the rest of the prints, at a rate of $0.85 per print. We could divide here, but it's easier to work with it this way: 10 additional prints would cost 10 times as much or $8.50, so 20 additional prints must cost 2 × $8.50, or $17.00. Now we can add on individual prints at $0.85 each: 21 additional prints cost $17.00 + $0.85, or $17.85, 22 additional prints cost $17.85 + $0.85, or $18.70. But this is more than the $18.35 Pete has available. So Pete can only afford 21 additional prints, **plus** the $1.65 first print, for a total of 22 prints.

20. 16

Find the total number of peanuts in the bag, then divide by the new number of children who will be sharing them. There are enough peanuts to give 12 peanuts to each of 20 children, so there are 12 × 20 peanuts, or 240 peanuts total.

After 5 children drop out, there remain 20 − 5 or 15 children to share the 240 peanuts. Each will get $\frac{240}{15}$, or 16 peanuts.

21. $4.00

If each adult's fare is twice as much as each child's fare, then 2 adults' fares cost as much as 4 children's fares. This, added to the 3 children's fares, gives us a total of 4 + 3, or 7 children's fares. This equals $14. If 7 children's fares cost $14, then the cost of each child's fare is $\frac{14}{7}$, or $2. The adult fare costs twice as much, or $4.

22. $3,000

The $250 that Doris spent on the carpet is one quarter of the one-third of Doris's savings that's left over after she buys the car, or $\frac{1}{4} \times \frac{1}{3} = \frac{1}{12}$ of her original savings. Therefore, her original savings must have been 12 × $250, or $3,000.

23. 3*n* − 14

Gheri is *n* years old. Carl is 6 years younger than Gheri, or *n* − 6 years old. Jean is 2 years younger than Carl, or *n* − 6 − 2 = *n* − 8 years old. The sum of their ages is then *n* + (*n* − 6) + (*n* − 8) = 3*n* − 14 years.

24. 13

We will get the maximum number of groups by making each group as small as possible. Each group must have at least 3 people in it, so divide 40 by 3 to find the number of 3-person groups. 40 ÷ 3 = 13 with a remainder of 1. So we have 13 groups with 1 person left over. Since each group must have at least 3 people, we must throw the extra lonely student in with one of the other groups. So we have 12 groups with 3 students each, and one group with 4 students, for a maximum total of 13 groups.

25. 30

Let *p* represent Philip's salamanders and *m* Matt's salamanders. If Philip has twice as many salamanders as Matt, we can write:

$$p = 2m$$

If Philip gives Matt 10 salamanders, then he will have 10 fewer, or *p* − 10, and Matt will have 10 more or *m* + 10. In this case Philip would have half as many as Matt, so:

$$p - 10 = \frac{1}{2}(m + 10)$$

We have two equations with two variables. (Note that although the number of salamanders each owns has changed, the variables p and m still have the same meaning: the original number of salamanders.) We can solve for p and m. Substitute our first expression for p, that is, $p = 2m$, into the second equation and solve for m.

$$2m - 10 = \frac{1}{2}(m + 10)$$
$$4m - 20 = m + 10$$
$$3m = 30$$
$$m = 10$$

Since $p = 2m$, if $m = 10$, then $p = 20$. The total number of salamanders is $p + m = 20 + 10$, or 30.

26. 48

If the average salary of the 60 workers is \$80, the total amount received by the workers is 60 × \$80 or \$4,800. This equals the total income from the \$75 workers plus the total income from the \$100 workers. Let x represent the number of \$75 workers.

Since we know there are 60 workers altogether, and everyone earns either \$75 or \$100, then $60 - x$ must earn \$100. We can set up an equation for the total amount received by the workers by multiplying the salary by the number of workers receiving that salary and adding:

$$75x + 100(60 - x) = 4,800$$

Solve this equation to find x, the number of workers earning \$75.

$$75x + 6,000 - 100x = 4,800$$
$$-25x = -1,200$$
$$25x = 1,200$$
$$x = 48$$

There are 48 workers earning \$75.

PERCENT, RATIO, AND RATES WORD PROBLEMS TEST
ANSWERS AND EXPLANATIONS

1. 20%

The percent profit equals the amount of profit divided by the original price of the stock (expressed as a percent). On each share a profit of $12 − $10 or $2 was made. Each share originally cost $10. The percent profit equals $\frac{2}{10}$, or 20%.

2. 18

The subway will pass $\frac{60}{10}$ or 6 times as many stations in one hour as it passes in 10 minutes. In 10 minutes it passes 3 stations; in 60 minutes it must pass 6 × 3, or 18 stations.

We could also use the UCM. The train passes 3 stations every 10 minutes, or $\frac{3 \text{ stations}}{10 \text{ minutes}}$.

To convert this to hours, multiply by $\frac{60 \text{ minutes}}{1 \text{ hour}}$:

$$\frac{3 \text{ stations}}{10 \text{ minutes}} \times \frac{60 \text{ minutes}}{1 \text{ hour}} = \frac{18 \text{ stations}}{1 \text{ hour}}$$

The train passes 18 stations in one hour.

3. $16\frac{2}{3}\%$

The percent discount equals the amount of discount divided by the **original** price. The amount of discount is $120 − $100 or $20. The original price was $120. The percent discount equals:

$$\frac{20}{120} = \frac{1}{6} \text{ or } 16\frac{2}{3}\%$$

4. 36

Find the number of seconds in an hour, then multiply this by the distance **the car is traveling** each second. There are 60 seconds in a minute and 60 minutes in one hour; therefore, there are 60 × 60 or 3,600 seconds in an hour. In one second the car travels $\frac{1}{100}$ kilometers; in one hour the car will travel $3,600 \times \frac{1}{100}$ or 36 kilometers.

5. $13

This problem is not as hard as calculating how much each of them paid **and then subtracting** John's amount from Sally's—there's a shortcut we can use, since their discounts are percents of the same whole. If John buys the stereo at a

7% discount and Sally buys it at a 5% discount, the difference in the amount of the discount they get is 7% − 5%, or 2% of the original price of $650. The difference is 2% of $650, or $\frac{1}{50}$ of 650 dollars.

$$\frac{1}{50} \times 650 = \frac{650}{50} = \frac{65}{5} = 13$$

Sally pays $13 more.

6. 5m

How many 5-hour periods are in a 25-hour trip? 25 ÷ 5 or 5 periods. So the train will travel 5 times as far in 25 hours than it does in 5 hours. Since it goes *m* miles in 5 hours, the train must go 5 times as far in 25 hours, or 5*m* miles.

Or, just use the formula Distance = Rate × Time. Here the rate is *m* miles in 5 hours, and the amount of time traveled is 25 hours. Therefore:

$$\text{Distance} = \frac{m \text{ miles}}{5 \text{ hours}} \times 25 \text{ hours} = 5m \text{ miles}$$

So the train travels 5*m* miles.

7. $6

The difference we need is the price of the compact disk minus the price of the record, or the price of the compact disk minus 60% of the price of the compact disk, which is just 40% of the compact disk price. We need only to find 40% of 15 dollars. The fractional equivalent of 40% is $\frac{2}{5}$, so the difference is $\frac{2}{5} \times 15$ dollars, or 6 dollars.

8. 9

Since it travels at $\frac{2}{3}$ the speed of the horse, the mule covers $\frac{2}{3}$ of the distance the horse does in any given amount of time, leaving $\frac{1}{3}$ of the distance left to travel. So in the time the horse has travelled the entire distance, the mule has only gone $\frac{2}{3}$ of the distance. So if the horse goes the whole distance in 6 hours, the mule goes $\frac{2}{3}$ of the distance in 6 hours. The mule has $\frac{1}{3}$ of the distance to go. It takes him 6 hours to get $\frac{2}{3}$ of the way, so it will take him half this, or 3 hours to get the remaining $\frac{1}{3}$ of the way. Therefore the whole journey takes the mule 6 + 3 = 9 hours.

Alternatively, consider finding the mule's rate by taking two-thirds of the horse's rate. The horse travels 20 miles in 6 hours; therefore, the horse's speed is $\frac{20 \text{ miles}}{6 \text{ hours}}$. The mule travels at $\frac{2}{3}$ this speed: $\frac{2}{3} \times \frac{20 \text{ miles}}{6 \text{ hours}} = \frac{20 \text{ miles}}{9 \text{ hours}}$.

Now we can use this rate to determine how long it takes the mule to make the trip. The mule needs 9 hours to travel 20 miles.

9. $33\frac{1}{3}\%$

The first thing we must do is find a single unit to work with. Convert $1.20 to cents. (We could work with dollars, but by working with the smaller unit we'll avoid decimals.) There are 100 cents in a dollar, so $1.20 = 120 cents. The ice cream costs him only 90 cents per scoop. The ice cream seller makes 120 − 90 or 30 cents of profit on every scoop of ice cream he sells. His percent profit is the amount of profit divided by the cost to him, or $\frac{30}{90} = \frac{1}{3}$, or $33\frac{1}{3}\%$.

10. 38

Since the cars are traveling in opposite directions, the distance between the two cars equals the sum of the distances each car travels. The first car travels 20 minutes or a third of an hour, so it goes only $\frac{1}{3}$ the distance it would travel in an hour, or $\frac{1}{3}$ of 24 miles, or 8 miles. The second car travels 45 minutes or $\frac{3}{4}$ of an hour. It goes $\frac{3}{4}$ of the distance it would go in an hour, or $\frac{3}{4}$ of 40, or 30 miles. The two cars are then 8 + 30, or 38 miles apart.

11. $10

The salesman has lost out on 10% of the $100 difference between the original price of the encyclopedia and the reduced selling price. 10% of $100, or $\frac{1}{10}$ of $100, is $10.

12. 40

The average speed equals the total distance the car travels divided by the total time. We're told the car goes 60 kilometers in an hour before its piston breaks, and then travels another 60 kilometers at 30 kilometers an hour. The second part of the trip must have taken 2 hours (if you go 30 miles in one hour, then you'll go twice as far, 60 miles, in twice as much time, 2 hours). So the car travels a total of 60 + 60 or 120 miles, and covers this distance in 1 + 2, or 3 hours. Its average speed equals 120 miles divided by 3 hours, or 40 miles per hour.

Notice that the average speed over the entire trip is **not** simply the average of the two speeds traveled over the trip. (That would be the average of 60 and 30, which is 45.) This is because the car spent different amounts of time travelling at these two different rates. Be wary of problems that ask for an average rate over a trip that encompassed different rates.

13. 64%

If 20% of the apartments with smoke alarms were found to have smoke alarms that are not working, then the remaining 80% of the apartments with smoke alarms have smoke alarms that **are** working. Since 80% of all apartments in the city have smoke alarms, and 80% of these have working smoke alarms, 80% of 80% of all the apartments in the city have working smoke alarms. 80% of 80% equals (converting to fractions) $\frac{8}{10} \times \frac{8}{10}$ of all the apartments in the city, or $\frac{64}{100}$ of all apartments. $\frac{64}{100}$ is 64%.

Alternatively, since we are working with percents only, try picking numbers. Let the number of apartments in City *G* be 100. If 80% of these have smoke alarms, then 80% of 100, or 80 apartments have smoke alarms.

If 20% of these do not work, then 80% do work. 80% of 80 is $\frac{8}{10} \times 80 = 64$ apartments. If 64 of the 100 apartments in City *G* have working smoke alarms, then $\frac{64}{100}$, or 64%, have working smoke alarms.

14. $\dfrac{60}{n}$

This is simply a motion problem; it's just one in which the speeds are very slow. First find the speed at which the tree grew, in feet per year. It grew 5 feet in *n* years, so it grew at an average rate of $\dfrac{5 \text{ feet}}{n \text{ years}}$. Now we want the average distance it grew in 1 year.

$$\text{Distance} = \text{Rate} \times \text{Time}$$
$$= \frac{5 \text{ feet}}{n \text{ years}} \times 1 \text{ year}$$
$$= \frac{5}{n} \text{ feet}$$

But we were asked for the average amount it grew in inches per year, so we must convert. As we're told, there are 12 inches in a foot, so:

$$\frac{5}{n} \text{ feet} \times \frac{12 \text{ inches}}{1 \text{ foot}} = \frac{60}{n} \text{ inches.}$$

This is the average amount the tree grew in 1 year.

15.   **1,440,000**

During the year of the first increase, attendance climbed to 1 million plus 20% or $\frac{1}{5}$ of 1 million. $\frac{1}{5}$ of 1 million is 200,000, so attendance rose to 1,200,000, or 1.2 million. During the year of the second increase, attendance climbed to 1.2 million plus 20%, or $\frac{1}{5}$ of 1.2 million. $\frac{1}{5}$ of 1.2 million is 240,000. The attendance the year of the second increase must have been 1,200,000 + 240,000, or 1,440,000.

16.   **80**

If Bill mows $\frac{3}{4}$ of his lawn in one hour, then one hour must represent $\frac{3}{4}$ of the time he needs to mow the entire lawn. Therefore, 60 minutes must equal $\frac{3}{4}$ of the time he needs to mow the entire lawn.

$60 = \frac{3}{4} \times \text{(Total time)}$.

Now solve for the total time.

$$\text{Total time} = 60 \times \frac{4}{3} = 80$$

He will need 80 minutes to mow the whole lawn.

17. $300

A potential profit of 20% means the store will sell the camera for 20% more than they paid for it themselves.

The $360 price of the camera represents the cost plus 20% of the cost. Then:

$$\text{Selling price} = 120\% \text{ of cost}$$

$$\$360 = \frac{120}{100} \times \text{cost}$$

$$\$360 \times \frac{100}{120} = \text{cost}$$

$$\$300 = \text{cost}$$

18. $200

The amount of the discount will *not* be 20% of $800; it will equal 20% of the original price of the item. Therefore you need to find this original price. You know the original price minus 20% of the original price equals $800. That is, 80% of the original price equals $800. Calling the original price x we have:

$$\$800 = 80\% \text{ of } x$$

$$\$800 = \frac{8}{10} \times x$$

$$\$800 \times \frac{10}{8} = x$$

$$\$1{,}000 = x$$

The original price was $1,000. The new price is $800. The amount of the discount was 20% of $1,000, or $200. (Or just subtract: $1,000 − $800 = $200.)

19. $\dfrac{PR}{N}$

If John buys R pounds for N people, he is planning on feeding his guests cheese at a rate of:

$$\frac{R \text{ pounds}}{N \text{ people}} = \frac{R}{N} \text{ pounds per person.}$$

We need to know how much additional cheese John must buy for the extra P people. If John is buying $\frac{R}{N}$ pounds of cheese for each person, then he will need $P \times \frac{R}{N}$, or $\frac{PR}{N}$ pounds for the extra P people. We can check our answer by seeing if the units cancel out:

$$P \text{ people} \times \frac{R \text{ pounds}}{N \text{ people}} = \frac{PR}{N} \text{ pounds}$$

The other approach here is to get rid of all those annoying variables by picking numbers. Say John buys 10 pounds of cheese for 5 people (that is, $R = 10$ and $N = 5$). Then everyone gets 2 pounds of cheese. Also, say 7 people come, 2 more than expected (that is, $P = 2$). Then he needs 14 pounds to have enough for everybody to consume 2 pounds of cheese. Since he already bought 10 pounds, he must buy an additional 4 pounds. Therefore, the answer choice which equals 4 when we substitute 10 for R, 5 for N, and 2 for P is possibly correct:

$\frac{(5)(2)}{10} \neq 4.$ Discard

$\frac{5}{(10)(2)} \neq 4.$ Discard

$\frac{5+2}{10} \neq 4.$ Discard

$\frac{2}{(5)(10)} \neq 4.$ Discard

$\frac{(2)(10)}{5} = 4.$ Correct

Since only choice **(E)** gives 4, that must be the correct choice.

20. 20%

The easiest approach here is to pick a sample value for the cost of the watch, and from that, work out the profit and selling price. As so often with percent problems, it will be simplest to pick 100. If the watch cost the store \$100, then the profit will be 25% of \$100 or \$25. The selling price equals the cost to the store plus the profit: \$100 + \$25, or \$125. The profit represents $\frac{25}{125}$, or $\frac{1}{5}$ of the selling price. The percent equivalent of $\frac{1}{5}$ is 20%.

21. 14

If it takes 10 minutes to fill up $\frac{5}{12}$ of the hole, then each twelfth (there are 5 of them) takes only 2 minutes. If each $\frac{1}{12}$ takes only 2 minutes, then $\frac{7}{12}$ takes 7 times as long, or $7 \times 2 = 14$ minutes.

You can also set up a proportion:

$$\frac{10 \text{ minutes}}{\frac{5}{12} \text{ of a hole}} = \frac{x \text{ minutes}}{\frac{7}{12} \text{ of a hole}}$$

Cross multiplying, we get:

$$\frac{7}{12} \times 10 = \frac{5}{12}x$$
$$\frac{70}{12} = \frac{5}{12}x$$
$$70 = 5x$$
$$x = 14$$

22. $33

First find how much she paid for all the windows. She received a discount of 25%; that is, she paid 75% of the total price.

$$\text{Cost to builder} = 75\% \text{ of } \$1,200$$
$$= \frac{3}{4} \times \$1,200$$
$$= \$900$$

She received an extra $75 discount. That is, she paid $900 − $75 = $825. She bought 25 windows, so each cost her $\frac{\$825}{25} = \$33$.

23. 200

Since we only need to consider two rates, use the shortcut combined work formula where A and B represent the two rates.

$$\frac{AB}{A+B} = \frac{5 \times 10}{5+10} = \frac{50}{15} = \frac{10}{3} \text{ hours}$$

Working together, it would take them $\frac{10}{3}$ hours. But the question asks for the number of minutes. Since there are 60 minutes in one hour, just multiply the number of hours by 60.

$$\frac{10}{3} \times 60 = \frac{600}{3} = 200 \text{ minutes}$$

24. $33\frac{1}{3}$%

Pick a sample value for the size of one of the classes. The first class might have 100 students. That means there are 30% of 100 = 30 boys in the class. The second class is half the size of the first, so it has 50 students, of which 40% of 50 = 20 are boys. This gives us 100 + 50 = 150 students total, of whom 30 + 20 = 50 are boys. So $\frac{50}{150} = \frac{1}{3}$ of both classes are boys. $\frac{1}{3}$ equals $33\frac{1}{3}$%.

25. 20

We can again use the shortcut combined work formula:

$$\frac{AB}{A+B}$$

Since the question asks for the number of minutes, be sure to convert all amounts to minutes. We get:

$$\frac{30 \times 60}{30 + 60} = \frac{1,800}{90} = 20 \text{ minutes}$$

26. $\frac{17}{2}m$

Just apply the distance formula, Distance = Rate $\times$ Time, to the two segments of the trip. In the first 4 hours she drives $4m$ miles. In the next 6 hours she drives $6 \times \frac{3}{4}m = \frac{9}{2}m$ miles. The total number of miles she drives then is $4m + \frac{9}{2}m$ or $\frac{17}{2}m$ miles.

27. 16%

Since Joan spends 20% of her income on taxes, the remainder is 80% of her income. If we call Joan's income x, then the remainder after taxes is 0.8x. Now if she spends 20% of this remaining 80% on rent, she spends

$0.2(0.8x) = 0.16x$

Because 0.16x is 16 percent of x, 16 percent of her income goes to rent.

This is also a great problem to solve by picking numbers, as is any problem that deals with percents of an unknown quantity, in this case Joan's income. If Joan has an income of $100, then spends $20 on taxes, that leaves $80. And 20% of 80 is 0.2(80) = 16. And here's why we pick 100: 16 is 16% of 100.

This is also a great strategic guessing question. Since we take 20% of the income away for taxes before Joan pays her rent, she pays 20% of less than her total income. So that must be close to, but a little less than, 20% of that income. Answer **(C)** is the only one that fits the bill.

28. 20

First find how long the trip takes him at the two different rates, using the formula:

$$\text{Time} = \frac{\text{Distance}}{\text{Rate}}$$

He travels the first 10 km at 30 km per hour, so he takes $\frac{10}{30} = \frac{1}{3}$ hour for this portion of the journey.

He travels the remaining 30 km at 15 km per hour, so he takes $\frac{30}{15} = 2$ hours for this portion of the journey. So the whole journey takes him $2 + \frac{1}{3} = 2\frac{1}{3}$ hours. Now we need to compare this to the amount of time it would take to make the same trip at a constant rate of 20 km per hour. If he travelled the whole 40 km at 20 km per hour, it would take $\frac{40}{20} = 2$ hours.

This is $\frac{1}{3}$ hour, or 20 minutes, shorter.

29. 44%

First find what percent of the entire population play a varsity sport. We can do this by finding out what percent of all students are male students who play a varsity sport, and what percent of all students are female students who play a varsity sport, and then summing these values. 40% of the students are male, so 60% of the students are female.

First, what percent of all students are males who play a varsity sport? 50% of the males play a varsity sport, that is 50% of 40% = 20% of all the students.

Now for the women. 60% of the females play a varsity sport, that is 60% of 60% = 36% of all the students.

Sum the percents of males and females who play a varsity sport: 20% + 36% = 56% of the total student population.

The percent of all students who DO NOT play a varsity sport is 100% − 56% = 44%.

30. 15

If we can find how long either leg of the journey takes, we can use that time and the speed to find the distance. Since Tammy traveled 3 times as fast to the end of the racecourse as she traveled back home, it took her 3 times as long to return. If we say she took x hours to complete the course and $3x$ hours to return, then her total time is $x + 3x = 4x$. The question tells us that her total time is 2 hours, so $4x = 2$ hours. Therefore, x is $\frac{1}{2}$. In $\frac{1}{2}$ hour at 30 miles per hour, Tammy traveled 15 miles.

31. 300

We are only given one figure for any group of workers: 72 for the number of full-time workers who received bonuses. We can find the total number of workers if we knew what percent of the total number of workers these 72 represent. 20% of the workers are part-time, so 80% of the workers are full-time.

30% of the full-time workers received bonuses, and this amounted to 72 workers.

If E is the total number of workers employed by the company then 80% of E = the number of full-time workers, so

$$30\% \text{ of } 80\% \text{ of } E = 72$$
$$\frac{3}{10} \times \frac{8}{10} \times E = 72$$
$$\frac{24}{100} \times E = 72$$
$$E = 72 \times \frac{100}{24}$$
$$= 300$$

The company employs 300 workers.

32. 48

We are given two rates for the same job. So we can use the shortcut combined work formula to find the amount of time that it would take for both pipes to fill the *entire* tank first.

$$\frac{AB}{A+B}$$

Using the rates of 3 hours and 2 hours, we get:

$$\frac{3 \times 2}{3+2} = \frac{6}{5} \text{ hours to fill the entire tank}$$

Since we only need to fill $\frac{2}{3}$ of the tank, we multiply this time by $\frac{2}{3}$:

$$\frac{6}{5} \times \frac{2}{3} = \frac{4}{5} \text{ hours to fill } \frac{2}{3} \text{ of the tank}$$

The question asks for minutes, so convert hours to minutes by multiplying by 60:

$$\frac{4}{5} \text{ hours} \times \frac{60 \text{ minutes}}{1 \text{ hour}} = 48 \text{ minutes}$$

33. a 5% increase

Choose a sample value easy to work with; see what happens with 100 jobs. If the factory cuts its labor force by 16%, it eliminates 16% of 100 jobs or 16 jobs, leaving a work force of $100 - 16$, or 84 people. It then increases this work force by 25%. 25% of 84, is $\frac{1}{4}$ of 84, or 21. The factory adds 21 jobs to the 84 it had, for a total of 105 jobs. Since the factory started with 100 jobs and finished with 105, it gained 5 jobs overall. This represents $\frac{5}{100}$ or 5% of the total we started with. There was a 5% increase.

34. $\dfrac{y}{60x}$

Method I:

First figure out how many minutes it would take for y centimeters of snow to fall. The snow is falling at a constant rate of x centimeters per minute; set up a proportion to find how long it takes for y centimeters. The ratio of minutes passed to centimeters fallen is a constant.

$$\frac{1 \text{ minute}}{x \text{ centimeters}} = \frac{m \text{ minutes}}{y \text{ centimeters}}$$

Solve for m.

$$m \text{ minutes} = y \text{ centimeters} \cdot \frac{1 \text{ minute}}{x \text{ centimeters}}$$

$$m \text{ minutes} = \frac{y}{x} \text{ minutes}$$

Now we must convert from $\frac{y}{x}$ minutes to hours. Since hours are larger, we must divide the minutes by 60.

$$\frac{y}{x} \text{ minutes} \times \frac{1 \text{ hour}}{60 \text{ minutes}} = \frac{y}{60x} \text{ hours}$$

Always be sure to keep track of your units: as long as they are in the right places, you can be sure you are using the correct operation.

Method II:

First find out how long it takes for 1 centimeter of snow to fall. We will eventually have to convert from minutes to hours, so we might as well do it now. If x centimeters of snow fall every minute, then 60 times as much will fall in an hour, or $60x$ centimeters of snow. Then one centimeter of snow will fall in the reciprocal of $60x$, or $\frac{1}{60x}$ hours. We're almost at the end: 1 centimeter falls in $\frac{1}{60x}$ hours, so y centimeters will fall in y times as many hours, or $\frac{y}{60x}$ hours.

35. $300

Method I:

Find the cost of the stereo to the dealer, then subtract 40% of this to find the price it was sold for. The selling price equals the dealer's cost plus the profit. The dealer would have made a 20% profit if he had sold the stereo for $600; therefore, letting x represent the cost to the dealer,

$$600 = x + 20\% \text{ of } x$$
$$600 = 120\% \text{ of } x$$
$$600 = \frac{6}{5}x$$
$$x = \frac{5}{6} \cdot 600 = 500$$

Instead the dealer sold the stereo at a loss of 40%. Since 40% or $\frac{2}{5}$ of 500 is 200, he sold the stereo for $500 - \$200 = \$300.

Method II:

Let x represent the dealer's cost. Then we're told that $600 represents $x + 20\%$ of x or 120% of x. We want the value of $x - (40\% \text{ of } x)$, or 60% of x. Since 60% of x is one-half of 120% of x, the sale price must have been one-half of $600, or $300.

36. 96

Method I:

First, find how long it takes 4 men to complete the entire job, then from that we can find the time for 1 man, and then we can find how long it takes 1 man to do $\frac{2}{5}$ of the job.

If 4 men can do $\frac{2}{3}$ of a job in 40 minutes, they still have $\frac{1}{3}$ of the job to do. Since they have $\frac{1}{2}$ as much work left as they have already done, it will take them $\frac{1}{2}$ as much time as they've already spent, or another 20 minutes. This makes a total of 60 minutes for the 4 men to finish the job. One man will take 4 times as long, or 240 minutes. He'll do $\frac{2}{5}$ of the job in $\frac{2}{5}$ as much time, or $\frac{2}{5} \times 240 = 96$ minutues.

Method II:

First, determine how long it takes one man to do the job, and from this find how long it would take him to do $\frac{2}{5}$ of it.

If 4 men do $\frac{2}{3}$ of the job in 40 minutes, 1 man does $\frac{1}{4}$ of this work, or $\frac{1}{4} \times \frac{2}{3} = \frac{1}{6}$ of the job in 40 minutes.

Therefore, it takes him 6 times as long to do the whole job, or $6 \times 40 = 240$ minutes. Again, he'll do $\frac{2}{5}$ of the job in $\frac{2}{5} \times 240 = 96$ minutes.

37. 40%

Here, work with the portion of the job Bob completes in one hour when he and Alice work together. Bob can do the job in 5 hours; he completes $\frac{1}{5}$ of the job in 1 hour. So in the 3 hours they both work, Bob does $3 \times \frac{1}{5} = \frac{3}{5}$ of the job. Alice does the rest, or $1 - \frac{3}{5} = \frac{2}{5}$ of the job. The percent equivalent of $\frac{2}{5}$ is 40%. Alice does 40% of the job.

PROBLEM SOLVING TEST
ANSWERS AND EXPLANATIONS

1. $432

We are told that Robert's rent increases at a constant percent; use the chart to determine the rate. His rent goes up to $300 in 2009 from $250 in 2008, or it increases $50. In fractional terms, this is $\frac{50}{250}$, or $\frac{1}{5}$. (Remember: always divide the amount of increase by the original whole.) It isn't necessary to convert $\frac{1}{5}$ to a percent; all we care about is the rate of increase, not whether we express it as a percent or as a fraction. At this rate, his 2011 rent was $\frac{1}{5}$ more than his 2010 rent, or

$$\$360 + \frac{1}{5}(\$360) = \$360 + \$72 = \$432$$

2. 51

Since the season is half over, there are 80 games left in the season. If team *A* wins half of the remaining games, that's another 40 games, for a total of 60 + 40, or 100 games. Team *B* has won 49 games so far, so in order to tie team *A*, it must win another 100 − 49, or 51 games.

3. 44

We need to learn the man's overtime rate of pay, but to do this we have to figure out his regular rate of pay. Divide the amount of money made, $200, by the time it took to make it, 40 hours. $200 ÷ 40 hours = $5 per hour. That is his normal rate. We're told that the man is paid time-and-a-half for overtime, so when working more than 40 hours he makes $\frac{3}{2} \times \$5$ per hour = $7.50 per hour. Now we can figure out how long it takes the man to make $230. It takes him 40 hours to make the first $200. The last $30 are made at the overtime rate. Since it takes the man one hour to make $7.50 at this rate, we can figure out the number of extra hours by dividing $30 by $7.50 per hour. $30 ÷ $7.50 per hour = 4 hours. The total time needed is 40 hours plus 4 hours, or 44 hours.

4. 0.01

If 1 centimeter = 10 millimeters, then

(1 centimeter)² = (10 millimeters)²

= 100 square millimeters.

Therefore, 1 square millimeter = $\frac{1}{100}$ square centimeters = 0.01 square centimeters.

5. **6**

Find out how far team *X* has moved thus far. They pulled team *Y* forward 3 meters, so *X* moved backward 3 meters. Then they were pulled forward 5 meters and then a further 2 meters. In total then they have moved forward $(-3) + 5 + 2 = 4$ meters. They must be pulled a further 6 meters to be pulled 10 meters forward.

6. **80**

The student has done 30 of the 60 problems, and has used up 20 of his 60 minutes. Therefore, he has $60 - 30$, or 30 problems left, to be done in $60 - 20$, or 40 minutes. We find his average time per problem by dividing the time by the number of problems.

$$\text{Time per problem} = \frac{40 \text{ minutes}}{30 \text{ problems}} = \frac{4}{3} \text{ minutes}$$

Each minute has 60 seconds. There are more seconds than minutes, so we multiply by 60 to find the number of seconds.

$$\frac{4}{3} \text{ minutes} \times 60 \frac{\text{seconds}}{\text{minute}} = 80 \text{ seconds}$$

7. **200**

We need to find the respective lengths of paved and unpaved roads, so that we can find the difference between the two. Call unpaved roads *u* and paved roads *p*. Then the sum of the lengths of the unpaved roads and paved roads is the sum of the lengths of all the roads in the county. So:

$$u + p = 1,400$$

The sum of unpaved roads is $\frac{3}{4}$ the sum of paved roads. So:

$$u = \frac{3}{4} p$$

We have two equations with two unknowns so we can solve for *u* and *p*. Substitute the value of *u* from the second equation into the first:

$$\frac{3}{4} p + p = 1,400$$

$$3p + 4p = 1,400 \times 4$$

$$7p = 5,600$$

$$p = 800$$

Since $u = \frac{3}{4} p, u = \frac{3}{4} \cdot 800 = 600$.

So there are 800 miles of paved roads and 600 miles of unpaved roads.

There are $800 - 600 = 200$ miles more of paved roads.

8. $\dfrac{1}{7}$

Since 3 out of 24 students are in student organizations, the remaining 24 − 3, or 21 students are not in student organizations. Therefore, the ratio of students in organizations to students not in organizations is:

$$\frac{\text{\# in organizations}}{\text{\# not in organizations}} = \frac{3}{21} = \frac{1}{7}.$$

9. 14

A die has six faces, where the number of dots on opposite faces sum to 7. Since we can see the faces corresponding to 1, 2, and 4 dots in the picture, the ones we cannot see must contain 6, 5, and 3 dots respectively. Since 6 + 5 + 3 = 14, there are 14 dots hidden from view.

10. 24

We cannot find any individual score from the average, but we can find the sum of the scores. The difference between the sum of all the scores and the sum of the 4 highest scores will be the lowest score.

The average of all 5 tests is 72, so the sum of all the scores is 5 × 72 = 360.

The average of the 4 highest scores is 84, so the sum of the 4 highest scores is 4 × 84 = 336.

The difference between the sum of all the scores and the sum of the 4 highest scores will be the lowest score; that is, 360 − 336 = 24.

11. 6

He owns 3 pairs of trousers and 5 jackets. For every pair of trousers, he can wear 5 different jackets, giving 5 different combinations for each pair of trousers, or 3 × 5 = 15 different combinations of trousers and jackets. With each of these combinations he can wear any of his different shirts. The different combinations of shirts, jackets and trousers is (number of shirts) × 15. We are told this equals 90, so:

$$\text{number of shirts} = 90 \div 15 = 6$$

12. 220

Jean drives at an average rate of 70 kilometers per hour. That means that each hour, on average, she travels 70 kilometers. Therefore, in two hours she travels 2 × 70, or 140 kilometers. After driving for two hours, she still has another 80 kilometers to travel. Therefore, the total distance between the two towns is 140 + 80, or 220 kilometers.

13. $3.20

We want to find the greatest possible original price of the item. Since we are given the price after the discount, the greatest original price will correspond to the greatest discount. (If we had been told the **amount** of discount, the greatest original price would have corresponded to the **smallest** percent discount; for instance, 10 is 25 percent of 40, but is only 10 percent of 100.)

So to have the greatest original price, $2.40 must be the cost after a 25 percent discount. Then $2.40 is 100% − 25% = 75% of the original price, or $\frac{3}{4}$ of the original price. If the original price is p, then:

$$\$2.40 = \frac{3}{4}p$$
$$\frac{4}{3}(2.40) = \frac{4}{3} \cdot \frac{3}{4}p$$
$$\$3.20 = P$$

14. $\frac{5}{8}(N - S)$

The man earns $\$N$ a month and spends $\$S$ on rent; this leaves $N-S$ dollars for things other than rent. He spends $\frac{3}{8}$ of this amount on food, so the remainder is $1 - \frac{3}{8}$ or $\frac{5}{8}$ of the amount after rent. The amount left is $\frac{5}{8}(N - S)$.

15. 7

The answer choices let us know that the biggest this sequence could be is 11 numbers. That's not so many that we couldn't just start adding them by hand, stopping when we reach 63:

$$6 + 7 = 13$$
$$13 + 8 = 21$$
$$21 + 9 = 30$$
$$30 + 10 = 40$$
$$40 + 11 = 51$$
$$51 + 12 = 63$$

When we count the number of terms in the sequence from 6 to 12, we count 7 integers in total. Another efficient way to solve this problem would be to backsolve. Say you started with **(D)** and tested a sequence of 8 integers:

$$6 + 7 + 8 + 9 + 10 + 11 + 12 + 13$$

Using the formula for adding long strings of consecutive numbers,

$$\text{sum} = \frac{\text{first} + \text{last}}{2} \times \text{\# of terms}$$
$$= \frac{6 + 13}{2} \times 8$$
$$= \frac{19}{2} \times 8$$
$$= \frac{19}{1} \times 4$$
$$= 76$$

Notice that the number of terms in a sequence that runs from integer x to integer y is *not* $y - x$ but rather $y - x + 1$ ($13 - 6 + 1 = 8$). Many counting-based GMAT problems are based on this formula.

We need the sum to be 63, so we clearly have too many numbers. That leaves **(E)**, 7, as the only possible answer.

16. **18**

You don't need to know anything about physics to answer this one. We need to find the mass, so rearrange our equation to get m on one side.

$$K = \frac{1}{2}mv^2$$

$$2K = mv^2$$

$$\frac{2K}{v^2} = m$$

Now substitute in our values for K and v:

$$m = \frac{2 \cdot 144}{(4)^2}$$

$$= \frac{288}{16}$$

$$= 18$$

The mass is 18 kilograms.

17. **9**

Bill had a five, two tens, and a twenty, for a total of $45. Since he didn't receive any change after purchasing an item, he must have paid **exactly** the amount of the purchase. He didn't have to spend all his money, though, so the cost wasn't necessarily $45. What we do know about the purchase price is that since all of Bill's bills are in amounts that are divisible by five, the purchase price must also be divisible by five. The smallest denomination that Bill has is a five-dollar bill. So we can start with $5, and then count up all the possible distinct combinations of these bills. There are $5 ($5 bill), $10 ($10 bill), $15 ($5 + $10 bills), $20 ($20 bill), $25 ($5 + $20 bills), $30 ($10 + $20 bills), $35 ($5 + $10 + $20 bills), $40 ($10 + $10 + $20 bills), and $45 (all 4 bills). So, in fact, all prices that are multiples of $5 between $5 and $45 are possible; there are 9 of them in all.

18. **30**

We need the total number of dogs. We are given a ratio between all the cats and all the dogs, that is 5:3. So for every five cats we have three dogs. Therefore, out of every 8 animals, 3 will be dogs. This means the total number of dogs will be three-eighths times the total number of animals. So we need to find the total number of animals. The total number of animals is the sum of all the dogs living in Dog Only households, all the cats living in Cat Only households and all the animals living in Dog and Cat households. Now for any of these categories, we can say:

$$(\text{the average number of pets per household}) = \frac{(\text{the number of pets})}{(\text{number of households})}$$

Rearranging this we get that the number of pets in that category = the average number of pets × the number of households.

For Dogs Only, the number of dogs = 1.5 × 16 = 24 dogs.

For Cats Only, the number of cats = 1.25 × 24 = 30 cats.

For Dogs and Cats, the number of animals = 3.25 × 8 = 26 animals.

So the total number of animals is $24 + 30 + 26 = 80$.

Finally, the total number of dogs is $\frac{3}{8} \times 80 = 30$.

19. 20

If Jane knits 72 stitches to the line and uses $\frac{1}{4}$ inch of yarn per stitch, that means she uses:

$$72 \frac{\text{stitches}}{\text{line}} \times \frac{1 \text{ inch}}{4 \text{ stitch}} = 18 \text{ inches of yarn per line.}$$

But we need to find out how many lines she can knit with 10 **yards** of yarn. Since there are three feet in a yard and twelve inches in a foot, there must be $3 \frac{\text{feet}}{\text{yard}} \times 12 \frac{\text{inches}}{\text{feet}} = 36$ inches in a yard. So 18 inches is $\frac{18}{36}$, or $\frac{1}{2}$ yard.

Each line requires $\frac{1}{2}$ yard of yarn to knit; each yard of yarn is enough for 2 lines. Therefore, 10 yards of yarn is enough for 10×2, or 20 lines.

20. 50

This is best solved intuitively. The maximum number of bonds that can be bought is when all the bonds are in $50 denominations. Since Robert bought $2,000 worth of bonds, the maximum number of bonds he could buy is $\frac{\$2,000}{\$50} = 40$ bonds. If he bought 50 $50 bonds he would spend $50 \times \$50 = \$2,500$. This is too much. If he bought any $100 bonds he would spend even more money. So it is impossible to buy $2,000 worth of bonds by purchasing 50 $100 or $50 bonds.

21. 20

The **more** sugar you use, the **less** time it will last. So discard answer choices **(D)** and **(E)** straight away. We have increased the use by 50%, or $\frac{1}{2}$, so we are using the sugar at a rate $1\frac{1}{2}$ times, or $\frac{3}{2}$ of what it was. We will go through it in the inverse of $\frac{3}{2}$, or $\frac{2}{3}$ of the time, since the usage and the time are in an inverse relationship. The sugar will last $\frac{2}{3} \cdot 30 = 20$ days.

Or try picking numbers. Say we have 300 ounces of sugar, and we use it at a rate of 10 ounces per day. (The supply will last for 30 days. So we've satisfied the requirements of our question.) Now increase the rate by 50 percent; that means we would use $10 + 50\%(10)$, or 15 ounces per day. How long would our supply of 300 ounces last if we use 15 ounces per day? $\frac{300}{15} = 20$. So it's 20 days.

22. $\dfrac{1}{3}$

The **faster** we travel, the **more** distance we cover in a given amount of time. Drawing a diagram will help you calculate the distances. Bucky and Robin meet 2 miles from Amity; since Amity is 8 miles from Truro, they must be 8 − 2, or 6 miles from Truro.

Since they left at the same time, Bucky traveled 2 miles in the same time it took Robin to travel 6 miles. Since they traveled for the same length of time, the ratio of their average speeds will be the same as the ratio of their distances.

$$\frac{\text{Bucky's average speed}}{\text{Robin's average speed}} = \frac{\text{Bucky's distance}}{\text{Robin's distance}}$$

$$= \frac{2}{6}$$

$$= \frac{1}{3}$$

23. 1.5

Start by converting kilometers to meters. Since a meter is smaller than a kilometer, we must multiply. We are told that a length of 10 centimeters on the map represents 5 kilometers or 5,000 meters; therefore, 1 centimeter must represent $\dfrac{1}{10}$ as much, or 500 meters. We want to know how many centimeters would represent 750 meters.

We could set up a proportion here, but it's quicker to use common sense. We have a distance $\dfrac{3}{2}$ as great as 500 meters $\left(750 = \dfrac{3}{2} \times 500\right)$, so we need a map distance $\dfrac{3}{2}$ as great as 1 centimeter, or $\dfrac{3}{2} \times 1 = 1.5$ centimeters.

24. 46

Each tree is 1 meter in width, and we need 16 meters between every two trees. Starting at the first tree, we have 1 meter for the tree, plus 16 meters space before the next tree, for a total of 17 meters. The second tree then takes up 1 meter, plus 16 meters space between that tree and the third tree, or 17 more meters. So we need 17 meters for each tree and the space before the next tree.

The street is $\dfrac{3}{8}$ kilometer long. We change this to meters (since we've been dealing with meters so far) by multiplying $\dfrac{3}{8}$ by 1,000—the number of meters in a kilometer. This gives us 375 meters to work with. Each tree and space takes up 17 meters, so we divide 17 into 375 to find the number of trees and spaces we can fit in. $\dfrac{375}{17}$ gives us 22 with 1 left over. So is 22 the number of trees we can fit on each side of the street? No—this is the number of trees followed by a space. But we don't need a space after the last tree—we only need a space between a pair of trees; since there's no tree after the last one, there's no need to have a space there. So we use up 374 meters with 22 trees and spaces, and can then add one more tree in the last meter of space, for a total of 23 trees on each side. Since there are trees on both sides of the street, we can fit 46 trees in all.

25. 60

This is a cycles problem. To understand what's going on here, let's say that the first lighthouse blinks every 10 seconds. That means it blinks, then blinks again after 10 seconds, then again after 20 seconds from the first blink, then after 30 seconds, etc. Suppose a second one blinks every 15 seconds; then it blinks after 15 seconds, 30 seconds, 45 seconds, etc. They will blink together at each common multiple of 10 and 15, and the first time they will blink together again is at the least common multiple of 10 and 15, or after 30 seconds.

Now back to the problem. Start by converting everything to seconds. There are 60 seconds in a minute, so 5 times a minute is once every $\frac{60}{5}$ or 12 seconds. 4 times a minute works out to once every $\frac{60}{4}$, or 15 seconds. So we need to find the least common multiple of 12 and 15. You could work this out by finding the prime factors, but probably the easiest method is to go through the multiples of the larger number, 15, until you find one that is also a multiple of 12.

$$1 \times 15 = 15$$
$$2 \times 15 = 30$$
$$3 \times 15 = 45$$
$$4 \times 15 = 60 \text{ This is a multiple of 12: } 5 \times 12 = 60$$

The two lighthouses will blink together after 60 seconds.

26. 120

The vault has 130 ounces total of gold and silver. Each tablet of gold weight 8 ounces, each tablet of silver 5 ounces. Not all of the 130 ounces can be gold, since 130 is not a multiple of 8. There must be some silver in there as well. The largest multiple of 8 less than 130 is 16×8, or 128, but this can't be the amount of gold either, since this leaves only $130 - 128$ or 2 leftover ounces for the silver, and each silver tablet weighs 5 ounces. So let's look at the multiples of 8 less than 128 until we find one that leaves a multiple of 5 when subtracted from 130. Well, in fact, the next smallest multiple of 8, which is $15 \times 8 = 120$, leaves us with $130 - 120 = 10$ ounces of silver, and since $2 \times 5 = 10$, this amount works. We have 15 tablets of gold for a total of 120 ounces, and 2 tablets of silver, for a total of 10 ounces. So 120 ounces is the greatest possible amount of gold.

27. 24

This balloon distribution is an unending series of cycles (at least unending until we run out of balloons). Each cycle is 1 blue, 2 red, and 3 yellow, so each cycle runs for 6 balloons, and has 2 red balloons. How many cycles will we go through over a period of 70 balloons? The largest multiple of 6 that is less than 70 is 66, so we will go through 11 complete cycles, and then go through the first 4 balloons in the next cycle. Since each cycle has 2 red balloons, we will have distributed 2×11 or 22 red balloons by the 66th. After the 66th balloon, we go through the beginning of a new cycle, so the 67th balloon is blue, the 68th and 69th red, and the 70th yellow. This adds 2 more red balloons to our earlier 22, for a total of 24 in the first 70.

28. 56

Translate what we are given into equations, and then solve for the number of plums. p plums at 25 cents each $= 25p$. $(p - 6)$ nectarines at 28 cents each $= 28(p - 6)$.

These two quantities are equal, so:

$$25p = 28(p - 6)$$

Solve for *p*.

$$25p = 28p - 168$$
$$168 = 28p - 25p$$
$$168 = 3p$$
$$\frac{168}{3} = p$$
$$56 = p$$

29. 3.2%

We need to realize that each time the stock changes its price by a percentage of **different** wholes. For instance, in July the original price increases by 10%. When it declines in August, it declines by 20% of the new price. So the net change after August will not be 10% − 20%, or −10%; it's not that easy. The best way to work with percent change is to pick a number. Usually 100 is the easiest number to start with for percents—it's really easy to take a percent of 100.

So say the original July price is $100. It increases by 10% or $10, up to $110. In August it declines by 20% of $110, or $\frac{1}{5} \times \$110 = \$22$. So now it's down to $110 − $22, or $88. Then it goes up by 10% of $88, or $\frac{1}{10} \times \$88 = \$8.80$; this brings the price back up to $96.80, only $3.20 less than it started. The percent change equals the amount of change divided by the original whole (100 in this case), or $\frac{3.20}{100} \times 100\% = 3.2\%$.

30. $\frac{15}{2}$

Method I:

Get both tics and tocs in terms of the same number of tacs. Since we are given the value of tics in terms of 3 tacs, and tocs in terms of 2 tacs, let's use the LCM of 2 and 3, or 6. If 1 tic equals 3 tacs, then 2 tics equal 6 tacs. If 2 tacs equal 5 tocs, then 6 tacs equal $3 \times 5 = 15$ tocs. Therefore, 2 tics = 6 tacs = 15 tocs. We don't care about tacs anymore; just tics and tocs. Divide to get the ratio of units on one side, and the numbers on the other side.

$$2 \text{ tics} = 15 \text{ tocs}$$
$$\frac{1 \text{ tic}}{1 \text{ toc}} = \frac{15}{2}$$

Method II:

Use the units cancellation method. We are given tics in terms of tacs, and tacs in terms of tocs. Since we are only interested in the ratio of a tic to a toc, we must somehow eliminate the tacs from consideration. Write down the two ratios we are given.

$$1 \text{ tic} = 3 \text{ tacs} \qquad 2 \text{ tacs} = 5 \text{ tocs}$$
$$\text{or} \qquad\qquad \text{or}$$
$$\frac{1 \text{ tic}}{1 \text{ tac}} = \frac{3}{1} \qquad \frac{1 \text{ tac}}{1 \text{ toc}} = \frac{5}{2}$$

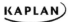

We have two ratios: in one, tacs are in the denominator, and in the other, they are in the numerator. If we multiply the two equations, the tac terms will cancel out, leaving us with the desired ratio:

$$\frac{1\,\text{tic}}{1\,\text{toc}} = \left(\frac{1\,\text{tic}}{1\,\text{tac}}\right)\left(\frac{1\,\text{tac}}{1\,\text{toc}}\right)$$
$$= \left(\frac{3}{1}\right)\left(\frac{5}{2}\right)$$
$$= \frac{15}{2}$$

31. $8

Let John's money $= J$ and Allen's money $= A$. John gives $5 to Allen so now he has $J - 5$ and Allen has $A + 5$. Allen gives $2 to Frank so now he has $2 less, or $A + 5 - 2 = A + 3$. They all have the same amount of money now, so

$$A + 3 = J - 5$$

or

$$A + 8 = J$$

Since Allen needs $8 to have the same as John, John has $8 more.

32. $30

First we have to find the number of sheets of paper in the pile, and then calculate the cost from that. If you have trouble working with very small numbers (or very large numbers) and can't quite figure out how to calculate the number of sheets, you may want to try it with some easier numbers, just to see which operation we need. Suppose we've got sheets of paper one meter thick, and need to stack enough for four meters. To calculate the number of sheets we divide one into four: dividing the thickness for each sheet into the total thickness, and we end up with the number of sheets: 4.

$$\frac{\text{Total thickness}}{\text{Thickness per sheet}} = \text{Number of sheets}$$

Here, of course, we use the same technique. We divide the thickness per sheet into the total thickness. First, we must change the meters to centimeters (we could change the thickness per sheet into meters, but we've got enough zeros as it is). There are 100 centimeters in a meter, so in 4 meters there are 4×100, or 400 centimeters. Now we can divide.

$$\frac{400}{0.08} = \frac{40,000}{8} = 5,000$$

So we have 5,000 sheets. If 500 sheets cost $3, then 5,000 sheets will cost ten times as much, or $30.

33. $25.00

Take this one step at a time. If Ms. Smith's car averages 35 miles per gallon, then she can go 35 miles on 1 gallon. To go 700 miles, she will need $\frac{700}{35}$, or 20 gallons of gasoline. The average price of gasoline was $1.25 per gallon, so she spent $20 \times \$1.25$, or $25 for the 20 gallons on her trip.

34. 9

Of the 7 people on committee *A*, 3 of them are also on committee *B*, leaving 7 − 3, or 4 people who are only on committee *A*. Similarly, there are 8 people on committee *B*; 3 of them are on both committees, leaving 8 − 3, or 5 people only on committee *B*. There are 4 people only on *A*, and 5 people only on *B*, making 4 + 5, or 9 people on only one committee.

35. $1

The important part of the money exchange is a person's **net** loss or gain. Carol is owed $3 by Bob, and she owes $5 to Anne. She needs a cash loss of $2 in order to settle all debts. Anne, on the other hand, is owed $5 by Carol and owes $4 to Bob. She must have a **gain** of $1. Since Carol settles all the debts, this $1 must come from Carol, and this is the answer. To finish the transactions, Carol has already given one of the two dollars in her net loss to Anne; she must give the other dollar to Bob. Since Bob is owed $4 and owes $3 for a net gain of $1, the $1 he gets from Carol makes all three of them solvent and happy.

36. 14 minutes

Since we only need to consider two rates, use the shortcut combined work formula where *A* and *B* represent the two rates.

$$\frac{AB}{A+B} = \frac{50 \times 20}{50 + 20} = \frac{1,000}{70} = 14.3 \text{ hours}$$

14.3 rounded to the nearest whole number is 14.

37. $2.47

Calculate separately the amount of usable beef, and the price at which he must sell all the beef to make a 25% profit, then divide the total price by the number of kilograms of usable beef.

Usable beef: he buys 240 kilograms, but 20% of this is unusable. This means the remainder, 80% of the beef, is usable. $80\% = \frac{4}{5}$, so $\frac{4}{5} \times 240 = 4 \times 48 = 192$. So he can sell 192 kilograms.

Total price: he wants a 25% profit. Since he paid $380 for the beef, he must sell it for 25% more than $380, or 125% of $380. $125\% = \frac{5}{4}$, so he has to sell it for $\frac{5}{4} \times \$380 = \$475$.

Price per kilogram: divide the total price ($475) by the number of kilograms (192):

```
          2.47
     192)475.00
         384
         910
         768
        1420
        1344
          76
```

The approximate price is $2.47 per pound.

38. $1.75

Since the vending machine dispenses gumballs in a regular cycle of 10 colors, there are exactly 9 other gumballs dispensed between each pair of gumballs of the same color. For example, gumballs 1 and 11 must be the same color, as must gumballs 2 and 12, 42 and 52, etc. To get 3 gumballs all of the same color, we get 1 of the chosen color, then 9 of another color before another of the chosen color, then 9 of another color before the third of the chosen color. That's a total of $1 + 9 + 1 + 9 + 1 = 21$ gumballs to get 3 matching ones. Since each quarter buys 3 gumballs, and we need 21 gumballs in all, we have to spend $21 \div 3 = 7$ quarters to get 3 matching gumballs; $7 \times 25¢$ = $1.75.

39. 450

In our ten-team league, each team plays the other nine teams 10 times each. $9 \times 10 = 90$, so each team plays 90 games. Since there are ten different teams, and $10 \times 90 = 900$, a total of 900 games are played by the ten teams. But this counts each game twice, since it counts when team A plays team B as one game and when team B plays team A as another game. But they're the same game! So, we must halve the total to take into account the fact that two teams play each game. $\frac{900}{2} = 450$. So 450 games are played in total.

40. $n - 4$

There are n people ahead of Eleanor in line. One of them is Henry. Three more of them are in front of Henry (since Henry is fourth in line). So that makes 4 people who are **not** behind Henry. All the rest, or $n - 4$, are behind Henry and in front of Eleanor, so $n - 4$ is our answer.

Chapter 6:
Data Sufficiency

About a third of the points available in the math section of the GMAT CAT appear in this format. The rest of the questions are in Problem Solving format. These questions ask you to solve a math problem and then look for the answer choice that matches your solution. But in Data Sufficiency you don't care about the solution to the question asked in the stem; you just need to decide whether you can answer it. As a result, most Data Sufficiency questions require little or no calculation. They're designed to be answered more quickly than Problem Solving questions, even though most people find them harder at first. It just takes a little practice to become comfortable with the format.

Data Sufficiency questions have a fixed format. The answer choices are the same for all Data Sufficiency questions. You're given a question stem followed by two statements that, taken together or separately, may or may not be sufficient to answer the question in the stem. You have to choose one of five options about the two statements.

Remember this: If a question asks for the value of a variable, for example x, and a statement leads you to an answer such as "$x = 2$ or $x = 5$", this statement alone is *not* sufficient. In this case, it must be possible to identify a *single* value of x in order for a statement to be sufficient.

DATA SUFFICIENCY—DIRECTIONS

Directions: In each of the following problems, a question is followed by two statements containing certain data. You are to determine whether the data provided by the statements are sufficient to answer the question. Choose the correct answer based upon the statements' data, your knowledge of mathematics, and your familiarity with everyday facts (such as the number of minutes in an hour or cents in a dollar). You must indicate whether:

- ◯ Statement (1) <u>by</u> <u>itself</u> is sufficient to answer the question, but statement (2) by itself is not;
- ◯ Statement (2) <u>by</u> <u>itself</u> is sufficient to answer the question, but statement (1) by itself is not;
- ◯ Statements (1) and (2) <u>taken</u> <u>together</u> are sufficient to answer the question, even though <u>neither</u> statement <u>by</u> <u>itself</u> is sufficient;
- ◯ <u>Either</u> statement <u>by</u> <u>itself</u> is sufficient to answer the question;
- ◯ Statements (1) and (2) <u>taken</u> <u>together</u> are <u>not</u> sufficient to answer the question.

Note: Diagrams accompanying problems agree with information given in the questions, but may not agree with additional information given in statements (1) and (2).

All numbers used are real numbers.

Example:

$$A \qquad B \qquad C$$

What is the length of segment *AC*?

(1) *B* is the midpoint of *AC*.

(2) *AB* = 5

Explanation: Statement (1) tells you that *B* is the midpoint of *AC*, so *AB* = *BC* and *AC* = 2*AB* = 2*BC*. Since statement (1) does not give a value for *AB* or *BC*, you cannot answer the question using statement (1) alone. Statement (2) says that *AB* = 5. Since statement (2) does not give you a value for *BC*, the question cannot be answered by statement (2) alone. Using both statements together you can find a value for both *AB* and *BC*; therefore you can find *AC*, so the answer to the problem is choice **(C)**.

THE KAPLAN THREE-STEP METHOD FOR DATA SUFFICIENCY

Example: Team *X* won 40 basketball games. What percent of its basketball games did Team *X* win?

(1) Team *X* played the same number of basketball games as Team *Y*.

(2) Team *Y* won 45 games, representing 62.5 percent of the basketball games it played.

1. Focus on the question stem.

Decipher the question stem quickly and think about what information is needed to answer it. Do you need a formula? Do you need to set up an equation? Do you need to know the value of a variable?

The sample question involves percents. (Hint: Percent × Whole = Part.) You're given the part (the number of games team *X* won) and asked for the percent (that is, the percentage of its games that team *X* won). What do you need? The whole—the total number of games team *X* played.

2. Look at each statement separately.

Remember, while determining the sufficiency of a particular statement, you must not carry over the other statement's information.

3. Look at both statements in combination only if necessary.

Proceed to step 3 only when statements (1) and (2) are both insufficient. This happens less than half the time. Note that if you reach this point on a problem, the answer must be either **(C)** or **(E)**. When considering the two statements together, simply treat them and the stimulus as one long problem and ask yourself: Can it be solved? *Stop as soon as you know if it can be solved! Don't carry out any unnecessary calculation.*

In the example problem, you will need statement (2) to determine the total number of games that team *Y* played. You will also need statement (1) to know that this is the same number of total games that team *X* played. Therefore, the answer to this example problem is choice **(C)**.

DATA SUFFICIENCY—PRACTICE TEST ONE

45 minutes—25 Questions

Choose the appropriate answer to each question from the answer choices at the top of the page.

(A) Statement (1) <u>by</u> <u>itself</u> is sufficient to answer the question, but statement (2) by itself is not;
(B) Statement (2) <u>by</u> <u>itself</u> is sufficient to answer the question, but statement (1) by itself is not;
(C) Statements (1) and (2) <u>taken</u> <u>together</u> are sufficient to answer the question, even though <u>neither</u> statement <u>by</u> <u>itself</u> is sufficient;
(D) <u>Either</u> statement <u>by</u> <u>itself</u> is sufficient to answer the question;
(E) Statements (1) and (2) <u>taken</u> <u>together</u> are <u>not</u> sufficient to answer the question.

1. Whose morning commute takes more time, Bob's or Nancy's?

   (1) Bob and Nancy do a crossword puzzle together on the morning train.

   (2) Nancy always arrives at her office five minutes before Bob arrives at his office.

   (A)   (B)   (C)   (D)   (E)

2. What is the selling price of a radio after its original price is reduced by 20 percent?

   (1) The price before the reduction was $120.

   (2) The price after the reduction is $24 less than the price before the reduction.

   (A)   (B)   (C)   (D)   (E)

3. Is $x > y$?
   (1) $x - y > 0$
   (2) $x + y > 0$

   (A)   (B)   (C)   (D)   (E)

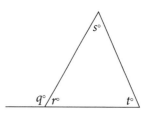

4. What is the value of q if $s = 50$?

   (1) $q > r$
   (2) $t = 80$

   (A)   (B)   (C)   (D)   (E)

5. What is the average production cost of a single x-car?

   (1) A total of 100 x-cars and 100 y-cars cost $2.2 million to produce.

   (2) The average x-car costs $2,000 more to produce than the average y-car.

   (A)   (B)   (C)   (D)   (E)

6. What is the value of x?

   (1) $x^2 - 6 = -x$
   (2) $x^2 = 4$

   (A)   (B)   (C)   (D)   (E)

(A) Statement (1) <u>by</u> <u>itself</u> is sufficient to answer the question, but statement (2) by itself is not;

(B) Statement (2) <u>by</u> <u>itself</u> is sufficient to answer the question, but statement (1) by itself is not;

(C) Statements (1) and (2) <u>taken</u> <u>together</u> are sufficient to answer the question, even though <u>neither</u> statement <u>by</u> <u>itself</u> is sufficient;

(D) <u>Either</u> statement <u>by</u> <u>itself</u> is sufficient to answer the question;

(E) Statements (1) and (2) <u>taken</u> <u>together</u> are <u>not</u> sufficient to answer the question.

7. Which does a rancher have a greater number of, cows or sheep?

   (1) The number of cows he has is less than 5 times the number of sheep he has.

   (2) One-fifth of the number of sheep he has is less than the number of cows he has.

     (A)   (B)   (C)   (D)   (E)

8. Is 6 a factor of $n + 3$?

   (1) n is even and divisible by 3.

   (2) n is divisible by 6.

     (A)   (B)   (C)   (D)   (E)

9. What is the average score of the bowlers in a bowling tournament?

   (1) Seventy percent of the bowlers average 120 and the other 30 percent average 140.

   (2) The 300 bowlers in the tournament all bowled 3 games.

     (A)   (B)   (C)   (D)   (E)

10. If 60 percent of the employees at Company X are female, does Company X have more than 100 female employees?

   (1) Company X has more than 150 employees.

   (2) Company X has 74 more female employees than male employees.

     (A)   (B)   (C)   (D)   (E)

11. What is the area of the figure above formed by a square and four semicircles?

   (1) The perimeter of the figure is 12π.

   (2) The perimeter of the square is 24.

     (A)   (B)   (C)   (D)   (E)

12. Does the average (arithmetic mean) of a, b, and c equal c?

   (1) $c - a = c + b$

   (2) $c = 0$

     (A)   (B)   (C)   (D)   (E)

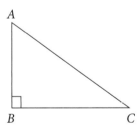

13. In $\triangle ABC$ above, what is the length of segment AB?

   (1) $AC = \sqrt{2}$

   (2) $AB = BC$

     (A)   (B)   (C)   (D)   (E)

(A) Statement (1) <u>by itself</u> is sufficient to answer the question, but statement (2) by itself is not;
(B) Statement (2) <u>by itself</u> is sufficient to answer the question, but statement (1) by itself is not;
(C) Statements (1) and (2) <u>taken together</u> are sufficient to answer the question, even though <u>neither</u> statement <u>by itself</u> is sufficient;
(D) <u>Either</u> statement <u>by itself</u> is sufficient to answer the question;
(E) Statements (1) and (2) <u>taken together</u> are <u>not</u> sufficient to answer the question.

14. Five years ago at laboratory B, the ratio of doctorate to nondoctorate researchers was 2 : 3. If no researchers have resigned, what is the current ratio?

    (1) In the last five years, twice as many doctorates were hired as nondoctorates.

    (2) 50 doctorates were hired during the last five years.

    (A)   (B)   (C)   (D)   (E)

15. In a certain country, the retail price includes a value added tax of $12\frac{1}{2}$ percent of the sum of the wholesale cost and the markup of an item. If the value added tax on a certain jacket is 6 shillings, what is the wholesale cost of a jacket in shillings?

    (1) The markup represents 50 percent of the wholesale cost.

    (2) The markup of the jacket is 16 shillings.

    (A)   (B)   (C)   (D)   (E)

16. If the ratio of integers a, b, and c is 1 : 2 : 3, what is the value of $a + b + c$?

    (1) $c - a = 8$

    (2) $b - a = 4$

    (A)   (B)   (C)   (D)   (E)

17. Every student graduating from Burgerville College is either a 4-year student or a transfer student. If Burgerville is graduating an equal number of 4-year students and transfer students, what fraction of the students who graduate with honors are transfer students?

    (1) Of the 700 transfer students graduating, 300 are graduating with honors.

    (2) Fifty percent more transfer students than 4-year students are graduating with honors.

    (A)   (B)   (C)   (D)   (E)

18. What is greater, x or $\frac{1}{x}$?

    (1) $4x^2 = 1$

    (2) $\left(x - \frac{1}{2}\right)(x + 2) = 0$

    (A)   (B)   (C)   (D)   (E)

19. In a certain law firm there are five senior partners and five junior partners, and all senior partners receive bonuses greater than those of the junior partners. Does senior partner Johnson receive the largest bonus of the lawyers at the firm?

    (1) Johnson receives a bonus greater than twice the average bonus for all the senior partners.

    (2) All partners receive some bonus, and Mr. Johnson receives five times the average given to all the partners.

    (A)   (B)   (C)   (D)   (E)

KAPLAN

(A)   Statement (1) <u>by itself</u> is sufficient to answer the question, but statement (2) by itself is not;
(B)   Statement (2) <u>by itself</u> is sufficient to answer the question, but statement (1) by itself is not;
(C)   Statements (1) and (2) <u>taken together</u> are sufficient to answer the question, even though <u>neither</u> statement <u>by itself</u> is sufficient;
(D)   <u>Either</u> statement <u>by itself</u> is sufficient to answer the question;
(E)   Statements (1) and (2) <u>taken together</u> are <u>not</u> sufficient to answer the question.

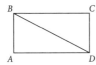

20.   What is the perimeter of rectangle *ABCD*?

   (1)   Diagonal *BD* has length 10.

   (2)   *BDC* has measure 30°.

   (A)   (B)   (C)   (D)   (E)

21.   A bag holds 3 gold rings, 7 silver rings, and 9 bronze rings. If John picks rings from the bag, does he pick more bronze rings than silver rings?

   (1)   John picks 15 rings.

   (2)   John picks 3 gold rings.

   (A)   (B)   (C)   (D)   (E)

22.   What is the sum of 5 evenly spaced integers?

   (1)   The middle integer is zero.

   (2)   Exactly 2 of the integers are negative.

   (A)   (B)   (C)   (D)   (E)

23.   Is quadrilateral *ABCD* a rectangle?

   (1)   The area of Δ*ABD* is one-half the area of *ABCD*.

   (2)   The area of Δ*ABC* is one-half the area of *ABCD*.

   (A)   (B)   (C)   (D)   (E)

24.   *S* is a set of positive integers such that if integer *x* is a member of *S*, then both x^2 and x^3 are also in *S*. If the only member of *S* that is neither the square nor the cube of another member of *S* is called the source integer, is 8 in *S*?

   (1)   4 is in *S* and is not the source integer.

   (2)   64 is in *S* and is not the source integer.

   (A)   (B)   (C)   (D)   (E)

25.   A piece of paper in the shape of an isosceles right triangle is cut along a line parallel to the hypotenuse of the triangle, leaving a smaller triangular piece. If the area of the triangle was 25 square inches before the cut, what is the new area of the triangle?

   (1)   The cut is made 2 inches from the hypotenuse.

   (2)   There was a 40 percent decrease in the length of the hypotenuse of the triangle.

   (A)   (B)   (C)   (D)   (E)

DATA SUFFICIENCY—PRACTICE TEST TWO

45 minutes—25 Questions

Choose the appropriate answer to each question from the answer choices at the top of the page.

(A) Statement (1) <u>by</u> <u>itself</u> is sufficient to answer the question, but statement (2) by itself is not;

(B) Statement (2) <u>by</u> <u>itself</u> is sufficient to answer the question, but statement (1) by itself is not;

(C) Statements (1) and (2) <u>taken</u> <u>together</u> are sufficient to answer the question, even though <u>neither</u> statement <u>by</u> <u>itself</u> is sufficient;

(D) <u>Either</u> statement <u>by</u> <u>itself</u> is sufficient to answer the question;

(E) Statements (1) and (2) <u>taken</u> <u>together</u> are <u>not</u> sufficient to answer the question.

1. What is the distance between City A and City B?

 (1) A nonstop train travels from City A to City B in 4 hours traveling at a maximum speed of 100 miles per hour.

 (2) A local train that makes 5 stops takes 7 hours to make the same run.

 (A)   (B)   (C)   (D)   (E)

2. If x is an integer, what is the value of x?

 (1) $14 < 2x < 18$

 (2) $5 < x < 10$

 (A)   (B)   (C)   (D)   (E)

3. Is the sum of five consecutive integers odd?

 (1) The first number is odd.

 (2) The average (arithmetic mean) of the five numbers is odd.

 (A)   (B)   (C)   (D)   (E)

4. What is the value of the fraction $\dfrac{x}{y}$?

 (1) $x - y = 14$

 (2) $2x = 5y$

 (A)   (B)   (C)   (D)   (E)

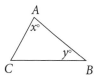

5. What is the length of side AC of triangle ABC?

 (1) $AB = 13$ and $BC = 5$

 (2) $x + y = 90$

 (A)   (B)   (C)   (D)   (E)

6. If y equals 75 percent of x, what is the value of y?

 (1) $x > 150$

 (2) $x - y = 74$

 (A)   (B)   (C)   (D)   (E)

7. In the figure above, does $a = b$?

 (1) $x = y$

 (2) $c = x$

 (A)   (B)   (C)   (D)   (E)

KAPLAN

(A) Statement (1) <u>by</u> <u>itself</u> is sufficient to answer the question, but statement (2) by itself is not;

(B) Statement (2) <u>by</u> <u>itself</u> is sufficient to answer the question, but statement (1) by itself is not;

(C) Statements (1) and (2) <u>taken</u> <u>together</u> are sufficient to answer the question, even though <u>neither</u> statement <u>by</u> <u>itself</u> is sufficient;

(D) <u>Either</u> statement <u>by</u> <u>itself</u> is sufficient to answer the question;

(E) Statements (1) and (2) <u>taken</u> <u>together</u> are <u>not</u> sufficient to answer the question.

8. If x and y are positive integers, is xy evenly divisible by 4?

(1) $y + 2$ is divisible by 4.

(2) $x - 2$ is divisible by 4.

(A)   (B)   (C)   (D)   (E)

9. What is the price of five apples and five pears?

(1) Two apples and ten pears cost $0.90.

(2) Two apples and two pears cost $0.50.

(A)   (B)   (C)   (D)   (E)

10. If Joe and Sam can complete a job in 2 hours working together, what fraction of the job was done by Joe?

(1) If Joe had worked alone, he would have completed the job in 3 hours.

(2) Sam did one-third of the job.

(A)   (B)   (C)   (D)   (E)

11. In Papersville, 6,000 people read at least one of the two papers, the Herald or the Tribune. How many people read both newspapers?

(1) Of the people in Papersville, 2,000 read the Herald only.

(2) Of the people in Papersville, 2,500 read the Tribune only.

(A)   (B)   (C)   (D)   (E)

12. A certain bread recipe calls for whole wheat flour, white flour, and oat flour in the ratio of $3 : 2 : 1$, respectively. How many cups of oat flour are needed to make a loaf of bread?

(1) A total of 30 cups of whole wheat and white flour are needed to make 3 loaves of bread.

(2) Two more cups of whole wheat flour than white flour are needed for every loaf.

(A)   (B)   (C)   (D)   (E)

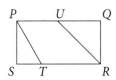

13. What is the area of triangle *PST* shown above?

(1) The area of rectangle *PQRS* is 40.

(2) The area of parallelogram *PTRU* is 32.

(A)   (B)   (C)   (D)   (E)

14. If x and y are positive integers such that $xy = 30$, what is the value of $x + y$?

(1) $1 < \dfrac{x}{y} < 2$

(2) $x > y$

(A)   (B)   (C)   (D)   (E)

(A) Statement (1) <u>by itself</u> is sufficient to answer the question, but statement (2) by itself is not;

(B) Statement (2) <u>by itself</u> is sufficient to answer the question, but statement (1) by itself is not;

(C) Statements (1) and (2) <u>taken together</u> are sufficient to answer the question, even though <u>neither</u> statement <u>by itself</u> is sufficient;

(D) <u>Either</u> statement <u>by itself</u> is sufficient to answer the question;

(E) Statements (1) and (2) <u>taken together</u> are <u>not</u> sufficient to answer the question.

15. How many kiloliters of water are in a reservoir?

(1) If the reservoir were filled to capacity, there would be 430 more kiloliters in the reservoir.

(2) The reservoir is normally 65 percent full.

(A)   (B)   (C)   (D)   (E)

16. During July, a mail order retailer received 3,300 orders for amounts less than \$100, and 1,100 orders for amounts greater than \$100. What was the average size of an order in July?

(1) The gross sales from the orders for amounts less than \$100 equaled the gross sales from the orders for amounts greater than \$100.

(2) The orders for amounts less than \$100 accounted for \$134,000 in gross sales.

(A)   (B)   (C)   (D)   (E)

17. In the figure above, what is the value of r?

(1) $c = 2$

(2) $c = d$

(A)   (B)   (C)   (D)   (E)

18. For all integers n, $n^* = n(n - 1)$. What is the value of x^*?

(1) $x^* = x$

(2) $(x - 1)^* = x - 2$

(A)   (B)   (C)   (D)   (E)

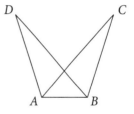

19. In the figure above, what is the ratio of the area of triangle ABC to the area of triangle ABD?

(1) The ratio of the height of triangle ABD to the height of triangle ABC is $4 : 3$.

(2) $AB = 8$

(A)   (B)   (C)   (D)   (E)

20. What is the number of students taking psychology?

(1) Twice as many students take psychology compared to history.

(2) Thirty students take both psychology and history.

(A)   (B)   (C)   (D)   (E)

(A) Statement (1) <u>by</u> <u>itself</u> is sufficient to answer the question, but statement (2) by itself is not;

(B) Statement (2) <u>by</u> <u>itself</u> is sufficient to answer the question, but statement (1) by itself is not;

(C) Statements (1) and (2) <u>taken</u> <u>together</u> are sufficient to answer the question, even though <u>neither</u> statement <u>by</u> <u>itself</u> is sufficient;

(D) <u>Either</u> statement <u>by</u> <u>itself</u> is sufficient to answer the question;

(E) Statements (1) and (2) <u>taken</u> <u>together</u> are <u>not</u> sufficient to answer the question.

21. How many cylindrical cans with a radius of 2 inches and a height of 6 inches can fit into a rectangular box?

    (1) The volume of the box is 230 cubic inches.

    (2) The length of the box is 3 inches.

    (A)   (B)   (C)   (D)   (E)

22. Mr. Daniels deposits $10,000 in a savings certificate earning p percent annual interest compounded quarterly. What is the value of p?

    (1) During the term of the certificate, he earns $18 more than he would if the interest were not compounded.

    (2) He withdraws all the money six months after depositing it.

    (A)   (B)   (C)   (D)   (E)

23. If company Y's profits decreased $1.5 million from last year to this year, what was the percent decrease in profits?

    (1) If the profits had decreased by $2 million, there would have been a 40 percent decrease.

    (2) This year's profits were $3.5 million.

    (A)   (B)   (C)   (D)   (E)

24.

In the given diagram, $\angle ABC$ is a right angle. What is the value of z?

    (1) The value of y is three times the value of z.

    (2) The value of x is $\frac{1}{2}$ the value of z.

    (A)   (B)   (C)   (D)   (E)

25. If A, B, and C are digits between 0 and 9, inclusive, what is the value of B?

    (1) AB
            $+$ BA
            —————
             AAC

    (2) $A = 1$

    (A)   (B)   (C)   (D)   (E)

DATA SUFFICIENCY TEST 1
ANSWERS AND EXPLANATIONS

(A)   Statement (1) <u>by</u> <u>itself</u> is sufficient to answer the question, but statement (2) by itself is not;

(B)   Statement (2) <u>by</u> <u>itself</u> is sufficient to answer the question, but statement (1) by itself is not;

(C)   Statements (1) and (2) <u>taken</u> <u>together</u> are sufficient to answer the question, even though <u>neither</u> statement <u>by itself</u> is sufficient;

(D)   <u>Either</u> statement <u>by</u> <u>itself</u> is sufficient to answer the question;

(E)   Statements (1) and (2) <u>taken</u> <u>together</u> are <u>not</u> sufficient to answer the question.

1. (E)

To find out whose morning commute takes longer, we might expect some information on the distance traveled, the average speed, etc. Unfortunately, we get nothing like that in the two statements. You might find the first few Data Sufficiency questions somewhat bizarre, especially if the information is insufficient.

Statement (1) tells us that Bob and Nancy do a crossword puzzle together on the train. Social of them, but not very helpful. That tells us that they ride the same train, but it does not imply that they ride the same distance on the train, or leave from the same place. Statement (1) is insufficient.

Statement (2) tells us Nancy arrives at her office 5 minutes before Bob arrives at his office; this tells us nothing about when they leave relative to each other. Statement (2) is insufficient; the answer is either choice **(C)** or choice **(E)**. If we put the statements together, we see that Nancy arrives at work before Bob, and that they ride on the same train, but we still don't know who leaves earlier in the morning. If we knew they left together, or that Bob leaves earlier than Nancy, we could answer the question, but we can't with what we're given. Both statements together are insufficient.

2. (D)

To find the selling price after a 20 percent reduction, we need either the amount of the reduction or the original price. Statement (1) tells us the original price; this is sufficient.

Statement (2) tells us the difference between the original price and the sale price; this is the same as telling us the amount of the reduction. Statement (2) is also sufficient.

3. (A)

There is not much we can do here before we look at the statements. Statement (1) tells us that the difference $x - y$ is greater than 0; we can add y to either side of the inequality and get that $x > y$. This answers the question.

Statement (2) tells us that the sum of x and y is positive; this tells us nothing about the relative values of x and y, so statement (2) is insufficient.

4. (B)

We're given the value of s here, and want the value of q. Since q and r are supplementary, they must sum to 180, so if we know r we can find q. If we are given t, then we have two angles of a triangle; we can find the third, and from that find q. So we should be looking for either the value of r or the value of t.

(A) Statement (1) <u>by itself</u> is sufficient to answer the question, but statement (2) by itself is not;

(B) Statement (2) <u>by itself</u> is sufficient to answer the question, but statement (1) by itself is not;

(C) Statements (1) and (2) <u>taken</u> <u>together</u> are sufficient to answer the question, even though <u>neither</u> statement <u>by itself</u> is sufficient;

(D) <u>Either</u> statement <u>by itself</u> is sufficient to answer the question;

(E) Statements (1) and (2) <u>taken</u> <u>together</u> are <u>not</u> sufficient to answer the question.

Statement (1) merely tells us that q is greater than r. This is not sufficient to give us a specific value of q; we can deduce that q must be greater than 90, but that isn't too helpful. Statement (1) is insufficient.
Statement (2) tells us the value of t, which is sufficient. Statement (2) is sufficient.

5. (C)

Here we might look for information on the cost of producing a group of x-cars, and the number of x-cars in the group. Statement (1) tells us the cost of producing a group of x-cars and y-cars; since there is no way to determine how much of the money is due to the x-cars, statement (1) is insufficient.

Statement (2) tells us the difference in cost between producing an x-car and a y-car; this is also insufficient. If we put the statements together, we have the total cost of 100 x-cars and 100 y-cars, and we have the difference in cost between the two types of cars. We can express the information in equation form as

(1) $100x + 100y = 2.2$ million

(2) $x = 2{,}000 + y$

This gives us two equations with two unknowns, which are solvable. Both statements together are sufficient.

6. (C)

We can't predict what kind of information they will give us; there are too many possibilities.
In statement (1), we can move the x to the left side and find that $x^2 + x - 6 = 0$; since this is not a perfect square (it factors into the product $(x + 3)(x - 2) = 0$), there are two solutions to the equation. Statement (1) is not sufficient.

Statement (2) gives us another equation involving the square of x; it too has two solutions ($x = 2$ and $x = -2$) and is not sufficient. Using the two statements together, we find that only one value satisfies both equations (x must be 2). Both statements together are sufficient.

7. (E)

Statement (1) can be translated into algebraic form as $c < 5s$, where c is the number of cows and s is the number of sheep. Unfortunately, we are not asked to compare the number of cows to 5 times the number of sheep. Statement (1) is insufficient.

Statement (2) can be translated as $\frac{1}{5}s < c$; if we multiply both sides by 5, we find that $s < 5c$, and we see that statement (2) is just as useless as statement (1) was. Putting the statements together, we find that each value is less than 5 times the other value, but this is still not enough to tell us which is greater. Both statements together are insufficient.

(A)   Statement (1) <u>by itself</u> is sufficient to answer the question, but statement (2) by itself is not;

(B)   Statement (2) <u>by itself</u> is sufficient to answer the question, but statement (1) by itself is not;

(C)   Statements (1) and (2) <u>taken together</u> are sufficient to answer the question, even though <u>neither</u> statement <u>by itself</u> is sufficient;

(D)   <u>Either</u> statement <u>by itself</u> is sufficient to answer the question;

(E)   Statements (1) and (2) <u>taken together</u> are <u>not</u> sufficient to answer the question.

8. (D)

Suppose 6 *is* a factor of $n + 3$. Then $n + 3$ is a multiple of 6. Since any multiple of 6 is also a multiple of 2 and a multiple of 3, $n + 3$ must be a multiple of both 2 and 3. Then n itself is 3 less than a multiple of 3, which makes n also a multiple of 3, and n is 3 less than a multiple of 2, which makes n an odd number. Now we can go to the statements and see whether this is true.

Statement (1) tells us n is even and divisible by 3. We already determined that for 6 to be a factor of $n + 3$, n must be odd and a multiple of 3. Therefore, statement (1) is sufficient to answer "No" to the question.

Statement (2) tells us n is divisible by 6. Since $n + 3$ is only 3 more than a multiple of 6, 6 cannot be a factor of $n + 3$. The answer again is "No." Statement (2) is also sufficient.

9. (A)

To find the average score, we need the number of bowlers and the sum of their scores. Statement (1) tells us the average scores of two groups, and what fractions of the whole the parts represent. We could use a weighted average here to find the average of the whole group. Statement (1) is sufficient, and the answer is either choice (A) or (D).

Statement (2) tells us how many games each bowler bowled. While this may be of interest to other bowlers out there, this tells us nothing about their scores. Statement (2) is insufficient, and the answer is choice 1.

10. (B)

We know what percent of the employees are female, so if we are given the number of employees, we can determine whether 100 employees are female. In statement (1) we're not given the actual value; only a lower limit. This could be enough, however, since we're not asked for the actual value, only whether it is greater than 100. Since 60 percent of 150 is 90, we only know that there are at least 90 female employees, and statement (1) is insufficient.

Statement (2) tells us the difference between the two parts: the male and female employees. Since we're told in the question stem what percent of the employees are female, we can deduce the percent that are male. We have two parts that together make up the whole, we have the percent each part represents, and we have the actual value of the difference, so we can find any other value we want, including the number of women. Statement (2) is sufficient.

11. (D)

The diameter of each of the semicircles is the same as a side of the square. Both squares and circles are regular figures; knowing almost anything about them is sufficient to tell us everything. Just about anything we're told here about either the square or the semicircles will enable us to find the area of the whole figure.

(A)   Statement (1) <u>by</u> <u>itself</u> is sufficient to answer the question, but statement (2) by itself is not;

(B)   Statement (2) <u>by</u> <u>itself</u> is sufficient to answer the question, but statement (1) by itself is not;

(C)   Statements (1) and (2) <u>taken</u> <u>together</u> are sufficient to answer the question, even though <u>neither</u> statement <u>by</u> <u>itself</u> is sufficient;

(D)   <u>Either</u> statement <u>by</u> <u>itself</u> is sufficient to answer the question;

(E)   Statements (1) and (2) <u>taken</u> <u>together</u> are <u>not</u> sufficient to answer the question.

Statement (1) tells us the perimeter of the figure. The perimeter is made up of four of the semicircles; from the perimeter of the figure we can find the perimeter of each semicircle, from which we can find the diameters and all the areas. Statement (1) is sufficient, and the answer is either choice (A) or (D).

Statement (2) tells us the perimeter of the square; this is sufficient to find the area of the square. The length of a side of the square is the same as a diameter of one of the semicircles, so from the perimeter of the square we can find the area of both the square and the semicircles, which gives us the whole figure. Each statement alone is sufficient.

12. (C)

When will the average of a, b, and c equal c? Think of average in terms of a balance. The three numbers balance at c. If we remove c from the group, it won't change the balance any. Therefore, a and b must also balance at c, and the average of a and b must be c as well. Therefore, the average of a, b, and c equals c only if the average of a and b is c.

We can cancel c from both sides of the equation in statement (1): this leaves us with $-a = b$. If we then add a to both sides, we find that $a + b = 0$. This tells us that the average of a and b is 0, but not whether $c = 0$. We still need to know the value of c to answer the question. Statement (1) is insufficient.

Statement (2) tells us the value of c, but it says nothing about either a or b. It is insufficient, and the answer is either (C) or (E). If we put the statements together, we know the value of $c = 0$, and we know that $a + b = 0$, so we know that the average of a and b equals c. Therefore, both statements together are sufficient.

13. (C)

We know that ABC is a right triangle, but not what specific kind of right triangle. We should look for either the type of triangle and one of the sides, from which we can find the other sides; or the lengths of two of the sides, from which we can use the Pythagorean theorem to find the third side.

Statement (1) tells us the length of one side, but not the side we want. This is insufficient.

From statement (2) we learn that two of the sides are equal. This tells us we have an isosceles right triangle, but we cannot find a particular length without some other length. Statement (2) is also insufficient. Using both statements together, we know ABC is an isosceles right triangle, and we know the length of one side. Using this information we can find the length of any other side. Both statements together are sufficient.

14. (E)

We know the ratio from five years ago and want the ratio now. We're probably going to need some sort of actual values for the number of researchers five years ago and at the present. Statement (1) gives us neither of these; since we don't know any numbers, we don't know how the ratio has been affected. Were 2 new doctorates hired or 200? Statement (1) is insufficient.

(A)   Statement (1) <u>by itself</u> is sufficient to answer the question, but statement (2) by itself is not;

(B)   Statement (2) <u>by itself</u> is sufficient to answer the question, but statement (1) by itself is not;

(C)   Statements (1) and (2) <u>taken together</u> are sufficient to answer the question, even though <u>neither</u> statement <u>by itself</u> is sufficient;

(D)   <u>Either</u> statement <u>by itself</u> is sufficient to answer the question;

(E)   Statements (1) and (2) <u>taken together</u> are <u>not</u> sufficient to answer the question.

Statement (2) at least gives us a number, but we can't get very far with it. We still need to know how many nondoctorates were hired, and how many doctorates there were originally. The statement is insufficient, and the answer is either choice (C) or (E). Using both together, we still don't how many doctorates were there originally. Were there 10 or 100? We need to know that before we can determine the new ratio. Both statements together are insufficient.

15. (D)

The tax is $12\frac{1}{2}$ percent of the sum of the wholesale cost and the markup. Since we know the tax on the jacket, we can find that sum. To find the wholesale cost, we need to know what fraction of the sum is the wholesale cost and what fraction is the markup.

Statement (1) tells us what we need: the markup is one-half of the wholesale cost. Then one-third of the sum is the markup, and two-thirds is the wholesale cost, so we can find the wholesale cost. This is sufficient.

Statement (2) tells us the amount of the markup. Since we know we can find the sum, we can subtract this markup from the sum, and be left with the wholesale cost. This is also sufficient.

16. (D)

Since we know the ratio, finding the value of any of the integers will tell us the value of all of them, from which we can find the sum. Statement (1) tells us the difference of two integers. We know the ratio of a to c, so given their difference we can find their actual values. Statement (1) is sufficient.

Similarly, statement (2) gives us another difference; we can find the actual values from this too. Each statement alone is sufficient.

17. (B)

We need the total number of honors graduates and the number of transfer students graduating with honors. Statement (1) tells us something close to this but very different; it gives us the fraction of transfer students graduating with honors, not the fraction of honors graduates who are transfers. We still need the total number of honors students. Statement (1) is insufficient.

Let x be the number of 4-year students graduating with honors. The number of transfer students graduating with honors must be 50 percent greater than x; in other words, $x + 0.5x$, or $1.5x$. The total number of students who graduate with honors is $1.5x + x = 2.5x$. Then the fraction of students who graduate with honors who are transfer students is $\frac{1.5x}{2.5x} = \frac{1.5}{2.5}$. There is no need to simplify this fraction. Knowing that we can find the fraction required is enough. Statement (2) is sufficient.

(A)   Statement (1) <u>by itself</u> is sufficient to answer the question, but statement (2) by itself is not;

(B)   Statement (2) <u>by itself</u> is sufficient to answer the question, but statement (1) by itself is not;

(C)   Statements (1) and (2) <u>taken</u> <u>together</u> are sufficient to answer the question, even though <u>neither</u> statement <u>by itself</u> is sufficient;

(D)   <u>Either</u> statement <u>by itself</u> is sufficient to answer the question;

(E)   Statements (1) and (2) <u>taken together</u> are <u>not</u> sufficient to answer the question.

18. (B)

A number is greater than its reciprocal if the number is greater than 1, or if it is between 0 and -1. (Never forget negative numbers!) If it is between 0 and 1, or less than -1, then the reciprocal is greater than the number. For instance the reciprocal of $\frac{1}{2}$ is 2, and $2 > \frac{1}{2}$.

Statement (1) gives us an equation for x; if we divide both sides by 4 we find that $x^2 = \frac{1}{4}$. There are two possible values for x: $\frac{1}{2}$ and $-\frac{1}{2}$. If x is $\frac{1}{2}$, then $\frac{1}{x}$ will be greater than x; if x is $-\frac{1}{2}$, then x will be greater than $\frac{1}{x}$. We need more information, and the answer is either choice (B), (C), or (E).

Statement (2) tells us the product of two binomials is zero; therefore, one of the terms is zero. Either $x - \frac{1}{2} = 0$, in which case $x = \frac{1}{2}$; or $x + 2 = 0$, in which case $x = -2$. In either case, though, the reciprocal of x will be greater than x itself. If $x = \frac{1}{2}$, then $\frac{1}{x} = 2$; if $x = -2$, then $\frac{1}{x} = -\frac{1}{2}$. The second statement is sufficient to answer the question.

19. (B)

There isn't much we can do here before we look at the statements. From statement (1) we can deduce that Johnson must receive a larger bonus than at least some of the partners, but not necessarily bigger than all of the other partners. For instance, if Johnson and another senior partner each receive bonuses of $10,000 and the other three each receive bonuses of $1,000 then the average bonus will be $4,600. This fits the statement, but Johnson does not receive the largest bonus. The statement is not sufficient.

Statement (2) is more helpful. To see this, first look at what the sum of the bonuses must be in terms of Johnson's bonus. Johnson's bonus is five times the average bonus of all the other partners. The sum of all the bonuses is the average bonus times the number of bonuses. Here we have 10 partners, so the sum is 10 times the average. But if Johnson's bonus is five times the average, then Johnson has one-half of all the bonus money. How does that help us? Well, the largest bonus anyone other than Johnson could have is the other half of the bonus money—any more and the sum will be more than 10 times the average. But we're told that everyone gets at least some bonus, so no one partner could have the other half of the sum all to him or herself—that would leave nothing for the other partners. Therefore Johnson must have the largest bonus. Statement (2) is sufficient.

(A)   Statement (1) <u>by itself</u> is sufficient to answer the question, but statement (2) by itself is not;

(B)   Statement (2) <u>by itself</u> is sufficient to answer the question, but statement (1) by itself is not;

(C)   Statements (1) and (2) <u>taken together</u> are sufficient to answer the question, even though <u>neither</u> statement <u>by itself</u> is sufficient;

(D)   <u>Either</u> statement <u>by itself</u> is sufficient to answer the question;

(E)   Statements (1) and (2) <u>taken together</u> are <u>not</u> sufficient to answer the question.

20. (C)

To find the perimeter, we need the length and the width. Statement (1) gives us neither, only the length of a diagonal. If *ABCD* were a square, that would be sufficient, but we need more information for a rectangle. Statement (1) alone is insufficient.

Statement (2) gives us the measure of angle *BDC*. This is also insufficient, since it tells us nothing about the lengths. Putting both statements together, we know the length of the diagonal, and we know the measure of angle *BDC*. Since the figure is a rectangle, all the angles are right angles, so Δ*BDC* is a right triangle with a 30 degree angle. The other angle must have measure 60 degrees, making this a 30-60-90 triangle. We know the length of *BD*, which is the hypotenuse of Δ*BDC*, and since we know what kind of triangle it is, we can find the lengths of the other two sides. This gives us the length and width of the rectangle, from which we can find the perimeter. Both statements together are sufficient.

21. (E)

Statement (1) tells us that John picks 15 rings. He could pick more bronze rings than silver rings, but he could also pick all 3 gold rings, all 7 silver rings, and only 5 bronze rings. We need more information.

Statement (2) tells us that John picks 3 gold rings. This by itself tells us nothing about the number of silver or bronze rings, and is not sufficient. Using the statements together, we know that 15 − 3, or 12 of the rings are either silver or bronze, but we still don't know which is greater. Both statements are insufficient.

22. (A)

Whenever you see the term *evenly spaced* you should think of averages. The average of evenly spaced numbers is always the middle number, so to find the sum, we need the average, or the middle term, or some way to find either.

Statement (1) tells us the value of the middle term. This is the same as the average, and is sufficient to tell us the sum.

From statement (2) we know that 2 of the integers are negative. This tells us nothing about the sum of the integers. If we knew they were consecutive integers, we could find the sum from this information, but we don't know that. Statement (2) is insufficient.

23. (E)

A rectangle is a quadrilateral with four right angles, and with diagonals of equal length. Statement (1) tells us that triangle *ABD* has one-half the area of the whole quadrilateral; this implies that *ABD* and *BCD* have the same area. This does not tell us anything about *ABCD*, however. It could be a rectangle, but it could also be a parallelogram.

Statement (2) is just as helpful as statement (1): not very. Here we just use the other diagonal to divide the figure. Using both statements together, we still don't know whether *ABCD* is a rectangle; it could be a parallelogram. Both statements together are insufficient.

(A) Statement (1) <u>by</u> <u>itself</u> is sufficient to answer the question, but statement (2) by itself is not;

(B) Statement (2) <u>by</u> <u>itself</u> is sufficient to answer the question, but statement (1) by itself is not;

(C) Statements (1) and (2) <u>taken</u> <u>together</u> are sufficient to answer the question, even though <u>neither</u> statement <u>by</u> <u>itself</u> is sufficient;

(D) <u>Either</u> statement <u>by</u> <u>itself</u> is sufficient to answer the question;

(E) Statements (1) and (2) <u>taken</u> <u>together</u> are <u>not</u> sufficient to answer the question.

24. (A)

First consider statement (1). If 4 is in *S*, and it is not the source integer, then it must be the square or cube of the source integer. Since 4 is not the cube of any positive integer, and it is the square of 2, 2 must be in *S* and must be the source integer. It follows that if 2 is the source integer, 4 is the square of 2, and 8 is the cube of 2. So 2, 4, and 8 would be in *S*. Statement (1) by itself is sufficient to answer the question.

Now look at statement (2). The statement "64 is in *S* and is not the source integer" must be considered in two cases:

1. If 64 is in *S* because it represents the square of 8, then 8, 64, and 512 are in *S*. In this case, 8 would be in *S*.

    OR

2. If 64 is in *S* because it represents the cube of 4, then we only know for sure that 4, 16, and 64 are in *S*. In this case, we cannot prove that 8 is in *S*. Therefore, statement (2) is insufficient to answer this question.

25. (D)

Here we need a diagram to see what we're doing. We're cutting an isosceles right triangle along a line parallel to the hypotenuse. This leaves us with a smaller triangle, but still an isosceles right triangle. (Since we're cutting parallel to one side, the two triangles are similar.) We know the area before the cut, so if we can find either the line ratio or the area ratio of these similar triangles, we can find the area of the smaller one.

(A)   Statement (1) <u>by itself</u> is sufficient to answer the question, but statement (2) by itself is not;

(B)   Statement (2) <u>by itself</u> is sufficient to answer the question, but statement (1) by itself is not;

(C)   Statements (1) and (2) <u>taken together</u> are sufficient to answer the question, even though <u>neither</u> statement <u>by itself</u> is sufficient;

(D)   <u>Either</u> statement <u>by itself</u> is sufficient to answer the question;

(E)   Statements (1) and (2) <u>taken together</u> are <u>not</u> sufficient to answer the question.

Statement (1) gives us the distance from the hypotenuse of the old triangle to the hypotenuse of the new triangle. Our question stem tells us the area of the original piece of paper was 25 square inches. The area of an isosceles right triangle is $\frac{1}{2} \times$ (the length of a leg)^2 so

$$\frac{1}{2} \times (\text{leg})^2 = 25$$
$$(\text{leg})^2 = 50$$
$$\text{leg} = \sqrt{50} = 5\sqrt{2}$$

The hypotenuse is $\sqrt{2} \times$ (leg), so hypotenuse = $5\sqrt{2} \cdot \sqrt{2}$ or 10. Now think of the hypotenuse as the *base* of the triangle.

$$\text{Area} = \frac{1}{2} \times 10 \times (\text{height})$$
$$25 = \frac{1}{2} \times 10 \times (\text{height})$$
$$5 = \text{height}$$

If the cut is made 2 inches from the hypotenuse, the height of the new triangle is 5 − 2, or 3. This gives us the line ratio of the similar triangles, 5 : 3, and that's enough to find the area ratio, and the area of the smaller triangle in turn. Statement (1) is sufficient.

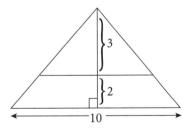

Statement (2) gives us the percent reduction in the length of one side. This is enough to determine the line ratio of the triangles (100% : 60% or 10 : 6 or 5 : 3), so this statement is also sufficient. Each statement alone is sufficient.

DATA SUFFICIENCY TEST 2
ANSWERS AND EXPLANATIONS

(A)   Statement (1) <u>by</u> <u>itself</u> is sufficient to answer the question, but statement (2) by itself is not;

(B)   Statement (2) <u>by</u> <u>itself</u> is sufficient to answer the question, but statement (1) by itself is not;

(C)   Statements (1) and (2) <u>taken</u> <u>together</u> are sufficient to answer the question, even though <u>neither</u> statement <u>by</u> <u>itself</u> is sufficient;

(D)   <u>Either</u> statement <u>by</u> <u>itself</u> is sufficient to answer the question;

(E)   Statements (1) and (2) <u>taken</u> <u>together</u> are <u>not</u> sufficient to answer the question.

1. **(E)**

To find out the distance between the cities, we might look for information such as the time it takes someone to travel between the cities, and the speed at which that someone travels.

Statement (1) tells us the time it takes for a train to make the trip; however, instead of giving us the train's *average* speed, they give us the *maximum* speed. The train could have been traveling at 100 miles per hour only for five minutes, and the rest of the time at 50 miles per hour. Statement (1) is insufficient.

Statement (2) tells us about a local train—again, we have the time for the trip, but are told nothing about the speed. Statement (2) is also insufficient.

2. **(A)**

The first statement tells us that twice *x* is between 14 and 18. If we divide all the terms in the inequality by 2, we are left with $7 < x < 9$. Since *x* is an integer, the only possible value of *x* is 8. Statement (1) is sufficient.

Statement (2) only tells us that *x* is between 5 and 10. There is more than one integer in this range, so the second statement is insufficient.

3. **(D)**

What do we know about an odd number of consecutive integers? We know the average of the integers is the middle term. Since we have 5 integers here, the middle term is one of the integers. The sum of the terms is the average times the number of terms, or here 5 times the middle integer. The product of two odd numbers is odd, so the sum will be odd only if the middle integer is odd.

Statement (1) tells us the first term is odd. That means the second term must be even, and the third term is odd. The third term is the middle integer; that is odd, so the sum must be odd. This is sufficient.

Statement (2) tells us the average (the middle integer) is odd; we've already seen that that is sufficient. Either statement alone is sufficient.

4. **(B)**

To find the value of the fraction we need either the individual values of *x* and *y*, or the ratio of *x* to *y*. Statement (1) does not give us the values, nor can we manipulate the equation to find the ratio of *x* to *y*. It is not sufficient.

Statement (2) does not give us the individual values either, but we can manipulate the equation to find the ratio. If we divide both sides by *y*, we find that $\frac{2x}{y} = 5$, and then dividing by 2 will leave us with just $\frac{x}{y} = \frac{5}{2}$. Statement (2) is sufficient.

(A)   Statement (1) <u>by</u> <u>itself</u> is sufficient to answer the question, but statement (2) by itself is not;

(B)   Statement (2) <u>by</u> <u>itself</u> is sufficient to answer the question, but statement (1) by itself is not;

(C)   Statements (1) and (2) <u>taken</u> <u>together</u> are sufficient to answer the question, even though <u>neither</u> statement <u>by</u> <u>itself</u> is sufficient;

(D)   <u>Either</u> statement <u>by</u> <u>itself</u> is sufficient to answer the question;

(E)   Statements (1) and (2) <u>taken</u> <u>together</u> are <u>not</u> sufficient to answer the question.

5. (C)

To find the length of the side, we need some information about the triangle, and some information about the other sides. Statement (1) tells us the lengths of two of the sides, but nothing about what kind of triangle it is. The most we can deduce is a range of values for *AC*, which is not what we want. Statement (1) is insufficient.

Statement (2) gives us the sum of two of the angles. We can deduce from this that the other angle must have measure 180 − 90, or 90 degrees; therefore, *ABC* is a right triangle. However, statement (2) tells us nothing about any side lengths; it is insufficient. Using both statements together we know we have a right triangle, we know which angle is the right angle, and we know the lengths of two of the sides. We can use the Pythagorean theorem to find the length of the third side. Both statements together are sufficient.

6. (B)

We have a percent; to determine the value of *y* we need an actual value. Statement (1) tells us that *x* is greater than 150; this is not sufficient to tell us a specific value of *y*, only a minimum value. Statement (1) is insufficient.

Statement (2) gives us an actual value: the difference between *x* and *y*. Since *y* = 75% of *x*, the difference between *y* and *x* must be 100% − 75%, or 25% of *x*. Since we know this difference, we can find the value of *x*, from which we can find the value of *y*. Statement (2) is sufficient.

7. (C)

If the two lines are parallel, then *a* and *b* will be equal. Statement (1) doesn't tell us whether the lines are parallel; if *x* and *y* are equal we know they must each be right angles, in which case *a* is also a right angle, but that tells us nothing about whether the two lines are parallel. Statement (1) is insufficient.

Statement (2) is not sufficient either. The angles *x* and *c* could each be 60 degree angles, for instance, in which case the lines would not be parallel; or they could be 90 degree angles, in which case the lines would be parallel. Statement (2) is also insufficient. Using both statements together, we find that *x* and *y* are right angles, as are *a* and *c*. Since *c* is a right angle, *b* must be a right angle, and *a* and *b* are equal. Both statements together are sufficient.

8. (C)

The product of *xy* is divisible by 4 if the factors of 4 are also factors of *xy*. There are two factors of 4 : 2 and 4. So 4 will be a factor of the product if it is a factor of either *x* or *y*, or if 2 is a factor of both *x* and *y*.

Statement (1) tells us that *y* + 2 is divisible by 4; this is the same as saying 4 is a factor of *y* + 2. Then *y* must be an even number; however, it is not divisible by 4—it is 2 less than a multiple of 4. Statement (1) is insufficient.

(A) Statement (1) <u>by</u> <u>itself</u> is sufficient to answer the question, but statement (2) by itself is not;

(B) Statement (2) <u>by</u> <u>itself</u> is sufficient to answer the question, but statement (1) by itself is not;

(C) Statements (1) and (2) <u>taken</u> <u>together</u> are sufficient to answer the question, even though <u>neither</u> statement <u>by</u> <u>itself</u> is sufficient;

(D) <u>Either</u> statement <u>by</u> <u>itself</u> is sufficient to answer the question;

(E) Statements (1) and (2) <u>taken</u> <u>together</u> are <u>not</u> sufficient to answer the question.

Statement (2) is similar: if $x - 2$ is divisible by 4, then x itself is even, and is not a multiple of 4. Statement (2) is insufficient. Using both statements together, we know that both x and y are even numbers; therefore, they each have 2 as a factor. This is enough to tell us their product is evenly divisible by 4. Both statements together are sufficient.

9. (B)

We need either the price per apple and the price per pear, or some other information that will allow us to find the price of 5 apples and 5 pears. Statement (1) gives us neither; we cannot find the individual cost per fruit, nor can we manipulate the information to find the cost of 5 apples and 5 pears.

We can manipulate statement (2) in such a way: if 2 apples and 2 pears cost $0.50, then 1 apple and 1 pear will cost one-half as much, or $0.25, and 5 apples and 5 pears will cost five times as much as *that*. Statement (2) is sufficient.

10. (D)

We know the time it takes Joe and Sam together to finish a job, so we might look for the time it takes Joe to complete the job alone, or some information that relates Joe's productivity to Sam's.

Statement (1) gives us Joe's time alone; from that we can find what fraction of the job he did. Statement (1) is sufficient.

Statement (2) tells us what fraction Sam did; Joe must have done the rest of the job, so statement (2) is also sufficient. Each statement alone is sufficient.

11. (C)

We're given the total number who read at least one of the two papers. Keep in mind that this includes people who read both papers. If we're given the number who read each of the two papers, we can find the number who read both.

Statement (1) gives us the number who read only the Herald. But we can't find what we want: the number who read both papers. The first statement is insufficient.

Statement (2) is similar to statement (1); it too gives us information on only one paper, while we need information on both. If we use both statements together, we have the number reading each, and we have the total number. If we add each of the individual numbers we get 4,500 total subscriptions. Since a total of 6,000 people subscribe to these papers, the difference or $6,000 - 4,500$ represents the duplication; the people who read both papers. This is exactly what we want. Both statements together are sufficient.

12. (D)

We have a three-term ratio, and want the value of one of the parts. If we are given the values of any of the parts, or of the sum of some of the parts, we can find all the terms in the ratio. Statement (1) gives us the total of wheat and white needed for 3 loaves; we can find the total needed for 1 loaf, and from that find the amount of oat flour needed. Statement (1) is sufficient.

(A) Statement (1) <u>by itself</u> is sufficient to answer the question, but statement (2) by itself is not;

(B) Statement (2) <u>by itself</u> is sufficient to answer the question, but statement (1) by itself is not;

(C) Statements (1) and (2) <u>taken together</u> are sufficient to answer the question, even though <u>neither</u> statement <u>by itself</u> is sufficient;

(D) <u>Either</u> statement <u>by itself</u> is sufficient to answer the question;

(E) Statements (1) and (2) <u>taken together</u> are <u>not</u> sufficient to answer the question.

Statement (2) gives us the difference between the amounts for two of the terms in the ratio; this too is sufficient to tell us each of the individual terms in the ratio. Statement (2) is also sufficient.

13. (C)

We are given a figure, quadrilateral *PQRS*, but we do not know what kind of quadrilateral it is. To find the area of *PST* we need the height and the base of the triangle, but keep in mind that the length of *QR* is not necessarily the same as that of *PS*, and that *PS* is not necessarily the height of the triangle.

We do learn in statement (1) that the figure is a rectangle, and we are given the area of the rectangle. This tells us nothing about the area of one part of the rectangle, the triangle. This is insufficient.

Statement (2) gives us information on part of the large quadrilateral: *PTRU* is a parallelogram. We know the area of the parallelogram, but this tells us nothing about the triangle. Statement (2) is also insufficient. If we use both statements together, a clearer picture results. Since *PTRU* is a parallelogram, *PT* and *UR* are of the same length, as are *PU* and *TR*. Since *PQRS* is a rectangle, *PQ* and *SR* are of equal length, and *PS* and *QR* are equal. So what we have is parallelogram *PTRU*, and triangles *PST* and *RQU*. The triangles have sides of equal length, so they are congruent and have equal area. The sum of their areas is the difference of the area of the rectangle and the area of the parallelogram; dividing this by 2 gives us the area of one triangle. Both statements together are sufficient.

14. (A)

We know the product of the integers; to find the sum, it would be helpful to find the individual values. What are the factor pairs of 30? 1 and 30, 2 and 15, 3 and 10, 5 and 6. We know that *x* and *y* make up one of these factor pairs; we can only hope the statements will pin them down further.

Statement (1) tells us the quotient $\frac{x}{y}$ is between 1 and 2. Only one of the factor pairs (5 and 6) is a possibility. Statement (1) is sufficient.

Statement (2) tells us *x* is greater than *y*; this doesn't pin down the factor pair any further. Statement (2) is insufficient.

15. (E)

Statement (1) tells us what the reservoir would look like if it were full. This doesn't tell us how many liters are currently in the reservoir.

Statement (2) tells us the reservoir is normally 65 percent full; also not very helpful. Using both statements together, we know how much more it would contain if it were full, and what percent of the reservoir is usually full. Take careful note of the word "normally" in statement (2); this does not imply that the reservoir is currently at its "normal" state. For all we know, the reservoir is at 98% of capacity now; or it could be almost empty. We need more information to find the current contents. Both statements together are insufficient.

(A)   Statement (1) <u>by</u> <u>itself</u> is sufficient to answer the question, but statement (2) by itself is not;

(B)   Statement (2) <u>by</u> <u>itself</u> is sufficient to answer the question, but statement (1) by itself is not;

(C)   Statements (1) and (2) <u>taken</u> <u>together</u> are sufficient to answer the question, even though <u>neither</u> statement <u>by</u> <u>itself</u> is sufficient;

(D)   <u>Either</u> statement <u>by</u> <u>itself</u> is sufficient to answer the question;

(E)   Statements (1) and (2) <u>taken</u> <u>together</u> are <u>not</u> sufficient to answer the question.

16. (C)

To find the average order, we need the number of orders and the total income. We know the number of orders for amounts less than $100 and the number of orders for amounts greater than $100; the total number of orders is just the sum of these two. We still need the total income.

Statement (1) tells us the totals from two types of sales were equal; however we still need the actual numbers. This is not sufficient.

Statement (2) gives us the income for orders for amounts less than $100; this still leaves us in the dark about the income for orders for amounts greater than $100. Using the statements together, we know the two types of sales account for equal income, we know the income from one type, and we know the total number of sales. This is sufficient to find the average sale. Both statements together are sufficient.

17. (B)

We know the line passes through the origin; to find the measure of the angle we need some information about the line; specifically its equation. Statement (1) tells us the value of c; we still need the value of d to find anything about the line. Statement (1) is insufficient.

Statement (2) tells us the coordinates of the point are equal; this is enough to tell us the line has the equation $y = x$. Then the point (c, d) is the same distance from the x-axis as it is from the y-axis; we could drop a perpendicular from the point to the x-axis and get an isosceles right triangle. This tells us the angle is a 45 degree angle. Statement (2) is sufficient.

18. (B)

The symbol means that we take the product of the number and one less than the number. Statement (1) tells us that the symbol of x gives us x. If we plug x into the equation, we find that:

$$x^* = x(x - 1) = x^2 - x.$$

This equals x, so we get the equation $x^2 - x = x$. This has two solutions: x could be 0 or it could be 2. Statement (1) is insufficient.

Statement (2) gives us the function for $(x - 1)$. If we plug in $(x - 1)$ for n in the original equation, we find:

$$(x - 1)^* = (x - 1)(x - 2).$$

We're told this equals $x - 2$, so

$$x - 2 = (x - 1)(x - 2).$$

Don't solve for x! Since some number times $(x - 2)$ leaves us with $x - 2$, we know that either $(x - 2) = 0$, or $(x - 1) = 1$. In either case we find that $x = 2$. Statement (2) is sufficient.

(A)   Statement (1) <u>by</u> <u>itself</u> is sufficient to answer the question, but statement (2) by itself is not;

(B)   Statement (2) <u>by</u> <u>itself</u> is sufficient to answer the question, but statement (1) by itself is not;

(C)   Statements (1) and (2) <u>taken</u> <u>together</u> are sufficient to answer the question, even though <u>neither</u> statement <u>by</u> <u>itself</u> is sufficient;

(D)   <u>Either</u> statement <u>by</u> <u>itself</u> is sufficient to answer the question;

(E)   Statements (1) and (2) <u>taken</u> <u>together</u> are <u>not</u> sufficient to answer the question.

19. (A)

The two triangles share a base; since the area is one-half the product of the base and height, if we find the ratio of the heights of the triangles, we know the ratio of the areas. Statement (1) tells us exactly what we need: the ratio of the heights. Therefore it is sufficient.

Statement (2) only gives us the length of the base; this is insufficient.

20. (E)

The number of psychology students is the number of students taking both psychology and history plus the number of students taking only psychology. Statement (1) tells us the ratio of psychology students to history students; this tells us nothing about the actual numbers.

Statement (2) tells us how many take both; this tells us little about the total number in psychology. (Some students may take psychology but not history.) Putting both statements together, we still have no way of finding the number of psychology-only students. Both statements together are insufficient.

21. (B)

The volume of a can is not relevant here; what is relevant is realizing that to find the number of cans that can fit in we need the actual dimensions of the box. Statement (1) doesn't give us the dimensions, only the volume: this is insufficient.

Statement (2) gives us the length; this would ordinarily be insufficient, except that since the length of the box is smaller than either the diameter or the height of the can, we can determine that *none* of the cans can fit into the box; it is too narrow. Statement (2) is sufficient.

22. (C)

To find the value of p, we need the amount of the interest, and the length of time that interest was earned. Statement (1) gives us some information about the interest, but since we don't know how long the *term of the certificate* is, we cannot find the interest from statement (1).

Statement (2) gives us the term of the certificate, but it gives us no information about the interest, so it is insufficient. If we use both statements together, we know how much less the certificate would earn if it were not compounded, and we know how long the money was earning this interest. We know the interest accrued in the first quarter is the same regardless of whether the interest is compounded; the difference is the second quarter interest. This extra interest is one-quarter of p percent of the interest earned in the first quarter. The first quarter interest is one-quarter of p percent of $10,000; therefore,

$$18 = \frac{p}{4} \text{ percent of } \frac{p}{4} \text{ percent of } \$10,000$$

This is a bit of a nasty equation, but we can solve it for p. Both statements together are sufficient.

(A)   Statement (1) <u>by itself</u> is sufficient to answer the question, but statement (2) by itself is not;

(B)   Statement (2) <u>by itself</u> is sufficient to answer the question, but statement (1) by itself is not;

(C)   Statements (1) and (2) <u>taken together</u> are sufficient to answer the question, even though <u>neither</u> statement <u>by itself</u> is sufficient;

(D)   <u>Either</u> statement <u>by itself</u> is sufficient to answer the question;

(E)   Statements (1) and (2) <u>taken together</u> are <u>not</u> sufficient to answer the question.

23. (D)

We know the amount of decrease; to find the percent decrease we need the original whole. Statement (1) doesn't tell us the original whole directly, but since it does give us another part and percent, we can find the whole. Statement (1) is sufficient.

Statement (2) tells us this year's profits; using addition we can find last year's profits, which is the original whole. Statement (2) is sufficient.

24. (C)

Statement (1) compares the values of y and z. Because these values are not compared to x, and no exact values are provided for either y or z, there are many possibilities for y and z. Given only statement (1), the values of y and z respectively could be 30° and 10°, 33° and 11°, 36° and 12°, etc. Since we cannot pinpoint an exact value for x, y, or z, statement (1) is insufficient.

The same reasoning holds true for statement (2). It only compares the values of x and z and does not provide any exact value of any of the three variables. Statement (2) alone is also insufficient.

Taking both statements together, however, we can write three equations and solve by substitution:

$$y = 3z$$
$$x = \frac{z}{2}$$
$$x + y + z = 90$$

Substituting the values of y and x from the first two equations into the third equation and solving, we get:

$$\frac{z}{2} + 3z + z = 90$$

We can find the value of z. Statements (1) and (2) taken together are sufficient. The answer is choice **(C)**.

25. **(A)**

From statement (1), we know that a two-digit number plus another two-digit number gives a three-digit number. Therefore, the first digit of the three-digit number must be 1 (otherwise the sum would be over 200, impossible for the sum of 2 two-digit numbers). So $A = 1$. Our addition now looks like

$$
\begin{array}{r}
1B \\
+\ B1 \\
\hline
11C
\end{array}
$$

The only possibility for B is 9; anything less would not add up to more than 100. Statement (1) is sufficient.

Statement (2) only tells us the value of one of the digits; this is not enough to tell us anything about either B or C. Remember, we don't know the information from statement (1). Statement (2) is insufficient.

GMAT* STRATEGY SHEET

Use this sheet to help you remember important formulas and math rules for success on Test Day.

Strategies and Test Day Tips:

Picking Numbers:
Pick numbers that are permissible and manageable.

Backsolving:
Start with choice (B) or (D).

Equations and Variables:
n distinct linear equations are needed to solve for *n* variables.

DATA SUFFICIENCY
1 (A) #1 is Suff.; #2 is Not Suff.
2 (B) #2 is Suff.; #1 is Not Suff.
T (C) #1 is Not Suff.; #2 is Not Suff.; #1 AND #2 are Suff.
E (D) #1 is Suff.; #2 is Suff.
N (E) #1 is Not Suff.; #2 is Not Suff.; #1 AND #2 are Not Suff.

Triangles:

$x + y + z = 180°$ (Interior angles)

$a + b + c = 360°$ (Exterior angles)

$a = y + z; b = x + z; c = x + y$

$\text{Area} = \frac{1}{2} \text{base} \times \text{height}$

Sum of any 2 sides × 3rd side

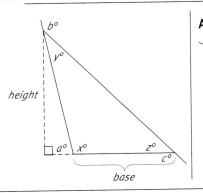

Angles:

$a + b = 180$

l_1 and l_2 are parallel

Right Triangles:

Equilateral 60°

Isosceles

45° 45° x $x\sqrt{2}$

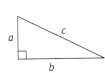
60° 30° x $2x$ $x\sqrt{3}$

Side Ratios
(Pythagorean Triples)
3:4:5
5:12:13
7:24:25
8:15:17
9:40:41

$a^2 + b^2 = c^2$

Circles:

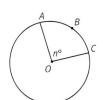

$d = 2r$
$C = 2\pi r$ or πd
$A = \pi r^2$
360° around

$\dfrac{n}{360} = \dfrac{\text{Arc } ABC}{\text{Circum.}} = \dfrac{\text{Area of sector } OABC}{\text{Area of circle } O}$

Order of Operations:
PEMDAS—Parentheses, Exponents, Multiplication and Division, Addition and Subtraction

FOIL:
First, Outer, Inner, Last
$(a + b)(c + d) = ac + ad + bc + bd$

Quadrilaterals: Sum of interior angles = 360°

s
$A = s^2$

w l
$A = lw$

b h
$A = bh$

b_1 h b_2
$A = \dfrac{1}{2}(b_1 + b_2)h$

Uniform Solids:

$V = \pi r^2 h$
$SA = 2\pi r^2 + 2\pi rh$

$V = lwh$
$SA = 2(lw + lh + wh)$

Other Formulas and Things to Know:

$\text{Speed} = \dfrac{\text{Distance}}{\text{Time}}$ $\text{Average} = \dfrac{\text{Sum of the terms}}{\text{Number of terms}}$ $\text{Average Speed} = \dfrac{\text{Total Distance}}{\text{Total Time}}$ $\text{Rate} = \dfrac{\text{Quantity of } A}{\text{Quantity of } B}$

$\text{\% Increase} = \dfrac{\text{New Amount} - \text{Original Amount}}{\text{Original Amount}} \times 100\%$ $\text{\% Decrease} = \dfrac{\text{Original Amount} - \text{New Amount}}{\text{Original Amount}} \times 100\%$

Exponent Rules:

$x \cdot x = x^2$ $(x^a)^b = x^{ab}$

$x^{-a} = \dfrac{1}{x^a}$ $\dfrac{x^a}{x^b} = x^{a-b}$

$x^0 = 1$ (negative)^{odd} = negative

$x^a x^b = x^{a+b}$ (negative)^{even} = positive

Radical Rules:

$\sqrt{a}\,\sqrt{b} = \sqrt{ab}$

$\dfrac{\sqrt{a}}{\sqrt{b}} = \sqrt{\dfrac{a}{b}}$

$a\sqrt{c} + b\sqrt{c} = (a+b)\sqrt{c}$

$\sqrt{a} + \sqrt{b} \neq \sqrt{a+b}$

$(\sqrt{a})^2 = a$

Numbers:

0 is an even integer.
1 is *not* prime.
2 is the lowest prime number and the only even prime number.
Mode: the most common number(s) in a set
Median: the middle term in a set of ascending or descending numbers; when the set has an even number of numbers, the average of the two middle terms
Only (odd) × (odd) and (odd) + (even) yield odd numbers.

Miscellaneous:

$ab + ac = a(b + c)$

$x\%$ of $y = y\%$ of x

$\dfrac{a+b}{c} = \dfrac{a}{c} + \dfrac{b}{c}$

$|-x| = |x|$

Work Formula:

$T = \dfrac{ab}{a+b}$

Coordinate Plane: In the *xy*-plane, the *y*-axis is vertical, and the *x*-axis is horizontal.

Standard form of a line: $y = mx + b$
(where *m* is the slope, and *b* is the *y*-intercept)

$\text{Slope} = \dfrac{\text{rise}}{\text{run}} = \dfrac{y_2 - y_1}{x_2 - x_1}$